spotlight

A CLOSE-UP LOOK AT THE ARTISTRY AND MEANING OF STEPHENIE MEYER'S TWILIGHT SAGA

BY JOHN GRANGER

This book has not been approved, licensed or sponsored by any person or entity that created or produced the *Twilight* books or films.

Spotlight

Allentown, PA

For information, contact Zossima Press www.Zossima.com

Zossima Press titles may be purchased for business or promotional use or special sales.

Cover design by J. Odell

10-9-8-7-6-5-4-3-2-1

ISBN 0-9822385-9-2
ISBN-13 978-0-9822385-9-2

Table of Contents

Part Two

Twilight as an LDS Midsummer Night's Dream

Reading as Dream Interpretation

Introduction to Spotlight
Why Read This Book?

Reading is an investment. We only have so much time and mental focus in any given day so we try to get the most return on those tasks we do with the cranial energy at hand between breakfast and bedtime. If you're like me, then, before picking up a book, whose every page represents a claim of substantial time and maybe a cash payment to boot, you want to know what *exactly* you're going to get out of reading it.

Let me be as clear as possible about what benefits you will get by reading *Spotlight* start to finish:

First, you will have an answer to several puzzling questions. If you're a serious reader of Stephenie Meyer's *Twilight* books, *Spotlight* answers the question, "Why do I like these books so much?" If you're not a fan but someone you know well cannot talk about anything else, reading *Spotlight* will explain to you, "What is my friend (spouse, child) seeing and experiencing in these young adult and vampire adventures that I'm missing?"

Spotlight's answer to these questions is the common sense one but, because it is very much out of step with the answers usually given, I'll share it straight up.

People Love These Books Because They're Good Books.

Not very mysterious, right?

If a book sells millions of copies – and Mrs. Meyer's *Twilight* novels have sold more than 70 million copies to date and will sell probably twice that before the movies are all released – I think the starting point for the discussion of *why* they are selling so well should be the obvious one: they do what books are supposed to do. The four and one-half novels of the Forks Saga deliver meaning in such a way that readers are engaged, edified, and eager for more.

In brief, the books succeed as books. They are well written, they touch readers in their hearts, and they profoundly confirm and perhaps even re-shape their readers' core beliefs.

Even *Twi*-hards, the most devout of *Twilight* readers, though, often blush when they admit they love Edward and Bella's adventures. Sad but true, it is something of a given that these books are "trash" or "just for teen girls." Let me explain why, then, I think the idea that Mrs. Meyer is a hack writer and her readers are idiots is nonsensical. However widespread and accepted this idea, it flies in the face of all evidence and experience.

Reading requires effort; longer books require greater and more sustained effort. The *Twilight* novels, at well over 2,000 pages when read beginning to end, represent at least a week's worth of any normal person's reading time. Does anyone, not to mention tens of millions of "anyones," spend that much time with any book that isn't delivering on the promise of a story well told?

I'm confident that American readers of all ages, both sexes, and from every region, would rather have a tooth filled or sleep under the bridge than be compelled (as we were in school, by the violence of "assignments") to read books that mean nothing to us. Mrs. Meyer is not writing schlock, whatever her critics say and believe – even if they *have* convinced most folks and many of her admirers that she has no talent.

The default reasons why readers love specific books and why any book sells very well are that the story is well written, delivers profound meaning in an entertaining way, and that it answers important questions about what it means to be human. These are the working assumptions of *Spotlight* about Mrs. Meyer's Bella Swan novels.

Five Reasons Critics Dismiss *Twilight* and Mrs. Meyer

Why do I think most people don't want to take these novels seriously as literature? Five quick reasons.

Prof. James Thomas of Pepperdine University, author of *Repotting Harry Potter: A Professor's Book-by-Book Guide for the Serious Re-Reader,* said in a *Time* magazine interview that the reason Ms. Rowling's *Harry Potter* books weren't accepted by scholars as "literature" were "the three 'Deathly Hallows' of these books: they are too current, too popular, and too juvenile."[1]

The same is at least as true of Mrs. Meyer's writing. The myopia of academics and media mavens makes them blind to the artistry and wagonload of meaning in genre fiction, i.e., anything other than the "modern novel." Being wildly popular, selling well *today* rather than years ago, and being a hit with younger as well as more mature readers are three strikes to the shadow shaper-umpires in the caves where we live.

Beyond the three "failings" of being commercially successful, accessible to readers of almost all ages, and much loved, Mrs. Meyer herself, by being the person and writer she is, has created two more road blocks to critical acceptance or even serious consideration: she writes Young Adult fiction and she is a married woman and mother who is not ashamed of her religious beliefs. Genre revulsion, institutional misogyny, and what I call "Sarah Palin Syndrome" mean any writer of Mrs. Meyer's description is going to be dismissed and beaten down by our self-anointed cultural gate-keepers. [2]

Spotlight answers the mystery of the *Twilight* books' popularity with the unjaundiced, common sense view that they are popular because they are good books. By 'good,' I mean they are **deliberately crafted**, they **deliver meaning** well beyond the narrative line, and, via this artistry and allegory, they **delight readers** profoundly.

In the first book about Mrs. Meyer as a writer-to-be-taken-seriously-as-artist, I will look at *Twilight* from two very different critical perspectives. The first and most important part of *Spotlight*, I think, is a reading of the Forks Saga as literature, a reading which reveals the choices Mrs. Meyer made in designing and telling her tales and why these choices work as well as they do.

---

1 James Thomas, *Time* magazine, Joanne Rowling: Person of the Year (Runner-Up), January 2008; http://www.time.com/time/specials/2007/personoftheyear/article/0,28804,1690753_1695388_1695436,00.html

2 See Lev Grossman, 'Good Books Don't Need to be Hard,' *Wall Street Journal*, 29 August 2009 on genre and the modern novel (http://online.wsj.com/article/SB10001424052970203706604574377163804387216.html) and Forks High School professor, 'Twilight and the Future of the Novel,' http://fhsprofessor.com/?p=233

Four Ways of Knowing: Four Layers of Meaning

The first benefit we get, then, from reading *Spotlight* is the literary answer to "why are these books so popular?" The second benefit is the practice we get in thinking about what all books mean, both as literature per se and as works of imagination. The first and longer part of *Spotlight* is an exercise in what Northrop Frye called "iconological criticism,"[3] which, though it sounds daunting, is really just looking at a story in the four different ways people know things. These ways of knowing anything – as information or data, opinion, knowledge, and as wisdom – when laid over a text are called its surface, moral, allegorical, and anagogical or mythic meanings. A book doesn't have to be Deuteronomy or be written by Dante to have these multiple layers; it just has to be written by someone human to be read by another human.

We'll walk through the layers step-by-step, spelling out the choices made by Mrs. Meyer at each level to give her series the "wow" resonance it has with millions of readers.

- We'll explore the **Surface** of the *Twilight* story first to clarify the fundamentals of the narrative: what effect, individually and taken together, do Mrs. Meyer's choices in her story formulas and narratives devices have on the reader? We'll look at Bella as narrator, the narrative drive being a combination of "boy meets girl" Harlequin piece and Blockbuster adventure thriller, and the way Mrs. Meyer joins the genres of Young Adult Romance with Paranormal fiction.
- Next, we'll unwrap the **Moral** meaning implicit in the surface story, which involves identifying the Gothic touches she uses to deliver postmodern messages about the evils of prejudice and the critical importance of choice.
- Then we'll look *at* the surface story as a transparency to see the **Allegorical** meaning looking back at us from the other side. Beyond the satirical points Mrs. Meyer scores via zombies in *New Moon* and some pointed Christian Church caricatures in *Breaking Dawn,* the overarching allegory of the Saga is a re-telling of the Garden of Eden story with Edward and Bella playing the parts of God and Man in a Medieval "Everyman Drama."

3 Northrop Frye, *Anatomy of Criticism,* Princeton University Press, Princeton, 1957, page 10.

- Finally, we'll step *into* the surface story as a translucency to experience its **Anagogical** or transcendent meaning. Here we will discuss the hero's journey, the many circles in the story, the literary alchemy, and the importance of eyes and a "shared vision" or conscience. This is Mrs. Meyer at her best.

Looking at her books on these layers of meaning will uncover Mrs. Meyer's neglected artistry and her answers, both traditional and postmodern, to life's big questions. In the Preface to Part One you will have in hand simultaneously two benefits from this book; it explains in large part the popularity of the Cullen Clan's story while also serving as an introduction for many readers to seeing beneath and within the story-line, a technique they can use to 'get at' the greater meaning and artistry of any book they read.

Reading *Twilight* as a Mormon Woman's Midsummer Night's Dream

Spotlight's first chapters are about what the *Twilight* Saga means to *everyone*, using the most traditional and just-human way of thinking about books to open them up. The second part of this book is quite different. Because of the specific inspiration Mrs. Meyer had to write about Bella and Edward and because of the restricted audience for whom she wrote the first books, *Spotlight* is obliged to read the series using the tools of *dream interpretation* to open their latent and more challenging meaning.

That's just crazy enough to require some extra explanation.

Mrs. Meyer's Cinderella story is almost as well known as Ms. Rowling's but, in case you missed it, here is a very brief re-cap.

On the night of 2 June 2003, Mrs. Meyer had a dream about a young couple in a meadow. The man was a vampire, the woman his girlfriend. He wanted to eat her up, quite literally, but his love for her held him back. The dream was so vivid that, when she woke up, Mrs. Meyer wrote down as much of the dream as she could remember. This scene became the pivotal chapter in *Twilight* and is the heart, not only of that book, but of each book in the series, all of which are Edward and Bella stories and all of which feature meetings and confrontations in mountain meadows.

Twilight, then, began as a dream. The saga's beginning and core is from Mrs. Meyer's unconscious mind. She wrote it out, she has explained many times, not because she expected to become the author of best-selling books that captivate the imaginations of millions. She wrote the story because she felt she had to, as if she "was guided through that process." [4] Her only audience members were a trusted sister and herself, which, inasmuch as her sister is as close to her own reflection in beliefs and ideas as another human could be, confirms she was writing as a psychological exercise and relief rather than for publication.

Serious readers of her books, consequently, I think are obliged to look at the books psychologically.

Let me say right away this doesn't mean I will be patronizing the author as a disturbed woman with mental issues and "putting her on the couch" to speculate about her sexual frustrations and unresolved issues with mom and dad. Far from it. I don't know Mrs. Meyer or her psychological history, I have no training in psychoanalysis that would qualify me for that kind of speculation, and I have never asked the woman or read her responses to questions that would make such speculation possible.

We do know, however, *exactly* when Mrs. Meyer had her dream. We know, too, that she is a Latter-day Saint (LDS) or Mormon, that she was raised in this church and considers LDS beliefs normative, and that she graduated from Brigham Young University, the LDS academic Mecca, with a degree in English Literature. And we have the books, the product of her dream's unconscious material, her deliberate artistry, and no little psychological energy.

Knowing these things and having read her books, I think a serious reading of Mrs. Meyer's books necessarily involves a close look at:

(1) the summer of 2003 to see what might have inspired a devout

---

4 See, for instance, her interview with William Morris at 'A Motley Vision: Mormon Arts and Culture,' http://www.motleyvision.org/2005/interview-twilight-author-stephanie-meyer/ in which she said:

In the beginning, I didn't even know that *Twilight* was going to be a *novel*. I had no expectations or direction. I was just writing because it felt wonderful and because I wanted to see where the story was going. Soon, I was also writing because I'd fallen in love with my characters and I felt like I was neglecting them when I wasn't writing. I didn't think of publishing until the moment that I wrote what I knew was going to be the very last line. ... I'm lucky *Twilight* wasn't a muddled catastrophe, because I had no outline or idea of where the plot would go while I was writing the last half (I wrote from the middle through to the end, and then went back and wrote the beginning until the two pieces matched up). To be honest, I feel like I was guided through that process.

and well-informed American Mormon woman to have the dream she did; and

(2) the books themselves to see how they reflect the manifest and latent meanings of this inspiration.

The second part of *Spotlight,* in contrast with the first part's exploration of what the *Twilight* Saga means to everyone and anyone, will be about what the Forks adventures mean just to Stephenie Meyer and to people very much like her. Which is to say, to Mormon women.

Not being a Mormon or a woman, how the heck can I know what these books mean to an LDS wife and mother? And why, if you aren't a Mormon woman, should you care?

Those are fair questions. About my knowing what they mean to a Mormon woman, the truth, right up front, is that I can't *know.* I can only guess.

I think my guesses are more than a stab in the dark, though, because even a non-Mormon or "gentile's" familiarity with the *Twilight* novels, the events of 2003, and with LDS history, theology, and culture reveal the books are largely about Mormon issues. The *Twilight* novels are an intelligent woman's expression of her love for, problems with, and experience of life as a Latter-day Saint.

I'm confident this is not over-the-top speculation for three reasons.

- As C. S. Lewis wrote, "To construct plausible and moving 'other worlds,' you must draw upon the only real 'other world' we know, that of the spirit."[5] The only real (or unreal, depending on your thoughts about Mormon revelation) "other world" that Mrs. Meyer knows, "that of the spirit," is the spiritual world of LDS doctrine and understanding. We can safely assume it informs her work.
- If we struggle with that, the author says as much herself. Not only is *The Book of Mormon* the most important book in her life,[6] but she also shares, point blank, that "I am also a member

5 C. S. Lewis, *On Stories and Other Essays,* Harvest: New York, 2002 page 12

6 **Q:** What book has had the most significant impact on your life? **A:** The book with the most significant impact on my life is *The Book of Mormon.* The book with the most significant impact on my life as a writer is probably *Speaker for the Dead,* by Orson Scott Card, with *Rebecca* by Daphne du Maurier coming in as a close second. http://www.amazon.com/exec/obidos/tg/detail/-/0316160172/ref=ase_stepheniemeye-20/104-0160833-2386318?v=glance&s=books

of the Church of Jesus Christ of Latter-day Saints, and that has a huge influence on who I am and my perspective on the world, and therefore what I write...."[7] And –

- As Edward Anaudin has written, Mrs. Meyer's books reflect specific LDS teachings about 'Milk Before Meat,' Agency, Sexuality and the Law of Chastity, Marriage, Family, Conversion, Harmful Language: Lying, Profanity, and Gossip, Diet and the Word of Wisdom, and Persecution and Tolerance."[8]

Reading *Twilight* as a Mormon novel is not a stretch, but just common sense. As fantasy fiction written by a faithful LDS believer, what else could her books reflect? Buddhism? Secular humanism? Hardly.

Artist, Apologist, and Apostate: The Mountain Meadows Metaphor

I take the step from "reading *Twilight* as a Mormon novel" to interpreting it as a dream or poem expressing what Mrs. Meyer believes *about* her church because of the LDS relevant events of 2003 and their expression in her stories. In brief, 2003 saw three books published with national exposure and distribution that focused on the Mountain Meadows Massacre of 1857, in which tragedy faithful Mormons in Southern Utah executed more than 120 men, women, and children on their way to California.[9] All three books paint LDS beliefs and history unsympathetically, to say the least, and as a group their publication caused a strong reaction from and a new awareness of Mountain Meadows in the Mormon community.

---

7 Originally on her StephenieMeyer.com website biography, since removed, but still posted at various sites online, cf., http://search.barnesandnoble.com/The-Twilight-Saga/Stephenie-Meyer/e/9780316043120#TABS

8 Edwin B. Arnaudin. 'Mormon Vampires: The Twilight Saga and Religious Literacy. A Master's Paper for the M.S. in L.S degree.' April, 2008; http://etd.ils.unc.edu/dspace/bitstream/1901/469/1/Mormon+Vampires+-+The+Twilight+Saga+and+Religious+Literacy.pdf. See also Eric W. Jepsen, 'Saturday's Werewolf: Vestiges of the Pre-mortal Romance in the Stephenie Meyer Twilight Novels' at http://www.motleyvision.org/readinguntildawn/ojs/index.php?journal=readinguntildawn&page=article&op=viewFile&path%5B%5D=5&path%5B%5D=24

9 *Blood of the Prophets: Brigham Young and the Mountain Meadows Massacre* (Bagley), *American Massacre: The Tragedy at Mountain Meadows, September 1857* (Denton), and *Under the Banner of Heaven: A Story of Violent Faith* (Krakauer)

That is not the only Mormon crisis or gentile assault on LDS beliefs in 2003 and the years just prior but it is the one most obviously reflected in Mrs. Meyer's dream and books. *Twilight* and the subsequent novels, especially *Breaking Dawn*, are best understood in depth after examining them in the context of the three Mountain Meadows books and the challenge they made to Mormon believers like Mrs. Meyer. I will argue that the Forks adventures are largely her metaphorical response as an LDS artist, as a Mormon apologist, and, significantly, as a feminist apostate.

This involves reading *Twilight* as a wish fulfilling dream in which almost every figure, group, setting, and conflict acts as a story transparency to deliver a sympathetic presentation of core LDS beliefs and a defense of controversial ideas that divide Mormons and their gentile neighbors. Mrs. Meyer's dream answers the objections every intelligent Latter-day Saint knows nonbelievers have about Mormonism in her portrayal of the Cullen vampire clan as her ideal Mormon family (even Father, Mother, Son, and Holy Spirit), the Quileute werewolves as the Salt Lake City Church, and Bella as her idealized Seeker for the restored faith and personal, individual immortality.

She answers in non-discursive images and stories those Americans who believe that:

- Joseph Smith was a fraud and the religion he founded just so much nonsense;
- Man-Child marriage and polygamy are Mormon horrors;
- The Latter-day Saints are a cult rather than a valid means to salvation;
- The Mormons have a 'magic world view,' not a sanctifying means of grace;
- Native American genetic evidence proves *The Book of Mormon* is hooey;
- The Mountain Meadows Massacre was caused by LDS doctrines of blood atonement, by their unquestioning obedience to the first president, and by their group oaths to take revenge for martyred Mormon prophets;
- Mormon men are misogynists and their women little more than slaves;

- Mormons as a rule are patronizing and condescending to non-believers because they think their temple-recommends make them not just a "peculiar people" but "perfect people," far better than others;
- Mormons believe they can be shamelessly dishonest with potential converts or when speaking with anyone about their church because they are "lying for the Lord" or just giving "milk before meat" to save souls; and
- The Latter-day Saints are racists and homophobes.

On all these points. Mrs. Meyer as a story artist is an able apologist for her religious beliefs. She leaves the reservation, though, on women's issues, of which Bella is very much aware. Mrs. Meyer goes so far in her fantasy saga to create a wish fulfillment resistance piece for Mormon women in the conclusion of *Eclipse* and the married life of Edward and Bella.

More hauntingly, in Leah, who like Mrs. Meyer has a brother named Seth, she gives us a self-portrait of the thinking Mormon woman in painful isolation because of her independence, intelligence, and will. In Edward's doubts about the soul and vampire transcendence, she leaves on the table the question of LDS life after death.

I will explore Mrs. Meyer's dream-epic in three steps.

First, I'll be obliged, because most readers will be unfamiliar with *The Book of Mormon* and LDS theology, to explain how Mrs. Meyer's beliefs inform her dream, the way everyone's conscious way of thinking shapes their sleeping thought.

Then I will review how the *Twilight* Saga is a Mormon's wish fulfillment exercise that glosses and gilds problematic LDS history and beliefs to put them in the best possible light.

Finally, I will discuss the several points of friction between Mormon practice and postmodern sensibilities where Mrs. Meyer's wish fulfillment takes the side of feminists and critical gentiles contra the Salt Lake City hierarchs and Temple conventions. Her story significantly reforms the "restored faith."

So what? Again, good question. This matters to Mrs. Meyer and her sister for obvious reasons. Why, if we're not Mormon women, should we care?

This is meaningful even if you aren't a Mormon woman or if you do not care to know anything about LDS history and beliefs because seeing how Mrs. Meyer's faith shapes and colors her stories reveals, beyond what we learned from looking at the books as layered texts, why they are so popular.

Getting Beyond the Author: Why Books *Really* Sell

Just as *Spotlight*'s iconological look at her books gives us both the theory and experience of reading books beneath the narrative line, so this dream interpretation of her novels helps us practice a psychological, even spiritual perspective in reading. As a rule, I am not a fan or exponent of what C. S. Lewis called the "Personal Heresy," i.e., examining poems, plays, and novels simply as an author's personal or ego excrescence rather than vehicles of artist-transcending meaning.

Reading an author's work psychologically, however, here means something completely different than searching for tit-for-tat correspondences with events from the author's childhood or his or her individual neuroses. What we are after here is the identification and understanding of the "other world" and spiritual beliefs this author is smuggling, intentionally or unconsciously. In this larger meaning, dream interpretation and a psychological reading explain why books sell.

Mircea Eliade wrote that in a secular culture like our own, entertainments, especially novels and films, serve a religious and mythic function.[10] This is an observation I will return to again and again in *Spotlight* as its core premise. Human beings, in brief, have a capacity for spiritual or transcendent experience; deprived of same in a godless and god-denying environment, we seek it where we can find it. Many people find it in their religious community and private devotions. *Everyone* gets it by "suspending disbelief" and skeptical self-awareness when we enter into story.

I have two corollaries to Eliade's "religious function of fantasy" thesis. The first is just the fairly obvious point that the more otherworldly or transpersonal meaning a book or drama has, the more aptly it will fill this religious function, and the more popular it will be (assuming of course the content is artfully presented, the Gospel "smuggled" as Lewis put it, rather than written like a tract or altar call). Think of *The Lord of*

10 Mircea Eliade, *The Sacred and the Profane: The Nature of Religion*, Harcourt: New York, 1957, page 204.

the Rings, *The Chronicles of Narnia*, and Joanne Rowling's *Harry Potter* novels,[11] their relatively transparent and profound Christian content, and their unmatched and enduring popularity.

My second addenda to Eliade is that to resonate profoundly in readers' hearts a work must reflect, either openly or opaquely, some spiritual truth or reality, and, simultaneously, the core beliefs of the historical period in which the readers are living. Ms. Rowling pulled off this conjunction by delivering postmodern themes using alchemical scaffolding and re-animating traditional symbolism from the English literature backlot.

I suggest here that Mrs. Meyer succeeds largely because of her religious beliefs themselves, Mormonism being born in the crucible of the early nineteenth-century, the dawn of Modernism, reflect conventional beliefs about the sovereignty of the individual, the myth of progress, and a faith in visible works rather than grace. Reading psychologically to find the hidden treasure in *Twilight* with our own "seeing-stones", if I may be forgiven an LDS metaphor, will reveal the substance of Mrs. Meyer's writing because it will bring to surface the beliefs, both Mormon and apostate, that give these stories their life and depth.

I close *Spotlight* with a hat-tip to the "For Dummies" guidebooks and their signature finales with my own "Chapter of Tens." In it, I will give a bullet item review of *Spotlight*, point to further reading, fiction and non-fiction, to deepen appreciation of Ms. Meyer's artistry and meaning, and a few "frequently asked questions."

Why I Wrote *Spotlight*: An Invitation

My ambition in writing this introduction has been to give you enough of an explanation of what you can get out of reading this book that you feel compelled to actually read it. I hope as well that I have not said so much that you don't think you need to read further to see if I succeed in delivering what I have promised!

Now that I've said what's in it for you, I'll close this introduction by saying why I have written *Spotlight* and by extending an invitation.

---

11 See my *How Harry Cast His Spell* for the Christian symbolism and themes of the Potter novels, so well smuggled that many Christians to this day still think of them as demonic or "gateways to the occult."

I have enjoyed the research, reading, and writing I have had to do for *Spotlight* because all of it has taken place at the intersection of what matters most to me, namely, faith, literature, culture, and the discovery of meaning. Mrs. Meyer's *Twilight* books have been exciting to explore since few people, for the five reasons mentioned at the start of this introduction, think they deserve serious reading. This has meant I have had the field of play largely to myself, if, to strain the sports metaphor, the stadium is filled with the millions of serious *Twilight* readers who want to know more about the books they love.

While I do think I am breaking relatively "new ground" here, I know mine will not be the last word. Even I am already putting together another book, *Bella Swan's Bookshelf,* in which I will tour the twelve books whose influence shines through individual *Twilight* Saga stories or the whole series. I know that at least one Latter-day Saint *Twilight* fan, too, is writing her critical exegesis of Mrs. Meyer's novels as the work of a Mormon feminist. My hope is that *Spotlight* fosters the serious critical discussion of Bella's Forks Adventures and moves us past the status quo of dismissal and disdain in which the *Twilight* books are held by serious readers.

As with my explanations of Ms. Rowling's *Harry Potter* series, the greatest pleasure in talking and writing about the *Twilight* Saga is in the friends I have made in person and online. Most everything you read in the pages that follow are ideas that came about in or were much improved during conversations and correspondence with the internet community at Forks High School Professor (fhsprofessor.com). Thanks to Elizabeth Baird Hardy, Deborah Chan, and Jennifer St. Hilaire for your help and especially for your kindness while correcting my mistakes.

I hope you will join that community's ongoing conversation or write to me at the email address below to let me know what you think of *Spotlight* and to share your questions, comments, and corrections. Thank you for reading *Spotlight* and, in advance, for letting me know what you think.

Fraternally in the love of a good book,

John

john@FHSProfessor.com

Preface to Part 1: On Iconological Criticism

Why We Love Bella

In Defense of a Close-Up Reading of Stephenie Meyer's Twilight *Books*

I read *Twilight* for the first time very much against my will. A serious reader of Harry Potter and good friend, Ann-Laurel Nickel, wrote to me for more than a year asking me what I thought of *Twilight* and urging me to read the series.

I couldn't have been less interested.

My thinking was, in essence, "life is too short for cheap beer or for reading Young Adult Romance with vampires."

Ann-Laurel persisted. She even teased me with the possibility of speaking at a June 2009 *Twilight* symposium she was sponsoring in Forks.[1] I politely blew her off, if you will, until March of 2009, when I was totally burned out after writing a book against near impossible deadlines.[2] Unable to do anything requiring more concentrated intellectual focus than peeling an orange, or, on good days, attempting a novice's Sudoku puzzle, I assumed I was in just the right state of mind for *Twilight*.

Even then I think I only picked up the "apple in hands" paperback because my 16 year old daughter Sophia had read the whole series that month in quick succession and had been almost unnerved by how much she liked them. Hence, the books were at hand and required no effort to acquire them, and, I now knew two serious readers who had been swallowed up by the books much as two Pevensie children and Eustace

---

1 Summer School in Forks, a Literature Inspired Fan Event sponsored symposium, 25-28 June 2009

2 John Granger, *Harry Potter's Bookshelf: The Great Books Behind the Hogwarts Adventures* (Penguin, 2009)

Scrubb were taken into the painting of the Narnian ship in *Voyage of the Dawn Treader.*

As you probably have guessed, I had much the same experience on reading *Twilight* as Mrs. Nickel, Sophia, and millions of other readers have had. I enjoyed it, quite despite myself, and finished all four published books and the incomplete *Midnight Sun* online in rapid order. Again, despite no little internal resistance, I found myself thinking about Edward, Bella, and company, their struggles and stories, and why these books are as gripping as they are.

You may have had this experience yourself. If you're reading this book, I assume you have or that someone you know and love has had it and, as important, you're at a loss to understand the fascination. Smart people aren't supposed to become so involved in this kind of book or any kind of book really. Are we stupid? I've asked myself that question, too, believe me. What makes my *Twilight* immersion and initiation experience different than most people's is only that I'd been there before. Sort of. And I know the answer to the question.

How I Became a Potter Pundit: From Resistance to Celebration

In the year 2000, a co-worker at Whole Foods Market had told me I had to read about a boy wizard and "this incredible school where he goes to study witchcraft." I explained to her that not only didn't I *have to* read this book, I almost certainly wasn't going to. Sorcery wasn't anything I was interested in or that I thought would be edifying reading for my seven children. I asked my wife that night if she had ever heard of 'Harry Potter.' She hadn't either, but we agreed that "Sorcery School" wasn't for us.

My oldest daughter, Hannah, then 11 years old, was given a copy of *Sorcerer's Stone* by our family pediatrician without our knowledge. She and her sister Sarah were reading it on the sly (walking around the house with the book held behind them) before I saw it. I took the book and told them I would read it myself that night and explain to them in the morning why we don't read trash like this.

Fast forward two years and I have written and friends have published *The Hidden Key to Harry Potter* (Zossima Press, 2002), the first sympathetic look at the Potter novels as literature in print.

That book was greeted with something like the reactions people have to "Man Bites Dog" stories in newspapers. Everyone *knew* then that the Harry Potter books were children's books of no substance greater than Nancy Drew and the Hardy Boys, and, more ominously, they were convinced that the books were "spiritually questionable." My assertion in *Hidden Key* that the popular novels were built on a Shakespearean scaffolding called 'literary alchemy' and were stuffed with traditional symbolism and edifying Christian content was almost universally considered risible projection of my own beliefs and the forcing of my own thinking into the text.

Fast forward again, this time to 2009. There are now well over 100 books exploring the artistry and meaning of Ms. Rowling's work, courses on the Christian content of the series are being taught at Yale and Princeton, and Penguin publishes my book on the literary antecedents of Harry in the Schoolboy novel, Gothic, and Fantasy traditions of English letters. No one remembers the disbelief that *Hidden Key to Harry Potter* met back in the day.

Having lived through it, though, and come out the other side as a Potter Pundit invited to speak about the Hogwarts Adventures at Universities and at Fan and Academic Conferences across North America, reading *Twilight* gave me the feeling of *déjà vu*. I've definitely been in this situation before.

- Resist reading books.
- Read them and love them.
- Discover the smart readers in schools and media critics have uniformly dissed the books (along with its author and her admirers) as, at best, a "beach read" and more often as second-rate slop.
- Explain how the book works as literature. And
- Get laughed at by all those who know better (and applauded by those who have loved the books).

If the parallels continue, of course, in a few years no one will recall the dismissive laughter or the disdain of Ivory Tower mavens in the landslide rush to think seriously about *Twilight* and publish companion books to the Forks Saga themselves.

The joke in scientific circles is that there are three stages of acceptance for a bold, new theory. First, derision: "This is absurd and unworthy of serious consideration or research money." Then, skepticism: "This idea is anything but accepted or demonstrated and requires a host of research before it can be thought of as anything more than irresponsible conjecture." Finally, acceptance (with a sneer): "We've always known that." This progression is as true, in my experience, in literary criticism as it is with hard science.

Taking Bella Seriously: The 'Blush Factor' Elephant in the Room

I understand if you are skeptical about my thesis that the *Twilight* books are as popular as they are because they are well written and deliver significant meaning. As I mentioned in the Introduction, because the books are *simultaneously* popular, current, aimed at younger people, and because they were written by a woman, not to mention one *without* academic credentials from a significant university (i.e., Ivy League or the equivalent) but *with* a faith in God, no one in professional academia takes the *Twilight* books seriously enough to do more than look down their nose at them and the readers who enjoy them. This despite the fact that the novels dominate Best Seller lists more than a year after the last book in the series was published[3] and have sold millions of copies – and despite the turn-around these same people have done with Joanne Rowling's writing.

Go figure.

Before I begin explaining why we love Bella, which is the substance of this book, I am obliged to speak very clearly about the Elephant in the Room during any such discussion. I do not know any serious readers, adult or teen, who reads or has read *Twilight* that is not to some degree embarrassed and defensive of their having read the four books in the series. Smart people aren't supposed to like this sort of books or think they're anything but entertaining pablum.

I call this Elephant the "Blush Factor" because readers everywhere are embarrassed about being engaged by the Forks Saga. Carrying one in one's hand is not unlike wearing clothes only appropriate for children or for the beach. Before we can explore the levels of meaning and the artistry of the books, then, I need to explain more than I have above why

3 Carol Memmot and Ann Cadden, 'Twilight Series Eclipses Potter Records on Best Selling List,' *USA Today*, 3 August 2009; http://www.usatoday.com/life/books/news/2009-08-03-twilight-series_N.htm, cf., also http://fhsprofessor.com/?p=76

it is that critics object so vehemently and uniformly to taking *Twilight* seriously. It is the universality and harshness of this criticism that has created, after all, the consensus that Mrs. Meyer's readers are all sex-consumed tweenie girls of negligible taste and intelligence and that she is a hack writer.

If you doubt that this is the case, I offer as a 'for instance' the opinions of Stephen King on *Twilight*. Mr. King, recipient of the National Book Foundation's Medal for Distinguished Contribution to Letters and author of *On Writing* in addition to numerous horror genre best sellers, said about Mrs. Meyer:

> In the case of Stephenie Meyer, it's very clear that she's writing to a whole generation of girls and opening up kind of a safe joining of love and sex in those books. It's exciting and it's thrilling and it's not particularly threatening because they're not overtly sexual. A lot of the physical side of it is conveyed in things like the vampire will touch her forearm or run a hand over skin, and she just flushes all hot and cold. And for girls, that's a shorthand for all the feelings that they're not ready to deal with yet.... Stephenie Meyer can't write worth a darn. She's not very good... [She is like Erle Stanley Gardner, the pulp mystery writer;] *He was a terrible writer, too, but he was very successful.*[4]

The irony of a horror genre writer who has been dismissed by heavy hitters like Harold Bloom as "an immensely inadequate writer on a sentence-by-sentence, paragraph-by-paragraph, book-by-book basis"[5] talking disdainfully about Ms. Meyer is just too rich, no? The point I want to make here, though, is not about Mr. King's self-blindness and self-importance but just that there is close to a zero-tolerance policy among critics about *Twilight*.

Lev Grossman, author of *The Magicians* and book critic for *Time* magazine, wrote an article in *The Wall Street Journal* called 'Good Books Don't Have to be Hard.' In that article, he made the seemingly

---

4 Lorrie Lynch, 'Exclusive: Steven King on J. K. Rowling and Stephenie Meyer,' USA Today, 2 February 2009; http://blogs.usaweekend.com/whos_news/2009/02/exclusive-steph.html Mr. King has since acknowledged that Mrs. Meyer writes "good stories," if his comments about her as terrible writer are unchanged (*Entertainment Weekly* Fall TV Preview '09, 'What's Next for Pop Culture?' September, 2009).

5 Harold Bloom, 'Dumbing Down American Readers,'*Boston Globe*, 24 September 2003, http://www.boston.com/news/globe/editorial_opinion/oped/articles/2003/09/24/dumbing_down_american_readers/

undeniable argument that the sort of books taken seriously by critics and academics, the 'literary' or 'modern' novel, is a dinosaur on life-support because it is a genre that neglected plot and readability for psychological depth, aesthetics, and nuance readers didn't enjoy or appreciate.[6]

In his arguments that plot is not only a good thing but that better literary novelists are now writing in genres that celebrate rather than avoid plot, Mr. Grossman compared the one year sales of a critically well-received literary novel (15,000 copies) with Mrs. Meyer's first quarter sales for the *Twilight* saga (8 million books). The comparison made his point. It also became the line-item focus of literary critics' counter-attacks on the *Wall Street Journal* article. It was, simply, unbelievable, in their collective opinion, that Mr. Grossman was offering *Twilight* as an example *in any way* for serious writers to follow.[7]

In response to the outrage of all those who invested their lives and lucre in advanced degrees so they could always dismiss "genre fiction," i.e., anything not by Saul Bellow, Phillip Roth, or a Faulkner disciple, Mr. Grossman discussed the *Twilight* books in a frank interview with Josh Jasper at Publisher Weekly's *Genreville* weBlog.

> Jasper: **You're implying that you think Stephenie Meyer is a good writer.**
>
> Grossman: Well, I think that one's a yes and no. I think it would be more accurate to say that I'm interested in the fact that tons and tons of people read her (I'm one of them), in numbers that make the number of people who read literary fiction a borderline statistically insignificant number. I want to know why that is. Obviously there are a lot of things the *Twilight* books do, and don't

6 Lev Grossman, 'Good Books Don't Have to Be Hard: A novelist on the pleasure of reading stories that don't bore; rising up from the supermarket racks,' *Wall Street Journal*, 29 August 2009; http://online.wsj.com/article/SB10001424052970203706604574377163804387216.html

7 For examples of the online vituperation Mr. Grossman received, see http://mumpsimus.blogspot.com/2009/08/its-plot.html, http://nielsenhayden.com/makinglight/archives/011593.html#011593, http://www.conversationalreading.com/2009/08/as-far-as-self-promotion-disguised-as-general-theory-of-the-novel-goes-lev-grossman-could-learn-a-thing-or-two-from-jonathan.html, and http://www.cheryl-morgan.com/?p=6070. For defenses of Mr. Grossman see Michelle Kern's 'The Nasty Debate over the Future of Fiction' in *Book Examiner* (http://www.examiner.com/x-562-Book-Examiner%7Ey2009m9d13-The-nasty-debate-over-the-future-of-fiction) and my own comments at *Forks High School Professor* (http://fhsprofessor.com/?p=233).

> do, that you can point to and say, good books do/don't do those things, therefore the *Twilight* books are ass. But — hear me out — millions of people love them. All those millions of people might be idiots or have bad taste. But I think it's kinda intellectually lazy to say that. Meyer is doing something very very well, or at least giving people something they really really want, and I don't think we have a good critical vocabulary yet for talking about what that something is. But I'm interested in it.[8]

I'm afraid, as refreshing as Mr. Grossman's honest desire for thoughtful people to reflect on the popularity of Mrs. Meyer's work is, that his naiveté in sharing the view that the literary novel Emperor is wearing no clothes and could use a few fashion tips from Mrs. Meyer will cost him his Critic's Guild card. He is, though, absolutely right that it is "intellectually lazy" for critics to assume that millions of readers are wrong, stupid, and have no taste because they love the books they do – and he points to the reason for this critical laziness or blind spot as well.

The tools and "critical vocabulary" in vogue today tell us little to nothing about why readers love certain books and what longing in the human person reading satisfies. The approach I will be using in *Spotlight* is diametrically opposed to the three literary pigs of deconstruction, genre hierarchy, and aesthetic criticism and is probably unfamiliar to most readers, so, before jumping into this approach, let's talk about the Medieval skeleton key for unlocking texts and how to use it.

Forward to the Past: Helpful Tools from the Middle Ages

Why do we read books, especially fiction? What do we get out of stories that keeps us coming back? Prof. Ralph Wood, the giant of Tolkien studies at Baylor University, once said that fantasy fiction wasn't about escaping *from* reality, but entering *into* it. I think he put his finger on the existential, even metaphysical delight we have in reading.

Reading serves, as Eliade said, a religious or mythic function in a secular culture. By entering into a story, any story really, the reader "suspends disbelief," which is to say, "escapes skeptical thoughts focused on the ego person." Whatever the substance or morality of the tale or drama entered into, the reader or audience member in suspending individuality has burst the greatest bond keeping him or her from spiritual life. Reading is the right orientation of person *away from* ego.

8 http://www.publishersweekly.com/blog/400000640/post/1310048531.html

That is true for *any* reading, even the debasing kind or immoral, I think. But the reading that we love, the books and poems we re-read endlessly, are those that not only free us from our ego concerns but which also foster and stimulate via an imaginative experience, our atrophied conscience, inner heart, or spirit. Love stories, tales of adventure, especially those with sacrificial heroism in the fight of good against evil, and mysteries in which the truth finally wins out – all of these act simultaneously as levers to break the inertia of ego and pumps to lift up our hearts.

The literary tools of our time, born as they are from a spiritless idea of man whose conscience is just super-ego, obscure rather than illumine why we love reading and what we get from better stories. To understand what works in books, poems, and plays, what artistry and meaning causes the hearts of readers to resonate resoundingly, we need conceptual helps and approaches from a different time, when the culture reflected a consensus that conscience was King or Lord.

The tools we need to understand the continued lure of reading and the pull of great writing comes from an age when this traditional and spiritual idea of person was the rule rather than an extraordinary exception. That time? The Middle Ages and early Renaissance. The tools? What Northrop Frye called "iconological criticism."

"Iconological" is a big word but its meaning is pretty straightforward. It means to read critically the way you look at a picture. Not just any picture, though. Iconological "looking" is about the way we look at, understand, even *enter into* an icon or sacred picture. This is where it gets a little tricky because we don't understand the world or ourselves the way traditional and theocentric people do.

To us, a picture is a snapshot or film in which physical reality at a moment of time is captured or frozen. Thinking of ourselves as essentially visible, physical realities, i.e., bodies with brain housing-groups and chemical minds, the picture's surface is its meaning. That's not the way an icon works.

An icon has a surface meaning or depiction, certainly, but it doesn't look very much like reality as we experience it. There are halos, for one thing, right? These nimbuses of light around saints' heads reflect their inner light or identity with conscience, their inner heart. Then there is the distortion in proportion and perspective. People, events, things, and physical space in icons just don't look like their equivalents in profane reality.

This is because icons aren't trying to capture profane, surface reality but spiritual or sacred time and space, eternity and a greater being rather than mundane existence. The icon serves first as a **transparency** through which the pure in heart can see something of that world-not-like-our-world, and, ultimately, as a **translucency** through which that reality and Light will shine through into the viewer's heart. The icon is not an object per se that the subject looks at as something 'other;' the sacred painting acts as a portal through which the subject's greater Self or inner heart experiences its reflection and in which subject and object elide as in a mirror.

Iconological criticism of a written text is looking at it to grasp how the reader responds to it in the way the religious believer experiences an icon. That may sound pretty heavy or "airy fairy" but fortunately it is pretty easy and common sensical. Reading iconologically, the way they did in the Middle Ages, means reading at four levels, what they called the four "senses," which correspond to the four ways human beings know anything in the world.

The surface of the story corresponds to the knowledge we have through our senses, knowledge we call "information" or "data." Just the facts, ma'am. The moral sense of what we read reflects the knowledge we call "opinion," that is, information as filtered through our understanding or perception of right and wrong. The first two layers of meaning or senses of any text, the surface and moral levels, are pretty much what anyone "gets" consciously on first reading a book or poem.

The third layer, allegory, is where we begin to see the text as an icon or portal to something higher or 'other' than ourselves. Here the meaning corresponds to the knowledge we call "science" from a lab or "demonstrated knowledge" like geometry proofs. Here, one thing corresponds or reflects another thing as a transparency through which I understand the one thing better or more profoundly. Think of how a scientific theory or mathematical equation in which real world objects and how they work are represented help us to understand those things. In a written work, the allegorical meaning is the truth or greater reality represented that our eye of the heart sees and understands in the characters and their struggles.

The fourth sense of a book, its sublime or anagogical meaning, corresponds to the kind of knowledge we call "wisdom." Unlike information, opinion, and science, wisdom is knowledge that is more than something that we have in our heads. It is a knowing from the spirit in our hearts that transforms everything that we are. We talk about the "wise man," sage or saint, as someone who is much more than "smart;" we think of and describe him or her as "illumined" or "enlightened," quite literally as "light bearers," because they have become **translucencies** through which the light of conscience shines on us.

The anagogical or sublime meaning of a text is that layer of artistry, almost always beneath our conscious experience on first and even after multiple readings, that corresponds with, stimulates, and fosters our spiritual orientation and transformation. C. S. Lewis said a great book was one you liked very much and one the reading of which made you "better, wiser, and happier."[9] This depth of change, becoming wise and experiencing joy, is a function not of mechanical morality in a plot but cathartic identification with and experience of the allegorical and anagogical depths of story.

Plato's Cave Allegory as a Model of Iconological Understanding

That's pretty heady stuff and quite a departure from the usual way of thinking about human beings and stories. This is so important to understanding why we love *Twilight,* though, that it's worth running through again from a different perspective. Namely, Plato's perspective. Whitehead famously observed that all philosophy existed as a series of footnotes to Plato. I think the same could be said of literary criticism, at least if you are trying to read the way you look at an icon.

The good news, if the idea of philosophy gives you hives, is that Plato doesn't write philosophy the way Kierkegaard, Arendt, or Kant did. He even insisted in the *Seventh Letter* that he had never written a word of philosophy in his life. His genre of choice was the dialogue, after all, the ancient world equivalent of a screenplay, rather than dry treatises. Plato wrote philosophical dramas featuring Socrates, his teacher, in dynamic question and answer sessions with fascinating people, many of whom were well known Athenians. Plato is more like Shakespeare and Steven Spielberg than Spinoza or Spengler. He doesn't dictate doctrine; he tells stories and asks his friends what they think (and then some more questions about what they think...).

9 "Does it make you better, wiser, *and* happier? And do you *like* it?" (Mark Koonz, "George Sayer on C.S. Lewis' Definition of a Great Book: Excerpts from our Conversation," *CSL: The Bulletin of the New York C. S. Lewis Society,* December, 2006).

One of his better stories and probably the most famous is the Cave Allegory (*Republic*, VII; 514a–520a). It's very short and you can read it online in a few minutes.[10] The story is a short course in seeing the world as a transparency and translucency – and about not being deceived by the surface appearances of things. It goes something like this:

Imagine human beings in a cave with their heads and necks bound in such a way that they can only look straight ahead and at a wall opposite the entrance. Their light doesn't come from the entrance but from a fire "burning far above and behind them." In front of this fire there is a wall that acts like a puppet show box. On the top of the wall, people who are not chained down carry figures of men, animals, and other things so their shadows are projected on the far wall. These shadows are the only things the cave prisoners can see and know. The shadows are their reality. "Such men would hold that the truth is nothing other than the shadows of artificial things."

Socrates, who tells the Allegory to Glaucon, then describes a prisoner who is liberated by force and dragged out from the wall of shadows and his chains, past the fire and wall over which the figures are held, and up to the cave entrance and out into the light. This is not a happy man. At first, he is unable to see things at the wall and fire as they are because he only recognizes image-shadows as reality.

Then, in the light outside the cave, he is all but blinded, "his eyes full of [the sun's] beam and... unable to see even one of the things said to be true." Slowly, though, his eyes would adjust to the light and he would be able to see shadows, reflections, objects, people, and finally the stars, moon, sunlight, and the sun itself. Finally, he could understand the sun is "the source of the seasons and the years, and the steward of all things in the visible place, and is in a certain way the cause of all those things he and his companions [in the cave] had been seeing."

In the book in *The Republic* just previous to the Allegory of the Cave, Socrates has explained to Glaucon a "metaphor of the Sun" in which the sun is a natural cipher for "the Idea of the Good" or God, "what provides the truth to the things known and gives the power to the one who knows" (*Republic*, VI; 508 e). The prisoner able to see and know the sun in the Cave Allegory experiences the truth behind the shadow images in the cave's darkness.

---

10 Try http://webspace.ship.edu/cgboer/platoscave.html

Socrates also makes it clear that this "enlightened" or "illumined" prisoner is in for a very hard time. He's quite happy now that he sees things as they are and feels nothing but pity for his friends back in the hole. But what happens if he goes back into the cave?

First, it's clear that would be something he'd try to avoid having to do at all costs. Better a slave in the sunshine than a king in what C. S. Lewis called "the Shadowlands." But if he did go back, he'd be in a fix. While his eyes adjusted, for one thing, he'd seem a moron whose eyes were damaged by his time outside the cave. If he tried to free the other prisoners and help them escape, Socrates is confident that the slaves would kill him rather than question the reality of the shadows.

"Don't be surprised," therefore, that the prisoners who have come back "aren't willing to mind the business of human beings" who think shadows are reality and truth. "Their souls are always eager to spend their time above."

Socrates, of course, finally spells out for Glaucon what the Allegory is about. *We* are the people in the cave. Our understanding of reality, the ephemeral quantities of matter and energy we think of as "real things," are just shared beliefs about shadows on the cave wall. The Good, the True, and Beautiful, the greater reality of things, are only knowable in escaping the cave and knowing the Idea of the Good itself, "what provides the truth to the things known."

What does this have to do with literature?

Good question.

The first part of the answer is in realizing that this isn't just Plato's otherworldly fantasy. This story for shadow-landers like you and me about the nature of reality and how we know (or don't know) is pretty much the Christian consensus from Pentecost up to and into the so-called Enlightenment and Age of Empiricism we live in now. As English literature, like it or not, is a Christian show, *Beowulf* to Joyce's *Ulysses*, in which Christian writers write for a Christian audience for their greater life in Christ, novels, poems, and plays almost have to be understood in light (sic) of Plato's Cave Allegory.

Believe it or not, the four levels of meaning correspond not only with traditional Jewish and Christian reading of revealed texts at four layers but also with Plato's four levels of knowledge he describes just before the Cave Allegory in his Divided Line Analogy (*Republic*, VI; 509d-513e) about the visible and intelligible worlds.[11]

11 See the Divided Line page on Wikipedia for a helpful introduction (http://

Stories in the western tradition can be sorted pretty much into two piles; a heap for those that reinforce the delusions of the shadows projected on the cave wall and another for the ones that make us feel our chains, stretch our necks, maybe even give us an imaginative experience of the noetic reality in the sunlight outside the cavern. Reading books is either an enlightening and liberating experience (and, yes, the Cave Allegory is one of the reasons we talk about "enlightenment" the way we do) or just entertainment to distract us from the darkness, smoke, and discomfort of life underground.

Either way, uplifting or dissipating, everything written is in some sense an allegory. The words on the page, the stories, sentiments, and sentience of them are not the things referred to themselves but signs that make us recall them or imagine them. And the meaning of everything written beneath the surface narration and morality, the first two iconological layers and the usual limit of contemporary criticism, is just a going deeper into the allegory and reflecting on what the story is calling up in us. If there are only two piles of books, I think we have to distinguish three types of reading we do:

1. *Novels Confirming the Shadows:* The shadows on the cave wall are the delusions, concerns, and blind-spots of our historical age. The biggest of these is usually tagged atheistic naturalism, the belief that the core reality is matter and energy quantities and that life is meaningless. Reading that confirms this view are the works celebrated by literary critics and despised by book buyers. Beautiful and majestic in language, these works bring our attention to our experience of the shadows on the wall and our chains, even our pathetic longing for a non-existent Edenic reality outside the cave.
2. *Novels freeing us from the agonies of our individual corner of the Cave:* Per Eliade, reading serves a mythic or spiritually liberating function in a secular culture because it frees us from our ego concerns and self-pre-occupation, flesh before spirit. A story well told or engaging film liberates us for a few hours from "me." If you're reading Fleming's *James Bond* adventures, Mickey Spillane mysteries, and Zane Grey westerns, the search pretty

---

en.wikipedia.org/wiki/Divided_line) and the chart detailing the Platonic understanding of soul faculties corresponding to visible and intelligible realities in the explanation of the 'Allegory of the Divided Line' in Allan Bloom's translation of *Plato's Republic*, Basic Books, 1968, p. 464.

much ends when the roller coaster comes to a stop; beyond story and moral (or lack of morals), it's time for another book.

But while reading, at least, the ugliness and darkness of the Cave was forgotten and the experience, consequently, awakens our spiritual faculty to reality beyond the shadows. *All popular reading* — to include Fleming, Spillane, and Grey — in a profane culture like our own serves a mythic or religious function because of our "suspension of disbelief" while reading or watching a movie. This disconnecting from our selfish concerns lifts us to, he thought, a better place something like religious ritual and sacraments are meant to take us.

3. *Novels taking us to the Cave mouth or into the Light:* The "good stuff," though, on second, third, and fourth readings reveals political and social commentary or allegory and, in real treasures, an escape from the cave via a truly mythic experience. There are books and story artists – poets, playwrights, and novelists – that deliberately or unconsciously take us up to the cave mouth and force us to look out into the Light. These works make us return again and again and again for a refresher course.

According to the "three literary pigs" of deconstruction, genre taxonomy, and literary aesthetics, though, a written work has value insomuch as it makes the shadows on the wall more rather than less real to us. Using book sales as a gauge of what we want to read tells us that thinking people not entirely hypnotized by televised images in the living room of our homes have had enough of these shadows. Human desire, as a consequence of human spiritual orientation, is all for the pursuit of illuminating and enlightening reading experience. We want those books that engage us most profoundly and orient us most surely to the Light outside the Cave's darkness and shadows.

Stephenie Meyer's *Twilight* Saga is one of those reading experiences.

Shadow Lands or Earthly Paradise? A Battle of Perspectives

Understanding the artistry of this sort of writing is the work of iconological criticism, and, as applied to the *Twilight* books, the heart of *Spotlight*. Iconological criticism differs from modern criticism in orientation – outside the Cave rather than on the wall's shadows and our chains – and, consequently, in method. To "get" the four layers of meaning unwrapped by traditional literary thinking requires thinking about thinking for a moment to understand how our knowledge or knowing works on four levels or senses.

The biggest difference in how individuals and civilizations see things is between those who believe in the shadows and others who think the light is more real. Swift wrote a very short and very funny book about this conflict called, appropriately, *The Battle of the Books.* Real quickly, in *Battle* the Ancients in a library, those books by Classical philosophers and traditional thinkers, come to life and have an overnight war with the Moderns, books by philosophers and thinkers of the 17th and 18th centuries for the most part. It's Aristotle, Homer, and Virgil against Hobbes, Descartes, and Wotton.

Their disagreement is fundamentally about which end of the telescope to look through. To the Ancients, to understand things – everything from a stone, to a person or an idea – we need to look outward to see intelligible rather than sensible things to grasp its inner principle or *logos*. To Moderns, this was so much nonsense, quite literally. Reality was solid and subject to sense perception. Rather than wisdom and communion with the principle of existence and nature, they sought scientific knowledge through examination of the hard surface facts of measurable matter and energy.

The Moderns win the day in the "real world" of history if not in Swift's story, but, as we've seen, the battle goes on. The best writers of the centuries before and after Swift have championed character over ego. To our great benefit, they have celebrated truth, beauty, and goodness before advantage, utility, and power against the always growing consensus that only matter and energy are real. As a rule, we see the world and our way of knowing it as Harry Potter does at his meeting with Dumbledore in *Deathly Hallows*; it's either "real" or "just in my head." Real knowledge is the facts we have of material things from sense perception and is objective; anything else is subjective, unverifiable delusion or just fantasy cooked up between my ears.

Writers of the classical and romantic traditions, in contrast, think like Headmaster Dumbledore. What is most real is the noetic or spiritual faculty "in your head" that is the same inner principle or *logos* as what brings every reality into existence. Things of matter and energy we can perceive through our senses are much less real because they are accidental combinations of their inner principles and relatively ephemeral stuff. Principles, in comparison and in themselves, are eternal.

Which brings us back to the four layers of interpretation.

The word "layers" suggests, inevitably and unfortunately, that there is separation or spaces keeping different meanings in air-tight compartments. Not true. The layers are experienced *simultaneously* in the surface story, albeit unconsciously.

The historical reason we have these four layers of literary interpretation and understanding is that traditionally scripture was read this way, beginning with Hebrew interpreters of the Old Testament in the 2nd Century, if certainly Plato's Cave Allegory points to a very similar perspective. The acronym for these four layers in Hebrew and Aramaic was P-R-D-S (frequently 'PaRDeS' or "Garden" in Hebrew): P standing for *pashat* or 'simple,' R for *remez* meaning 'hint,' D for *drash* meaning 'search,' and S for *sod* or 'hidden.'[12]

This tradition is not arbitrary or just a historical artifact. The reason it worked for interpretations of the world and man for Plato and for understanding the levels of meaning in Old and New Testament studies, is because reality itself has four dimensions and the human person has corresponding means of knowing these diverse aspects of the real as explained above. I've put our information, opinion, science, and wisdom into a chart so you can see the corresponding types of understanding, their objects, how we perceive them, and what we call this kind of knowledge:

---

12 See http://www.zworld.com.au/2006/04/03/pardes-the-four-levels-of-interpretation/ for a helpful introduction to 'Garden' thinking and Aquinas' *Summa Theologica* 1.1.10 for an exploration of its use in understanding Scripture: http://www.newadvent.org/summa/1001.htm#article10 (Article 10. Whether in Holy Scripture a word may have several senses?)

Under-standing	Realm	Object	Perception Filter	Way of Knowing
'P' Surface	Visible	Material Things, images	Senses	Information, data
'R' Moral	Visible	Good/Bad	Beliefs	Opinion, Argument
'D' Allegorical	Intelligible	Qualities, ideas, math	Logic	Demonstrated Knowledge
'S' Anagogical	Intelligible	Truth, Beauty, Virtue, inner principles	Intellect (Nous, Logos, Conscience)	Spiritual Knowledge, Wisdom

To simplify aggressively, as 'Moderns' we think the top two 'layers' of boxes in this chart are the core of reality. We sense real things and abstract our ideas from the data bank of our sensory perception, which abstractions become less real the less tangible or measurable they become. A thermometer gauging the temperature of water coming to boil is an indicator of something very real; your opinions about right and wrong, logic removed from sensory data, and religious beliefs and doctrines are increasingly *less* real.

Traditional philosophers, the best poets and story tellers of ancient times, and many of more recent centuries have seen things, in contrast, from the bottom of the chart up. They believed that the conscience or inner heart was of the same intellective substance as the creative principle and unity of existence. It was through this intellect or 'nous' that we know anything, "like" recognizing "like" as we recognize ourselves in a mirror. It perceived the eternal essences of things which are eternal the way a nose smells an aroma.

Working our way up the chart, then, from this traditional perspective, our knowledge has increasingly *less* dependable foundation the farther we move away from eternal and unchanging ideas and what we know is only more and more about ever changing things. Data and information about ephemera is useless, especially compared to wisdom or spiritual knowledge that is not conceptual but permeates the whole person, body and soul. Physical things, understood right side up, are accidental abstractions of substantive principles or ideas rather than "concrete" reality from which ideas are drawn out more or less arbitrarily.[13]

Hence our difficulty and skepticism, as Cave dwellers hypnotized by the naturalist shadows, about anagogical meaning. Rather than reading from the bottom up with the Ancients and artists, we view reality as empirical scientists and materialists say we should. We think 'anagogical meaning' has to be made up or "entirely subjective," maybe even projection or delusion, especially the further we get from the dependable, simple surface meaning.

Here is where literature comes in – and why cultural subversives from the Lake Poets to our day, the resistance fighters in the very real Battle of the Books against a dehumanizing materialism, have taken up arms against the empiricists with fairy tales, satire, and fantasy fiction. Every time we read a novel or watch a play,[14] we suspend our disbelief in spiritual reality and substance – and we experience them, almost always unconsciously, in the story we lose ourselves in. This experience is an immersion simultaneously in all the layers of meaning and, just as much as our atrophied noetic faculty permits or is capable of, we take in the anagogical layer with the allegorical, moral, and surface messages.

The skeptic can deny, consciously and discursively, both that there is a faculty of 'mind' that is not a function of the brain organ and that there is a spiritual meaning this relatively cardiac intelligence perceives. Deny it or not, as much as the skeptic suspends disbelief and enters into story, he or she is taking a mythic-meaning bath. Mircea Eliade's aside in *The Sacred and the Profane* that entertainments serve a mythic and religious function in a secular culture is precisely about this baptism of the imagination, willing or unwilling.

What better way, then, to attack the powerful and undermine their hold on the hearts and minds of people in the cave? Tell them stories about the light and the true, good, and beautiful to create in them, so

13 See James Cutsinger, "The Codifying of Unintelligence" on the deceptive appeal to "concrete" things as a basis of knowing: http://www.cutsinger.net/wordpress2/?p=150

14 This much less true of a television or movie experience because our imagination is not engaged here in the same way or depth it is in story that is heard or read. The realism of the experience does not allow us, in large part, to suspend our disbelief as profoundly or for as long a time, if, undeniably, it remains the greater part of self-less experience in our godless culture, hence our obsession with Hollywood and its mostly demeaning productions.

much as they are capable of it, an experience of life in the sunshine and an appetite for more of it.

True Art is Revolutionary but Never Didactic or Boring

In contrasting Milton and Shakespeare, Martin Lings argues that Shakespeare's greatness is the scope of his ambition as a playwright and how anyone and everyone in his audience benefitted from his edifying and uplifting artistry according to his capacity. Like John Ruskin, Lings tells us that story and setting trump sermons in delivering meaning:

> Now Shakespeare also seeks to justify the ways of God to man. That is, beyond doubt, the essence of his purpose in writing. But his justification is on an intellectual plane, where alone it is possible; and this brings us back to the theme of his plays, for the intellect is none other than the lost faculty of vision which is symbolized by the Holy Grail and by the Elixir of Life.
>
> In considering how Shakespeare conveys his message to us we must remember that the true function of art is not didactic. A great drama or epic may contain little or much teaching of a didactic kind, but it does not rely on that teaching in order to gain its ultimate effect. Its function is not so much to define spiritual wisdom as to give us a taste of that wisdom, each according to his capacity.
>
> We may quote in this connection a profound remark which has been made about sacred art in Christianity: 'it sets up against the sermon which insists on what must be done by one who would become holy, a vision of the cosmos which is holy through it beauty; it makes men participate naturally and almost involuntarily in the world of holiness.'
>
> In its original context it is the great Norman and Gothic Cathedrals, the sanctuaries in which the sermon is preached, which immediately spring to mind as examples of art which reveals a vision of the cosmos. But drama can also yield such a vision; and to reveal the beauty and thereby the harmony of the universe is to justify the ways of God.[15]

We get the iconological tool of literary "slow mining" from Aquinas and a medieval tool for interpreting scripture through artists like Dante and Shakespeare. Dante instructs Can Grande to read *The Divine Comedy* on four layers of meaning, says in the *Convivio* that his

15 Martin Lings, *Shakespeare's Window Into the Soul: The Mystical Wisdom in Shakespeare's Characters*, Inner Traditions, 2006, New York, pp 193-195

cantos "may be understood, and they must be explained by allegory," and even makes that argument again within Canto IX of the *Inferno*.[16] Medieval man and the great writers of this era see the world through the four-focaled vision of these ways of knowing and incorporate it into their work via allegorical symbols and hermetic artistry. The symbols and artistry then become the stuff and substance of English literature from Shakespeare to Rowling.

As I discuss in *Harry Potter's Bookshelf* and *The Deathly Hallows Lectures,* the setting and scaffolding of story, in Rowling's work the Hero's Journey formula and symbols of literary alchemy, speak to our spiritual faculty, the intellect or nous, in the language it understands just as a cathedral and play give us a taste of a greater reality and experience of life in it. It is this artistry and the symbolism of vision, the books' anagogical layer, that, in the end, make our hearts glad and our spirits rise when we read Harry's adventures.[17]

When a book takes off, that is, when journalists describe publication parties as a "mania" and there are lines of customers outside bookstores and theatres waiting for greater experience of story, that is when we need to be thinking about allegory and anagogical or sublime meaning. People's hearts are resonating with their reflection in a greater reality.

Conclusion: Reading *Twilight* At Four Layers

Hey, it's time to start unwrapping the four layers of meaning in Stephenie Meyer's *Twilight* books! To wrap up this preface, then, all reading is disengagement from ego and an escape from the delusion of persona into greater reality, not from the world but *into* the world, the. Better books, the ones we want to re-enter again and again, always foster our spiritual growth and transformation.

Reading them is an exploration and depiction of Spirit. In these poems, plays, and novels we experience some interface of rightly ordered or right-side-up soul with the Absolute, albeit only imaginatively. Our choice to join the protagonist, to identify with him or her in the journey, romance, mystery, or coming-of-age trial is our deliberate turning away from even our actively combating evil within ourselves, "evil" understood as that which keeps us from our shared knowing and illumination, our coming into the kingdom of heaven.

---

16 *Epistle to Can Grande*: paragraph 7, http://www.english.udel.edu/dean/cangrand.html; *Convivio* 11.1, *Inferno*, IX, 60-63

17 See *The Deathly Hallows Lectures*, Chapter 5, 'The Seeing Eye'

Reading is the secular person's inner *jihad* or crusade. It is not a distraction for the mindless or a confrontation with existential despair for the elect as literary critics would have us believe. Reading makes us more human; our pleasure in it is the best measure of any book's worth because that pleasure's depth signifies how profoundly we left ourselves and entered into the story and how much of the allegorical and sublime meaning we captured while our disbelief was suspended.

Do you blush when you talk about reading *Twilight*? You don't need to. The folks looking down their noses at Young Romance fiction have missed the substantial meaning at the surface, moral, allegorical, and anagogical layers that Mrs. Meyer has deliberately stacked in and with no little artistry. As you'll soon see, the Forks Saga is not magisterial in language or composition; but its romance, Eden allegory, story of soul's seeking and transformation or apotheosis is as engaging and ennobling as any of the Greats and far more accessible.

Let's start at the surface!

Chapter 1

The Surface Layer of Meaning:

How Mrs. Meyer's Choices about Voice, Plot, and Genre Engage Us

When I give talks at libraries, bookstores, churches, and schools about the layers of meaning in *Harry Potter*, the senses of the text, I find almost invariably a certain resistance to the idea that there are multiple meanings to the stories occurring simultaneously. This is a natural problem because every reader experiences consciously only one layer of meaning, the surface narrative, at least on first reading, through which layer all the other meanings filter in via the writer's artistry with character, plot, and symbols. Though it is the easiest sense of the story to get, consequently, and the only one each reader has in common with every other reader, it is easily the most important.

To risk a food analogy, if the novel is a cake, the surface layer of meaning is the icing of that cake. If we find the icing inviting and it brings up in us the desire to eat a piece of the cake, the odds are very good that we will eat at least a piece and enjoy it. Even though the icing is not the cake, however, if we do not enjoy it, even finding the sight of it repugnant, it is unlikely that we will make it through a whole piece of the cake or even try it.

The narrative line is, like the cake icing, the most important layer of artistry and meaning because the surface story is our point of entry and engagement with the story. All the other layers have to come through the surface story, so, if we're hooked by the narrative line and suspend our disbelief and skeptical faculties, the deeper meanings and artistry have a chance of reaching us.

The plot, character, and drama we share with friends who ask what the story we're reading is about is the surface layer of meaning or "narrative line." The artistry of the surface layer is how the writer chooses to tell this story. Unwrapping the meaning of the narrative line, then, is essentially just a review of the choices an author made in constructing his or her story and the effects of those choices, individually and collectively, on the reader.

The three surface story choices Mrs. Meyer made that I will lay out in this chapter for your reflection are about:

- "narratological voice," who tells the story,
- "plot," the pace, facts, and rhythm of the story, and
- "genre," the kind of story we're reading with the attendant conventions of such stories and our expectations for it as readers.

The specific choices Mrs. Meyer made and how the combinations work together are the ingredients of her story-cake's icing. If right, the story is devoured and reader begs for second and third helpings. If wrong, the reader will claim, if polite, that he or she is dieting and skipping desserts. Nothing but the compulsion of a school assignment will get the repulsed reader to try it or finish it (and most students today, I think, will read the Wikipedia synopsis of the story instead, the nutritional equivalent of taking a vitamin rather than eating real food).

Let's start with what may be the most important decision an author makes because it is the person we meet when we open the door of a book's cover: the "voice" in which the story is told.

Finding Our Voice: An Author's Choices for Who Narrates the Story

Because we get the book we read as a finished product, it's easy to overlook that it came into existence as only one of an indefinite number of possibilities and as the specific product of a series of choices made by the author. Of these choices, none affects our experience of the book more than the decision about "who" will be telling the story. This "who," in geek-speak the "narratological voice" or just "voice," is the greater part of our listening or hearing the tale being told because this voice, disembodied or personal, is our relationship or interface with the text. Almost everything about the sequence and manner of the storytelling, and, consequently, if we listen attentively, depends on who narrates the story.

An author has three basic choices for the voice he or she can frame the story to be told. *Moby Dick*, for example, is told from the perspective of Ishmael the survivor, not from the perspective of Herman Melville the author per se. Ishmael speaks for himself straight to the reader as "I" or "me," so this perspective is called "First person narration" (because in grammar "I" and "We" are first person, "you" singular and plural are second person, and "he/she/it" and "they" are third person).

Melville's Chase-the-Divine-White-Whale story would be completely different if another person told the story (Ahab? Queequeg?) from their equally limited first person perspective or if the story were told from high above the top sail from which God-like height everything can be seen. This God-perspective is called "Third Person, omniscient" because it is a "see all" perspective not restricted to any person's isolated view.

These are the two big options an author has when writing a novel. "Do I tell it from a narrator's experience of the tale a la Dr. Watson in the Sherlock Holmes cases? Or do I tell it as God sees it unfolding in time?" Open up any anthology of detective fiction and quickly check to see whether a story is told either by a fictional narrator in the "I saw this" and "then we did that" perspective or if the story comes from the author in the role of an all-seeing god. It's usually one or the other.

There are a few variants on these two options, the one readers today almost certainly know is the storytelling perspective Joanne Rowling borrowed from her favorite author and book, Jane Austen's *Emma*. This "narratological voice" is called "third person, limited omniscient view" which is a half-way point between one person telling the story as an 'I' and the author telling the story as an omniscient 'eye.' In *Emma* and the Potter Saga, the story is told from the view just above Emma's and Harry's heads. Neither one is telling the story but we never get to see what characters outside of his or her sight are doing. The surprise endings in each of Harry's adventures, as I explain in *Unlocking Harry Potter*, depends on how our attention is misdirected from important things because of what Harry sees, ignores, or never sees.

Mrs. Meyer's three possible voice choices, then, are:

- **First person:** Is it one person relating their experience?
- **Third person:** Is it an omniscient God with a view of everything happening that he shares?

- **Third person limited omniscience:** Or is it a view with a specific character focus but not in his or her voice?

The voices of *Twilight* are all one voice, albeit from different people. Bella Swan, our heroine, is the narrator for *Twilight, New Moon, Eclipse,* and three fourths of *Breaking Dawn*. Jacob Black, her furry friend, picks up the story-telling burden in that part of *Breaking Dawn* during which Bella is locked down in the Cullen household because of her difficult pregnancy. Edward Cullen is the narrator of *Midnight Sun*, Mrs. Meyer's aborted re-telling of *Twilight* from Edward's perspective.

You cannot get much more different than Bella, Edward, and Jacob (at least not in Forks) but *all* the stories are told in the same voice, namely, first-person narration. Bella and her two boyfriends each tell their part of the *Twilight* story exactly as they are experiencing it and we relate to it, consequently, exactly as much as we accept and begin to care about the story-teller.

I'll go so far, in fact, as to say that the test of a successful "voice choice" is the degree to which we readers identify with the hero or heroine. What does that mean for *Twilight*?

Bella is the narrator for the whole series except for the part of *Breaking Dawn* mentioned above, in which she is idle, and *Midnight Sun*. She is *the* character who tells us her story in the first person a la Ishmael, Dr. Watson, and Holden Caulfield. Does this voice choice work?

Oh, yeah, you wouldn't be reading this if it didn't. If readers for the most part didn't love Miss Swan, the series would have been deep-sixed after the first novel instead of becoming the international publishing phenomenon it has.

Face it, she's a likeable person. Bella Swan is a modest, self-conscious, sacrificial young woman with a self-deprecating sense of humor. Her conversation with the reader, her telling of the story, works as a narrative device because we like her and we want to hear her story and learn what happens to her. We enjoy her observations and company.

What's not to like? She's a good girl whose several moral and intelligence failings don't make reading her stories painful and yet these idiosyncrasies are substantial enough that we can sympathize with her struggles. Mrs Meyer wins sympathy of reader, too, going beyond just making her pleasant company, via making Bella something of an orphan. She has parents but Bella acts like a parent for both her parents and is left essentially with no one looking out for her interests except herself. Nothing wins a reader's heart more than the plucky orphan or latchkey kid in difficult circumstances; think Oliver Twist, Holden Caulfield, and Harry Potter.

Of course, there are a lot of readers who *can't stand* Bella and for them liking *Twilight* is as unlikely as our enjoying the cake whose icing makes us gag. I'm not sure if this is just a matter of not liking Bella or the way she tells the story or even her relationship with Edward. It seems possible that Bella-bashing is due in part at least to the type of story she is telling as much as it is to how she tells the story or who she is. We'll come back to this in our discussion of genre.

For now, though, it's enough to note that Mrs. Meyer's choice of Bella as her *Twilight* narrator works. Her readers listen to, care about, and identify with her eventually at sufficient depth to enter into her story and "suspend disbelief." The story hooks begin with Bella's voice. They go in much deeper with the Blockbuster Novel plot.

The *Da Vinci Code* with Vampires: *Twilight's* Blockbuster Novel Formula

Mircea Eliade's thesis that stories in a secular culture serve a mythic or religious function, as explained earlier, assumes that these fictions are sufficiently engaging that they pull our attention away from the shadows on the Cave wall. Great stories help us disengage from our pre-occupation with our individual ego concerns, the necessary first step in the spiritual life. Before we can believe, we have to be able to "suspend our disbelief" that there is nothing greater than ourselves and our pursuit of advantage.

Oddly enough, tales can serve this religious function even if they are implicitly or explicitly anti-religious. Philip Pullman, the United Kingdom's "Un-Lewis" and public atheist, comes to mind, as does Dan Brown, the author of *The Da Vinci Code* and other blockbuster novels with an anti-clerical message.

I went to the same prep school as Mr. Brown, though I never met him that I can remember. His father was a teacher at the school so he grew up on campus and still lives in town. Though I am not a fan of his work, I can say that he has been wonderfully generous as an alumnus with the bounty his books have earned him.

I bring this up because another one of my classmates sent me an article from *Godspy* about Mr. Brown's genesis as an author, a piece called 'My Lunch with an Old Friend of Dan Brown Proves Revealing About *The DaVinci Code*.'[1] Two writers are tossing story ideas back and forth in a restaurant when the article's writer, a Catholic, begins to complain about the atheism and anti-Papism of *Code*. His friend tells him that Brown is neither atheist nor artist but a hack formula writer without any convictions:

> But Ted didn't rise to the bait [of my rant about Brown]. He just shook his head. "Dan Brown's not anti-Christian. He's not anti-anything. I doubt he's pro-anything, either, except pro-Dan Brown. That book has as much of an agenda as *The Complete Idiot's Guide to Hockey*. Dan Brown doesn't have enough conviction to make a decent agnostic. He grew up a faculty brat in New England, and I don't think he set foot off campus until he was in his 20s."
>
> I perked up, and ordered another beer. "You know Dan Brown?"
>
> "I knew him for years. He started out as a joke-book author." Ted said, dunking a clam-strip in tartar sauce. "Some of the jokes were funny. But he wanted to be a novelist. He kept pestering me about it, so finally I gave him this paperback, *Writing the Blockbuster Novel*, by Albert Zuckerman. It's a paint-by-numbers guide on how to write a page-turner. One important part of the formula was: Find a villain your readers can safely hate."
>
> "A few months later, Dan brought me this manuscript to read – and it followed the formula precisely ... as if he'd poured Jello into a mold. In this case, the 'safe villain' was the National Security Agency, government spies. It sold pretty well, and he kept on pounding out books – each time with a different 'safe villain.' Eventually, he started running out – Communism was gone, the Nazis were all dead.... That pretty much leaves the U.S. government, drug cartels, and the Catholic Church."

That's a fun story with just enough truth to make it interesting. Mr. Brown was a "faculty brat," he did write two humor books, and he claims to have been inspired by a Sidney Sheldon thriller, which, as much as he enjoyed it, he felt he could better with a novel of his own.[2] No mention of the Zuckerman "paint-by-number's guide, though, so I

---

1 John Zmirak, May 2006; http://oldarchive.godspy.com/reviews/My-Lunch-with-an-Old-Friend-of-Dan-Brown-by-John-Zmirak.cfm.html

2 BBC News, 'Decoding the Da Vinci Code Author, 7 April 2006; http://news.bbc.co.uk/2/hi/entertainment/3541342.stm

think we'll have to assume that part of the story is apocryphal.

What makes this relevant to a discussion of Mrs. Meyer's surface story choices is that she, like Mr. Brown, could also be accused of studying from the step-by-step advice in *Writing the Blockbuster Novel*. Here are the "musts" for any Blockbuster Novel according to Mr. Zuckerman:

- **High stakes:** "The life of at least one major character is usually in peril" and it is much better if the fates and lives of whole countries are in play.
- **Larger-than-Life Characters:** "Characters in fiction, as in life, are defined by what they do, and in big novels the main characters do extraordinary things."
- **The Dramatic Question:** The plot of the Blockbuster may be long and complicated with many plot turns, but "the book's *spine* – the ongoing central conflict around which the major characters interact, the main issue that drives and unites its myriad scenes – couldn't be more basic and clear cut."
- **High Concept:** The Blockbuster has "a radical or seemingly outlandish premise." "Big books need to be built on highly dramatic situations, plots that include bizarre and surprising actions and that lead to one powerful confrontation after the next."
- **Multiple points of view:** "The story is ... expressed through the feelings, thoughts, and sensibilities of a small number of major characters."
- **Setting:** Big books feature "new, unfamiliar, and even exotic environments."
- **Story Points and Pacing:** Blockbusters are fast paced and action laden with "ten to thirty story points within a chapter – small and middling actions that ideally should mount in intensity and lead inexorably to your climax."[3]

Zuckerman, an award-winning novelist and playwright as well as famous literary agent and "book doctor," says aspiring Blockbuster authors must answer "yes" to these questions:

3 Albert Zuckerman, *Writing the Blockbuster Novel*, Writer's Digest Books, Cincinnati, 1993, pgs 15-20, 159-160.

> Is what's at stake monumental, at least for my main character? Am I creating a character (or maybe two) who is extraordinary in some way, even larger than life? Can the thrust of my novel be summarized in a simple but strong dramatic question? Is my plot built around a high concept conflict...? Am I developing at least one character (and preferably more than one with whom the reader will become emotionally involved)? Am I placing my characters in an environment that is in some way unusual or exciting, one that will cause the reader to feel she's entering a largely new world?[4]

For the record, I don't think Mrs. Meyer has read Zuckerman's book. If she's following anyone's formula for story writing, it is Orson Scott Card's, her favorite living author, who has written extensively about his craft.[5] But her books do conform in large part to the Zuckerman recipe for engaging plot with notable breaks. Run through the bulleted points and questions above.

Larger than Life Characters? Can you say "immortal vampires" and "heroic Native American shape-changers"? Check that one off.

Dramatic Question? "Will Bella survive to wed Edward?" Got it.

High Concept? "There are supernatural beings about us, some struggling with the urge to eat us for lunch (or just a snack)." As premises go, that's about as outlandish as you can get without a time machine or space ship.

Setting? Besides Forks, a rather mundane backwoods town on the Olympic Peninsula, we get high blood pressure road trips to Phoenix, Arizona, to Volterra, Italy, and to magical Mountain Meadows for revelations and confrontations. This isn't your standard high school novel. Check off "unfamiliar, even exotic settings." Just going to the Cullen House or Quileute reservation, knowing the secret lives of the locals is like "entering a whole new world."

---

4 Zuckerman, op. cit.; pgs 21-22; see also http://easywaytowrite.com/writing_a_blockbuster_formula.html

5 Books by Card she has almost certainly read (she claims to have read everything he has written) are *How to Write Science Fiction and Fantasy* (Writer's Digest, 1990) and *Characters and Viewpoint* (Writer's Digest, 1988)

Story Points and Pacing? Go ahead, look yourself if you have the books nearby. Open up a chapter and identify the defining idea or event it has and as many smaller ideas, "story points" or "story turns," as you can find. Mrs. Meyer, as a rule, I'm pretty sure you'll find, does not keep pace with a Tom Clancy, Sidney Sheldon, or Dan Brown and knock out "ten to thirty" story-turns a chapter. In a romance, that would be headspinning and, with only one narrator, close to bizarre. But the story moves right along, with every chapter building up the tension and preparing us for the frenetic finale.

Multiple Points of View? That's a fail. It's all about Bella until *Breaking Dawn*.

High Stakes? Zuckerman's ideal blockbuster is all about an adventure in which, at least, the outcome of an international war is in the balance. He allows, though, that outside of the espionage thriller and techno-military heart-pounder, a story can achieve "high stakes" with just a touch of peril if romance is in the air:

> In many major women's novels, however, the principal stake is not life and death but with personal fulfillment, as with Scarlett in *Gone With The Wind* or Meggie in *The Thorn Birds*. Although this stake – the consummating or the not consummating of a love relationship – may in itself seem mundane, no more than the stuff of everyday life, the heroine's lusts, longings, and passions are imbued by their creators with such fierce and unrelenting intensity that what is at issue for them strikes the reader as powerfully as mayhem, murder, or national catastrophe.[6]

Bella's life is always at risk (or so Edward tells us) and she certainly has her share of Near Death Experiences – in Phoenix, Italy, on the cliffs of the Peninsula, in the Mountain Meadows, even walking the streets of laid back Port Angeles! But the "high stakes" of her story are primarily of the romantic kind, although we have political or military moments. Check that off.

If you had to describe the plot of any one of the *Twilight* Saga books or the series as a whole, I think this last point about the "high stakes" of romance fitting in the Blockbuster novel mold reflects one of Mrs. Meyer's story strengths. She doesn't write books that neatly fit into one, neat genre-formula pigeon hole. Or even two. Or three.

6 Zuckerman, op.cit., pages 15-16

They've vampire and werewolf books, right? Well, they have vampires and characters that shape change into monster-sized wolves, *but* they don't conform to any of the rules of vampire-literature canon.

It's chick lit, no? Sort of. It is about a young woman coming of age, but it isn't a boy-meets-girl, three step walk-off (as I'll explain in a moment).

Twilight is Blockbuster adventure then? Well, we do get that last second rescue in Phoenix in the first book. There is the exciting race across the Atlantic Ocean and the Volterra city square in *New Moon,* not to mention the meeting in the circular tower with the Volturi. And *Eclipse* gives us the deep background and an experience of an honest-to-god vampire battle with Newborns, featuring a man-to-enraged-vampire-woman fight to the death at story's end. *Breaking Dawn* offers both Bella's transition to life as a vampire and mommy *and* an international face-off with vampires of X-Men like super powers.

But with vampire love as its "high concept" and its principal setting being the only high school in North America, public or private, without school sports, band, newspaper, yearbook, or homecoming, *Twilight* is a stretch for Blockbuster status except for the success of its plot in engaging the reader. Twilight has plot to spare as teen romance in every book shifts gears about halfway through to finish with a CGI heavy chase and battle.

We'll come back to Mrs. Meyer's genre double-coding in a second. Here we just need to note that, unlike Proust and Joyce remembrance and reflection classics, her Twilight books give us the super-sized story points and plot to take our minds off the Cave wall and perhaps give us the break we need from projected shadows to think of better things.

Surface Meaning Essential: Look at the Cover, Dummy!

Zuckerman's *Writing the Blockbuster Novel* does tell us a lot about plot, not to mention the formula writing that broke records in the late 90s and early 21st century. Dan Brown, Tom Clancy, and their imitators have either read his book or figured out the connect-the-dots program themselves.

But *Blockbuster Novel* has a few funny recommendations, funny, that is, in hindsight. He was convinced, for example, in 1994 that "coming-of-age novels, I believe, are a big no-no for the author who aspires to write a big book."[7] Good thing that Joanne Rowling and Stephenie Meyer decided to test that "big no-no" or a lot of book stores and publishers would be out of business today.

Mr. Zuckerman also had misgivings about books not set in the present day. "For a writer attempting a blockbuster novel now... I would not recommend a historical setting." The book clubs don't like historical novels "and the clubs do reflect the tastes of the hard cover fiction buying public."[8]

The only blockbuster books I read, though, are the mega-bestsellers by Louis Bayard, Matthew Pearl, and writers like Jeb Rubenfeld, whose page turners are historical pieces featuring writers (see Longfellow and friends in Pearl's *The Dante Club*), great books (revel in Tony Tim's grown-up adventures within Dickensian London in Bayard's *Mr. Timothy*), and giant thinkers (match wits with Freud and Jung in the *fin de siècle* murder mystery in New York by reading Rubenfeld's *The Interpretation of Murder*).

I won't mention the industry of Jane Austen re-writes or Regency romances that aren't even explicitly about Austen's books.

Still, having just finished both Pearl's and Bayard's books on Edgar Allen Poe[9] – and loved them for what each said about Poe as a gothic and mystery writer by featuring him in gothic-laden detective stories – it is hard to deny their conformity to the *Blockbuster* formula. And so what? The books are gripping page-turners and laden with artistry and meaning that is fuel for edifying reflection among us cave dwellers.

But beyond plot and voice, the key to grasping the surface level of meaning in any story is the first thing we learn about a book. In fact, as you might expect in looking for the sense of a book that is supposed to be right up-front, the biggest part of the surface meaning as often as not can be discovered on the book's flaps or back cover description.

That's where we learn what kind of story the book is, right? Fiction or non-fiction, mystery or romance, gothic horror or espionage thriller, the cover should clue us in to what the author is writing and the "high concept" grab that will move us to buy the book or keep looking.

When I was a boy, back in the pre-historical past of vinyl LP record albums, three television stations, and the Four Food Groups, the

7 Zuckerman, op. cit., page 21

8 Op. cit, page 20

9 Louis Bayard, *The Pale Blue Eye;* Mathew Pearl, *The Poe Shadow*

divisions in Mall book stores and in libraries between genres like science fiction and "chic lit" was as clear as the chasm and Dewey Decimal breaks between cookbooks and Self-Help guides. Now, of course, latter-day Norman Vincent Peales write cookbooks and every book category seems to be eliding into two or three other categories. This is especially obvious in popular fiction.

Take Joanne Rowling's *Harry Potter,* the most popular book of our time, even something of a global and cross generational "shared-text." In the book stores and gas station convenience stores where they're sold (where aren't they sold?), how are they categorized? In those bricks-and-mortar book pavilions that don't have a section devoted just to Potter-mania, my experience is that the books are shelved in the children's or Young Adult departments.

That makes a certain sort of sorting sense, but, then again, not really. Adults have been the predominant buyers of these books since the third adventure was out in 1999. Among the adult fiction books, then, where do the *Potter* books belong?

This is not a silly question. When I talk to Harry's legion of devotees and serious reading fans, the first thing I try to get across is just what kind of story Ms. Rowling is writing, because without that base of understanding, her conformity to and departures from formula are very hard to grasp. And these readers, many of whom have read the 4100 pages of the Hogwarts Saga more than a few times, struggle to get what the core story genre is.

They're not stupid. Ms. Rowling has just obscured her central story by overlaying this genre with ten other story types and creating something of a story-melange or casserole. Every one of the ten chapters in my *Harry Potter's Bookshelf: The Great Books Behind the Hogwarts Adventure,* in fact, is devoted to explaining a different story-type that is an important part of understanding Harry.

That being said, there is a core genre in those books – the School Boy Novel – that is the skeletal system or story scaffolding over which all the other categories of story are draped. If you don't know anything about the School Boy Novel and its conventions, a lot of the fun of what Ms. Rowling does is going to go right by you, from the "mischievous twins" and "daffy French teacher" (Trelawney!) to the centrality of school sports and a beloved Headmaster.

It's a Young Adult-Suspense-Romance-Horror-Comedy, Right?

Stephenie Meyer's *Twilight* Saga readers have a similar struggle in coming to terms with the Bella and Edward story. The booksellers shelve them with 'Young Adult' books but that isn't how they were conceived or written:

> **Q: Did you have a YA/Teen audience in mind when you started writing your novels? Are you surprised at the cross-over in popularity of the books?**
>
> **A:** When I first started writing, I was my only audience. A few weeks in, my older sister joined the audience. So the entire time I was writing Twilight, my audience was an average of thirty years old. I was more surprised at how well the book ended up suiting the YA audience than I was that older readers enjoyed it, too. I love the cross-over popularity.[10]
>
> **Q: Did you know from the beginning that *Twilight* would be a young adult (YA) novel? What authors or works in the genre are your favorites?**
>
> A: In the beginning, I didn't even know that *Twilight* was going to be a *novel*. I had no expectations or direction. I was just writing because it felt wonderful and because I wanted to see where the story was going. Soon, I was also writing because I'd fallen in love with my characters and I felt like I was neglecting them when I wasn't writing. I didn't think of publishing until the moment that I wrote what I knew was going to be the very last line.
>
> Even then, I didn't think YA. After all, I'd written the story just for myself (and my big sister, who was the only one allowed to know what I was doing), and I was 29. It wasn't until I started researching agents that I considered submitting the story to some who represented YA (because it was set in high school). I had it submitted as both adult and YA; it was a YA agent who first showed interest.
>
> My favorite YA authors are L.M. Montgomery (I still read the *Anne of Green Gables* series through every other year or so), C.S. Lewis, Louisa May Alcott... It's kind of hard to remember who is YA and who isn't — I read adult books before I went back for YA, so some books — like *Romeo and Juliet* and *Gone with the Wind* — I think of as YA because I read them before I was ten.[11]

---

10 Chapters.indigo.ca online bookstore interview; http://blogs.myspace.com/index.cfm?fuseaction=blog.view&friendId=454417681&blogId=494700862

11 William Morris, 'Interview: *Twilight* author Stephanie Meyer,' *A Motley*

These books aren't Judy Blume novels targeted at tweenies or adolescents. They were written for the author and her sister, a point we will have to return to because these two women are the *real* audience of the books, and neither of them was a "young adult."

Or a vampire or a vampire book fan. Ask 20 people on the street what sort of books these novels are, though, and my experience is 19 of them will say they're "vampire stories."

And they're wrong.

Of course, there **are** vampires in the *Twilight* books but that is where the conjunction of *Twilight* and vampire-fiction ends, be it classic horror as in Bram Stoker's *Dracula,* Hollywood schlock, or Anne Rice's *Interview* and postmodern *Buffy.* Mrs. Meyer hasn't read *Dracula* or ever seen a vampire movie.[12]

The central vampire characters, the Cullen family (they run around as a clan — three other couples plus Edward), are "vegetarians," meaning they feed on large animals instead of humans. Other vampires in the story feed on humans — there's one particularly gruesome scene in the second novel — but Edward and his family have taken an oath not to.

Meyer's vampires don't turn into bats or sleep in coffins. They don't have fangs, and they can even go out during the day, though they prefer darkness because they are simply too beautiful in the sunlight.

Essentially, she has created an entirely new vampire myth.

Vision: Mormon Arts and Culture, 26 October 2005; http://www.motleyvision.org/2005/interview-twilight-author-stephanie-meyer/

12 Gregory Kirschling, 'Stephenie Meyer's 'Twilight' Zone,' Entertainment Weekly, 10 August 2007; http://www.ew.com/ew/article/0,,20049578,00.html; see also Chapters.indigo.ca online bookstore interview, op.cit:; **Q: Do you have your favourite vampire movies and books? What are they and why?**
A: I have never seen a vampire movie. I think I read one Anne Rice novel a million years ago when I was in college, but I don't even remember which one it was. I'm not a horror person.
Q: Where does the mythology behind the Twilight Series come from? Do you find that you are influenced at all by the popular "vampire themed shows" like Buffy the Vampire Slayer, vampire novels and subculture, or, do you try your best to ignore this? Do you feel that your novels are a newer extension of this trend?
A: It's easy to be positive that I am not influenced by Buffy, because I've never watched an episode of *Buffy the Vampire Slayer.* I've never been into the horror genre, so I was fairly free of preconceived notions when I began constructing the Twilight mythology. I think the roots of my mythology are much more influenced by superheroes than by monsters.

"I haven't even seen *Interview with the Vampire.* I change the channel really fast when horror movies come on," she says. "I know the [traditional vampire] stories because everyone does, so I knew I was breaking the rules, but I didn't really think about it much until I started worrying. But vampire fans have been very open-minded." [13]

As we will see in the coming chapters, in addition to creating "an entirely new vampire myth" outside vampire literary canon's rules, Mrs. Meyer combines and re-shapes her core genre by grafting in elements of:

- Satire – think of the Zombie flick and zombie life Bella leads in *New Moon* (we'll get to this in Chapter 3)
- Hero's Journey – Bella's name means "beautiful swan" and her adventures are about her transformation from ugly duckling to goddess in something like apotheosis (see chapter 4)
- Gothic horror – think of the Volturi castle in Volterra and the lunch they enjoy just off stage (this plays into the morality of the books discussed in the next chapter)
- Alchemical drama – Mrs. Meyer, a big Shakespeare fan, includes hermetic imagery and symbolism as a hat tip to the Bard (chapter 4)
- Everyman Allegory – Bella and Edward, believe it or not, are stick-figure story stand-ins for, well, skip to chapter 3 on allegory for the details.
- Postmodern morality play – As all books, plays, and movies of our time, the central themes of the books are about the essential role of choice in escaping prejudice and becoming free. Mrs. Meyer is no exception as we'll discuss in Chapter 2.
- Mary Sue 'Coming of Age' tale – Bella's story could be re-titled *Jane Eyre with Vampires,* something like *Pride and Prejudice with Zombies,* because the resemblances are so heavy. We'll discuss in chapter 5 how much of *Twilight,* especially Mrs. Meyer's religious beliefs, are informed by her experiences and wish-fulfilling projection into story.

---

13 Megan Irwin, 'Charmed: Stephenie Meyer's vampire romance novels made a Mormon mom an international sensation,' *Phoenix New Times,* July 12, 2007, http://www.phoenixnewtimes.com/content/printVersion/481142

Again, as was true with the category-casserole and publishing juggernaut *Harry Potter*, so is it true that *Twilight* has a host of story elements that are grafted onto a single, core genre that supports the rest like a shop window mannequin. If you've ever been to a *Twilight* fan convention, book or movie release, where the teen girls show up in disproportionate numbers to wave their flags for 'Team Edward' or 'Team Jacob,' you know what the literary potato is in Mrs. Meyer's potato salad: Romance.

As she said when asked about the sort of story she is telling:

> **Q: If you pitched the first book to publishers as a "suspense romance horror comedy," which of those do you think your books are *most*?**
>
> **A.** I think that it's romance more than anything else, but it's just not *that* romance-y. It's hard to nail down, but romance tends to be my favorite part of any book or movie, because that's really the strongest emotion.

What's a romance? You know, a *love story.* One with a happy, Boy-Gets-Girl ending, too.

Romeo-Vampire Meets Girl, Vampire Loses Girl, Vampire Gets Girl

The romance story of 'Boy Meets Girl' formula, what Northrop Frye calls 'Comedy' in his four literary myths, is as old as Plautus in Rome, as venerable as Shakespeare's *Midsummer Night's Dream,* and as novel as the film *When Harry Met Sally*, originally titled *Boy Meets Girl.* The romantic formula that literature critics qualify as "comedy" even if it isn't just about being funny, goes something like this:

> The comedic plot usually follows this basic structure: a young man, the hero (*eiron*), wants a young woman but is prevented from having her because of an arbitrary rule or law put in place by an existent and undesirable society. The hero's desires can also be obstructed by a blocking character (*alazon*), who is sometimes a paternal figure such as the forbidding father type. Eventually a twist in fate, comic discovery (*anagnorisis*) or resolution occurs which enables the hero to have his way.
>
> The movement of the comedic plot leads the hero and heroine from one type of society to another. The existent society is likely to appear to the audience or reader as being absurd or oppressive

> and the new one desirable and correct. The existent society is thus replaced with the final society of the young lovers and is usually finalized with a festival or celebration of some sort. In many cases, as in Shakespeare's comedies, multiple weddings occur wherein several characters of the new society are paired off to achieve a traditional comic conclusion.[14]

"What does that mean in human language?" I hear you.

A love story is, first of all, the 'Boy Meets Girl, Boy loses Girl, Boy regains Girl' formula. The friction or necessary conflict in the 'Boy-loses-Girl' part comes from something conventional – a prejudice, a caste restriction, or just a Boyfriend-hating-daddy with a shotgun – that is keeping our lovers apart. The story is about Boy and Girl transcending whatever separates them and creating a new understanding or culture through the sacrifices and changes each make in love for their partner.

Think of the peace between warring Capulets and Montagues in the Verona of Romeo and Juliet after their union in death. But think of a happier ending for the couple, please! There aren't supposed to be any tragic endings in love stories like the ones Mrs. Meyer is writing.

The "boy" of each *Twilight* story is principally Edward, of course, and the girl, Bella. The exterior "blocking figure" in the four books that keeps them apart varies. Charlie Swan is a comic *alazon*, the forbidding father figure from the storytelling backlot of cardboard characters who appears for comic effect. He never really figures, though, as a real obstacle to Bella and Edward consummating their love.

What prevents their union, a love that is less about sex than it is a matter of Bella's being transformed into a vampire, are, first, the exterior obstacles of "what people think" – the Cullens, the Quileutes and their treaty – and of the natural fears and impediments to this cross-species relationship. The more important blocks, though, are the interior ones of love, pride, misunderstanding, and just plain 'eternal life' theological concerns, most notably, Edward's concern for Bella's soul. Not to mention his fear that he or a member of his 'family' will devour her!

---

14 Northrop Frye, *Anatomy of Criticism*, 1954, as summarized online by *Archetypal Pursuit*: "This site was created by Meaghan Campbell, Kyle Fredenburg and Craig Love as part of English 701 at the University of Waterloo;" http://artsweb.uwaterloo.ca/~mr2campb/Learning%20Object/spring.html

These interior blocks create the "boy loses girl" tension essential to this genre that creates our page-turning frenzy to find out if they reconcile and are joined in the end.

- In *Twilight*, vampire-loses-girl because he thinks he is bad for her, some of his family aren't happy about the relationship, and then she is hunted down by a tracker-vampire.
- In *New Moon*, vampire-loses-girl entirely of his own volition after Bella cuts herself and is attacked by Jasper at her birthday party.
- In *Eclipse*, the *Wuthering Heights* edition of these stories, Edward has to respect Bella's relationship with Jacob Black, a rival and capable "blocking figure."
- And in *Breaking Dawn*, after the Alchemical Wedding, Edward plays the melodramatic lover waiting for Camille's death – until she rises from the dead and their relationship is threatened by the Volturi, the ultimate blocking figures.

And what do we get at the end of the series? I mean, *besides* a marriage, a baby, and a happily ever after love feast between Bella and Edward?

We get the conjunction not only of humankind and vampires in Bella's father and mother being brought into the Cullen family sphere but, more importantly, we have a resolution in large part between Quileute shape-shifting man-wolves and Cullen vegetarian vampires. The friendship of Seth Clearwater and Edward, the imprinting of Jacob Black with Bella and Edward's daughter, and the respect everyone has for one another after the final confrontation with the Volturi in *Breaking Dawn*, turns the paranormal world of the Peninsula insideout.

The glue for and the drive toward this seismic change? It's all from Bella and Edward's love story.

Time to Move beneath the Surface

We'll return in each of the coming chapters to romance as the *Twilight* core genre and the opening it creates for the more profound moral, allegorical, and sublime meanings in the books. For now, it's enough if we note the fairly obvious point that *Twilight* is first and last a love story.

Yes, there's more to it than that – it's technically a Young Adult boy-meets girl romance with international thriller plot (Blockbuster!) with paranormal characters – but all the extras are wrapped around and work the way they do because the 'high concept' vampire-and-girlfriend love story is a winner. The 'wow' plotting and pacing and the hook sunk into the reader via Bella's credible, engaging first person voice used to tell the trials and victories of their romance do all that a reader can ask from the surface story.

This narrative line brings us inside the tale with sufficient suspension of disbelief and identification with hero and heroine that we can experience in it the meanings within and just beneath the surface. That richer content only gets to us, like water through a hose, if the greater meaning is present – water pressure! – and the surface invites us in – hose connected and water turned on!

Those people who don't like *Twilight* and those convinced that it is pablum, slop, or worse for the distraction of the mindless many are repelled from the surface, nine times out of ten. Bella is too good, not sufficiently feminist, or not the reader's type. More often, it is conventional critical and academic disdain for "juvenile literature," for blockbuster pacing and plots (especially those thrillers that become best sellers), and especially for love stories. There isn't anything lower than a Harlequin formula 'bodice wripper' in literary taxonomy. One written for 'Young Adults' and with hints of *Da Vinci Code* adventure doesn't stand a chance with the cognoscenti.

But millions of readers love them. To discover why that is, beyond the pleasures of the surface story, we begin with a look at the White Hats and Black Hats of the series in the moral layer of meaning.

Chapter 2

The Moral Layer of Meaning:

How Twilight's Vampires Deliver Traditional and Postmodern Values and Morality

The first of meaning "beneath" the surface of any story isn't cleverly hidden; it is within the story, like flavor is in our favorite ice cream. The moral message of the author or playwright is as plain as figuring out who the good guys and bad guys are.

Granted, in literary novels, the stories of gritty psychological realism and reflection celebrated in the Academy and in literary reviews, this protagonist-antagonist distinction is rarely clear. But not many people read these books. I suggest for your consideration in this chapter that the reason most of us don't care for the "there is no good and evil" morality of such stories is because we recognize the contradiction of this thinking and storytelling.

In brief, like the assertion that "there is no truth" contradicts itself (because the assertion is putting forward the idea as something objectively true while asserting this is not possible), so the silliness of saying "there is no morality" cuts its own hamstrings. The good guys in a "morality free" or relativist story are those who struggle with this truth; the bad guys are the morons who hang on in their ignorance to their false moralities – guns, religious fantasies, national identity, and sports fraternities. The relativist morality, though, obviously is still a good guy-bad guy morality, just not a very interesting or compelling one (outside of nihilist enclaves, that is).

To find the moral sense of a story that is not a Proustian exploration of the narrator's aesthetic thinking, memories, and feelings is a snap. Just figure out who the author wants us readers to like, who the bad guys are, and what their differences are about, that is, what distinguishes a good guy from a bad guy, and we have the moral sense of the story. With *Twilight,* Mrs. Meyer tells a tale that is in essence the history of two conflicts: of the Cullens with conventional vampires led by the Volturi and of the Capulet-Montague treaty-restrained antagonism between Cullens and Quileutes.

Looking at these relationships and how both conflicts are resolved through the love of Edward and Bella, we learn the postmodern and transcendent moral message of the books. In a nutshell, the difference between "good" and "evil" is what Mrs. Meyer and all Latter-day Saints call "free agency" and what we and all *Twilight* characters call "choice" and "conscience." The measure of one's fidelity to conscience, the hallmark of virtue, is the willingness to sacrifice life itself in love for another.

White Hats and Black Hats:
A Program of Heroes and Villains in *Twilight*

If you've watched the three *Lord of the Rings* movies by Peter Jackson, you know it's not very hard to tell good guys from bad guys in that tale. The protagonists or heroes are the ones who don't live in dark, creepy buildings with large fires and who don't have misshapen faces and black uniforms. I mean, who comes out of the theatre after watching any one of these movies and wants to be an Orc, a Ring Wraith, or a Mountain Troll? Not me.

Believe it or not, though, one of the criticisms of Tolkien's masterpiece when it was first published was that it was morally ambiguous. The thought was that there seemed to be little difference between good guys and bad guys in what motivated them to hate the other guys. Without the benefit of graphic CGI to help them see the scary difference, some readers said the "us versus them" antagonism of the books offered only a mechanical, even jingoistic or colonial morality. Aragorn seemed as much a power seeker as Sauron to these critics and, consequently, no moral guide.

W. H. Auden answered this charge in his review of *The Return of the King* in 1956:

> To present the conflict between Good and Evil as a war in which the good side is ultimately victorious is a ticklish business. Our historical experience tells us that physical power and, to a large extent, mental power are morally neutral and effectively real:

> wars are won by the stronger side, just or unjust. At the same time most of us believe that the essence of the Good is love and freedom so that Good cannot impose itself by force without ceasing to be good.
>
> The battles in the Apocalypse and "Paradise Lost," for example, are hard to stomach because of the conjunction of two incompatible notions of Deity, of a God of Love who creates free beings who can reject his love and of a God of absolute Power whom none can withstand. Mr. Tolkien is not as great a writer as Milton, but in this matter he has succeeded where Milton failed.
>
> As readers of the preceding volumes will remember, the situation in the War of the Ring is as follows: Chance, or Providence, has put the Ring in the hands of the representatives of Good, Elrond, Gandalf, Aragorn. By using it they could destroy Sauron, the incarnation of evil, but at the cost of becoming his successor. If Sauron recovers the Ring, his victory will be immediate and complete, but even without it his power is greater than any his enemies can bring against him, so that, unless Frodo succeeds in destroying the Ring, Sauron must win.
>
> Evil, that is, has every advantage but one – it is inferior in imagination. Good can imagine the possibility of becoming evil – hence the refusal of Gandalf and Aragorn to use the Ring – but Evil, defiantly chosen, can no longer imagine anything but itself. Sauron cannot imagine any motives except lust for domination and fear so that, when he has learned that his enemies have the Ring, the thought that they might try to destroy it never enters his head, and his eye is kept toward Gondor and away from Mordor and the Mount of Doom.[1]

The difference between good and evil is not that the white hats always do the right or virtuous thing and win or that the bad guys always are wicked and lose in the end because they are not virtuous. The difference between the two in Tolkien's epic, according to Auden, is one of imagination, and, ultimately, of choosing the good that imagination allows us to discern. Those who have chosen evil "defiantly" "can no longer imagine anything but" evil and, having become morally blind, can no longer chose the good or even to turn from vice.

As in Tolkien, so in *Twilight*.

---

1 W. H. Auden, 'At the End of Quest, Victory,' *New York Times*, 22 January 1956; http://www.nytimes.com/1956/01/22/books/tolkien-king.html

The cowboys in white hats we are meant to admire and want to be like are the Cullen vampires. As with Tolkien's *Fellowship of the Ring*, these seven vampires are idealized figures but not cardboard characters from the Hall of Heroes who lack personality and their individual failings and prejudices. The Cullens, like these heroes, differ from their foes, not in being saints, but in the choices they are able to make. The Olympic Coven of vampires have separated themselves from the vampire black hats of the *Twilight* Saga, that is, the human-eating immortals who are loosely led but strictly policed by the Volturi, in having imagined *and* chosen a life without murdering human beings.

The Cullens differ, then, from all their vampire brethren (except for one like-minded coven in Alaska) not only in having chosen their "vegetarian" alternative-lifestyle and in how this changes them but, more importantly, in their being capable of such a choice. Living on the blood of animals rather than human blood changes their nature sufficiently that they are able to live as a family and in proximity, even in service to human beings.

Volturi vampires, as a rule to which the Volturi themselves are exceptions, are nomads with few relationships even with other vampires; these hemophages are mystified, too, and confused or repulsed by the Cullen family's choice because the conventional vampire has chosen the evil of conformity and obedience to the vampire's "carnivorous" nature. Having chosen evil, per Auden (and human experience and history), they cannot imagine another life. To paraphrase Thomas Aquinas, "sin makes you stupid."

This vampire conflict is played out in the several *Twilight* battles between the vegetarian Cullens and conventional bloodsuckers, and, more meaningfully, in Edward's interior struggle not to act from his inner vampire and kill his beloved Bella.

Here is a Book by Book Look at these inside-outside battles:

- In *Twilight*, the outside battle comes in the climactic confrontation with James the Tracker, a vampire who decides he must hunt down and kill Bella if only because of the challenge after meeting her in the Mountain Meadow baseball game. The greater part of this book, though, and all of what we have of *Midnight Sun* is the story of Edward's agony in wanting simultaneously to love and to murder Bella Swan. The story ends with James being vanquished and Edward proving equal to tasting Bella's blood without losing his control: choice and love vanquish our animal nature and evil.

- In *New Moon,* the exterior vampire conflict is with James' mate Victoria, who hunts Bella to seek revenge and with the Volturi, who inadvertently learn that Bella knows the secret of vampire existence. The interior battle is about Edward's choice to leave Bella because he knows if he stays she must either become a vampire and lose her soul or be devoured either by a Cullen or another vampire. Neither of the exterior battles is won, though Victoria fails to kill Bella, and Edward, Alice, and Bella are allowed to leave the Volturi castle in Volterra. The interior battle is resolved in Edward's realization that living without the other is killing both Bella and himself, precipitating his return to Forks.
- In *Eclipse,* the visible vampire war comes to a pitch as Victoria creates an army of "newborns" that invade the Olympic Peninsula to kill Bella. Edward's interior battle is with his jealously and protectiveness, feelings spurred by Bella's relationship with Jacob Black. Edward and his family, with the help of the Quileute shape-changing wolves, vanquish Victoria and her army. Though not friends, Edward comes to respect and appreciate both Jacob and Bella's feelings for her best friend.
- In *Breaking Dawn,* the Volturi confrontation that we've been dreading since the end of *New Moon* finally comes to pass as our exterior conflict finale and Edward goes through the chrysalis of despair as the consummation of his marriage to Bella seems to have doomed her to an agonizing death in pregnancy and childbirth. He saves her during the throes of her labor, however, again through his self-restraint while tasting her blood, and the Volturi back down in the Mountain Meadow climax when confronted with the Cullen-Quileute alliance and various vampires not in their control.

The moral thrust of *Twilight,* then, is, in one word, 'choice.' Good guys can make virtuous and vicious choices because their imagination is still able to listen to conscience and see consequences. The Bad guys and Black hats are, having once chosen evil, morally blind and incapable of choosing the good, especially a sacrificial good.

The Morality of Edward and Bella's Love Story

In case you think I'm making this up, here are a few "choice comments" from Mrs. Meyer's various interviews in which she lays bare the importance of choice and "free agency" in her thinking and work:

> Of course, the fact that Edward has a strong urge to kill his girlfriend and suck her blood complicates things. His conflicted nature and constant struggle are part of what pushes the series forward.
>
> "There's something about overcoming the natural man," Meyer says. "Having free agency to decide what you're going to do with yourself is a gift. I think kids pick up on that — it doesn't matter if you're a vampire. You can choose what to do with your life. Conflicted heroes are the best kind. Edward really has to fight." [2]
>
> **Was it difficult to portray vampires sympathetically?**
>
> They ended up being vampires in the way they are because I have strong opinions on free will. No matter what position you're in, you always have a choice. So I had these characters who were in a position where traditionally they would have been the bad guys, but, instead, they chose to be something different—a theme that has always been important to me.[3]

Mrs. Meyer told *TIME* magazine's Lev Grossman that choice was the uniquely human freedom:

> Edward and the Cullens aren't ordinary vampires: they have renounced human blood on moral grounds, feeding instead on wild animals, which they hunt by night. He and Bella are instantly, overwhelmingly attracted to each other, but he is also wildly hungry for her blood.
>
> Resisting that temptation is a constant struggle. Edward's choice – and the willingness to choose a different way in general – is a major theme in Meyer's books. "I really think that's the underlying metaphor of my vampires," she says. "It doesn't matter where you're stuck in life or what you think you have to do; you can always choose something else. There's always a different path."[4]

And when asked about the meaning of the series' signature image, the apple being held out by the arms of a young woman, Mrs. Meyer

---

2 Charmed, op.cit; http://www.phoenixnewtimes.com/content/printVersion/481142

3 Rick Margolis, 'Stephenie Meyer talks about vampires, teen love, and her first novel, 'Twilight',' *School Library Journal*, 10/1/2005;http://www.schoollibraryjournal.com/article/CA6260602.html

4 Lev Grossman, 'Stephenie Meyer: A New J.K. Rowling?,' *Time*, Apr. 24, 2008; http://www.time.com/time/magazine/article/0,9171,1734838-1,00.html

quotes the *Genesis* epigraph that opens the first book and explains, "To me it says: *choice*."[5] The original idea for the book's title, one that Mrs. Meyer gave up begrudgingly, was *Forks*, because the word has the suggestion of "critical choices" (think "Fork in the road," the place of defining choice in the road to be taken).

I'm not making this choice bit up.

If Edward's inner struggle and the conflict with all other vampires consequent to the Cullens' peculiar food choices isn't enough to drive home that *Twilight* morality turns on choice, there is the love story at the heart of the drama. The love Bella and Edward feel for each other is born in their radical, even self-destructive choices.

Bella's big choice comes when she realizes, after her rescue in the high school parking lot by a superpowered Edward and what she is able to figure out about the Cullens from Jacob Black's comments at the beach, that the young man she loves is a vampire. It's the pivotal scene of the whole series because she chooses love, beauty, and what she knows is true (in the face of Edward's lies and what she has always been taught) over even life itself. Loving a vampire, after all, is not something your insurance agent is ever going to recommend. Bella's 'Big Scene', in full.

> Q: Could the Cullens be vampires?[5]
>
> A: Well, they were *something*. Something outside the possibility of rational justification was taking place in front of my incredulous eyes. Whether it be Jacob's *cold ones* or my own superhero theory, Edward Cullen was not ...human. He was something more.
>
> So then – maybe. That would have to be my answer for now.
>
> And then the most important question of all. What was I going to do if it was true?
>
> *If* Edward was a vampire – I could hardly make myself think the words – then what should I do? Involving someone else was definitely out. I couldn't even believe myself; anyone I told would have me committed.
>
> Only two options seemed practical. The first was take his advice: to be smart, to avoid him as much as possible. To cancel our plans, to go back to ignoring him as far as I was able. To pretend there was an impenetrably thick glass wall between us in the one

5 Emphasis in original; the question is the first on her website's FAQ page: http://www.stepheniemeyer.com/twilight_faq.html#apple

> class where we were forced together. To tell him to leave me alone – and mean it this time.
>
> I was gripped in a sudden agony of despair as I considered that alternative. My mind rejected the pain, quickly skipping on to the next option.
>
> I could do nothing different. After all, if he was something ... sinister, he'd done nothing to hurt me so far. In fact, I would be a dent in Tyler's fender if he hadn't acted so quickly. So quickly, I argued with myself, that it might have been sheer reflexes. But if it was a reflex to save lives, how bad could he be? I retorted. My head spun around in answerless circles.
>
> There was one thing I was sure of, if I was sure of anything. The dark Edward in my dream last night was a reflection only of my fear of the word Jacob had spoken, and not Edward himself. Even so, when I'd screamed out in terror at the werewolf's lunge, it wasn't fear for the wolf that brought the cry of "no" to my lips. It was fear that *he* would be harmed – even as he called to me with sharp edged fangs, I feared for *him*.
>
> And I knew in that I had my answer. I didn't know if there ever was a choice, really. I was already in too deep. Now that I knew – *if* I knew – I could do nothing about my frightening secret. Because when I thought of him, of his voice, his hypnotic eyes, the magnetic force of his personality, I wanted nothing more than to be with him right now. Even if ... but I couldn't think it. Not here, alone in the darkening forest. Not while the rain made it dim as twilight under the canopy and pattered like footsteps across the matted earthen floor. I shivered and rose quickly from my place of concealment, worried that somehow the path would have disappeared with the rain. ...

Bella looks at a life without Edward and chooses to love him regardless of consequences. Having made that choice, she feels strangely liberated, elated:

> That had always been my way, though. Making decisions was the painful part for me, the part I agonized over. But once the decision was made, I simply followed through - usually with relief that the choice was made. Sometimes the relief was tainted by despair, like my decision to come to Forks. But it was still better than wrestling with the alternatives.
>
> This decision was ridiculously easy to live with. Dangerously easy.[6]

---

6 Stephenie Meyer, *Twilight*, Chapter 7, pages 138-140

Edward's choice, oddly enough, takes place much less logically and systematically. Having saved Bella from Tyler's skidding van and put his family at risk of exposure, he learns through Alice's visions that there are only two futures for Bella: either Edward will lose control and kill her or she will become Alice's friend – and a vampire. Both possibilities seem catastrophes to him, and, with the image of Bella's crushed body in his mind, he thinks, echoing Mrs. Meyer's interview comments above:

> Alice's bleak vision filled my head, and I writhed internally with the agony it caused. Meanwhile, the monster in me was overflowing with glee, jubilant at the likelihood of his success. It sickened me.
>
> This could not be allowed. There had to be a way to circumvent the future. I would not let Alice's visions direct me. I could choose a different path. There was always a choice.
>
> There had to be.[7]

He makes that choice later that night in Bella's bedroom when he realizes it is too late for him to be able to leave her because he is already in love. He resolves to live in the mean between the futures Alice has seen; he will love her as best he can without either killing her or transforming her into a soulless immortal.

Note the enormity of these choices.

Bella all but says farewell to life. In accepting that she loves Edward and choosing to embrace this love though she knows he is a vampire, she has kissed her future goodbye. Any ideas about an education, raising a family, even continuing her relationships with Charlie and with Renee, hey, just staying alive – poof. Not with a vampire boyfriend, she's not.

Edward's choice is about as difficult. Choosing to spend time with Bella, to embrace the love he cannot deny he feels, gets him coming and going. His family is put at greater risk because he cannot guarantee the girl won't figure out and reveal their secret – or even that he won't lose control and kill her, also exposing the family. Inside, the burning desire to consume her wars with his love for her in a moment to moment battle for mastery. He isn't jesting when he tells her in the school cafeteria the day after making his choice that "I decided as long as I was going to hell, I might as well do it thoroughly."[8]

---

7 Stephenie Meyer, *Midnight Sun*, unpublished manuscript, Chapter 4, 'page 60'

8 Stephenie Meyer, *Twilight*, chapter 5, page 87

These choices are superhuman, frankly, and I think we're meant to ask, as this is the difference between good and evil in the series, where this ability comes from.

Conscience.

Edward gets his conscience and consequent powers of choice courtesy of having been "born" a Cullen. The defining principle of vegetarian vampire life is conscience. Carlisle Cullen was the son of a crusading 17th century Anglican priest in London, an "intolerant man" who "was enthusiastic in his persecution of Roman Catholics and other religions," not to mention leading "hunts for witches, werewolves, ... and vampires."[9] Carlisle, though, on one of these hunts is bitten by a vampire and makes the painful three day transformation in a basement under a pile of rotting potatoes.

As a man of faith, however, and one who has nothing but hatred for vampires, Carlisle heroically resists his thirst for human blood. He tries, in fact, to do something no Christian would try to do, at least not while human. He fails in these suicide attempts but discovers he can assuage his longing for human blood with animal blood. The "vegetarian principle" is born.

Edward describes this principle as Carlisle's "vision" and it is the way of life to which all the Cullens "commit" themselves. Edward had lived on what the Volturi refer to as their "natural food," i.e., humans, in a period of rebellion and independence as an "adolescent" vampire but found he was not "exempt from the ... depression ... that accompanies a conscience.... I began to see the monster in my eyes. I couldn't escape the debt of so much human life taken, no matter how justified."[10]

This conscience, the shadow of Carlisle's Christian faith and ethics, which is to say, his morality, is the engine of Edward's making the hard choice he does. He thinks it is wrong to kill human beings, though it is his inner self as a vampire, the monster within him. He thinks it at least as wrong to take away Bella's humanity and transform her into a soulless creature who cannot know eternal life. His conscience forces him, once he realizes he loves the girl, to choose staying with her and working to control his blood lust, the most difficult option he has. It seems clear that only decades of "fasting" from human blood and the self-control consequent to such deliberate abstinence and his sensitive conscience make this possible.

---

9 Meyer, *Twilight*, chapter 15, page 331

10 Op., cit., chapter 16, pages 342-3

And Bella? Where does she get her ability to make the choice she does?

Not from a church, certainly. Neither Charlie the Police Chief nor mother Renee have taken daughter Isabella to services of any kind with any consistency. Bella just seems naturally, maybe even unnaturally *good*. Edward catalogues her virtues while eavesdropping on a classmate's thoughts about Bella in *Midnight Sun*:

> [Mike Newton] hadn't observed the unselfishness and bravery that set her apart from other humans, he didn't hear the abnormal maturity of her spoken thoughts. He didn't perceive that when she spoke of her mother, she sounded like a parent speaking of a child rather than the other way around – loving, indulgent, slightly amused, and fiercely protective. He didn't hear the patience in her voice when she feigned interest in his rambling stories, and didn't guess at the kindness behind the patience.
>
> Through her conversations with Mike, I was able to add the most important quality to my list, the most revealing of them all, as simple as it was rare. Bella was *good*. All the other things added up to that whole – kind and self-effacing and unselfish and loving and brave – she was good through and through.[11]

When we first meet Bella, she is leaving the sunny Phoenix, Arizona, she loves for the dreary, backwoods town of Forks she loathes. She makes this choice because she thinks it is the right thing for her to do for her mother's happiness. Bella Swan, as Edward observed, is more mommy than daughter to her own mother – and her conscience is such that sacrifice and selfless love is something of a reflex.

Bella and Edward were born and bred for making absurdly hard choices.

It is interesting to note here that the Quileute shape-changing wolfmen are virtuous and use their paranormal powers only for good, but there is little choice or freedom in this virtue. As Jacob Black complains frequently, he didn't *choose* to become a lupine LaPush protector – the transformation is based in genetics and triggered by vampires in the area – and his "free agency," as Mrs. Meyer might put it, is anything but "free." He is subject to the pack's Alpha leader and group mind, like it or not.

11 Meyer, *Midnight Sun, op.cit.*, chapter 5, 'pages 62-63'

But Jacob Black is good, too, much in the way that Bella is, so he makes hard choices when he recognizes the right thing to do. In *New Moon,* he goes to Bella and, contrary to instructions from Sam Uley and tribe conventions, all but spells out their wolfman secret. More boldly, in *Breaking Dawn* he defies Sam's authority and Alpha commands when they are planning to attack the Cullens and kill Bella. He does this despite his hatred for the Cullens, his love and loyalty to his tribe and pack, and his own misgivings about Bella and baby.

That's conscience driving choice becoming heroic, sacrificial virtue. All of it seems to be spurred in these stories by love. A daughter's love for her mom, the love of Jacob and Bella as friends, and the romantic love of Edward and Bella jump start their conscience and selfless choices. Love and the consequent selflessness the lover feels foster conscience and virtuous choice which fosters love and self-transcendence in a loop.

Christian, Pagan, or Postmodern: What Kind of Morality is This?

The morality of these *Twilight* characters is something that many Christians, unlike the initial response to *Harry Potter* and Philip Pullman's *His Dark Materials* trilogy, have celebrated as a good thing. That Bella and Edward are not having casual sex and that they abstain from it both for prudential reasons and because of concerns about their souls, is a relatively uplifting, even spiritual message for the hook-up and "friends with benfits" generation.

And, as I'll discuss in chapter 4, there is a boatload of traditional Christian content in *Twilight,* much of it about conscience. C. S. Lewis explained in his essay 'The Seeing Eye' that the human conscience was sacred and continuous with the fabric of reality, something like our *logos* mind. As such, fidelity to the directions of conscience up to the point of identifying oneself with them is akin to obedience to a personal revelation and entering the "Kingdom of Heaven." That this requires a death to the ego persona or 'flesh' is the esoteric and individual meaning of John the Baptist's seemingly only historical observation that "I must decrease that He [Christ] may increase" (John 3:30). [12]

---

12 C. S. Lewis, 'The Seeing Eye, ' in *The Timeless Writings of C. S. Lewis,* Inspirational Press, New York: 2008, pages 290-296. Cf., John Granger, 'The Seeing Eye,' chapter 5 of *The Deathly Hallows Lectures,* Zossima Press, 2008, and chapter 4 of this book.

But what about Edward sleeping with Bella every night, abstinent or not, though her father knows nothing about it? What about the lies that the Cullens tell, the systemic dishonesty of their life as vampires? Yes, they have to hide their existence from humankind, but only because their vampire brethren are slaughtering innocent human beings like cattle around the world every day. Where is the Christian conscience in that? Watching a bus full of tourists march into the Volturi castle mess hall and knowing that they are about to be served as lunch sickens Alice, Edward, and Bella, but none of them raises a finger to save the human take-out meals.

What's up with that? The moral message seems a little confused.

Well, if we were expecting a *Focus on the Family* evangelical radio program like 'Adventures in Odyssey,' in which a Christian message is carried by each character on a sandwich board, *Twilight* had to be a disappointment. Here's a rule of thumb from the pool of literary common sense to prevent this kind of disappointment in the future: 'Every Great Work will simultaneously reflect human truths that transcend all ages and cultural boundaries *and* the prevalent beliefs of the historical period in which it was written – and first the prevalent beliefs.'

This is common sense because the defining ideas and blind spots of any age are by necessity going to color any work created in that period. If it were possible for a poet today to think and write like Milton, to hear his Muse (highly doubtful), it is a near certainty that no one other than literary antiquarians and Miltonians would read the epic this atavistic poet had published. Stephenie Meyer is a Latter-day Saint so her books are not vulgar, violent, or vicious for the sake of it, but expecting her 21st century books to reflect a Georgian or Victorian Christian morality is a big stretch.

Mrs. Meyer is a writer of her times and no other. Her books, consequently and inevitably, reflect our age's concerns and beliefs. If they didn't, they wouldn't sell; there would be no hook or resonance for their readers to connect with. As popular as the *Twilight* novels are, it is no surprise that what the good guys in them believe and the story reveals are the very beliefs we all share as members of our historical period, usually called post-modernity.

To grasp their temporal morality, then, before we move onto the transcendent truths of the books in the next two chapters, we need to take a minute and look at our own eyeballs for an idea of how we, to include Mrs. Meyer, see things. What is postmodern thinking? PoMo morality? After looking at the three chief qualities typical of the way people see things now, we will look at how this shapes our storytelling and how it is reflected in almost every story element of *Twilight*.

A Cultural Belief Contra Cultural Beliefs: The Big, Bad Metanarrative

Here is the bumper sticker version of what Postmodernism is about from one of the big thinkers of this age (Lyotard): postmodernism is "Incredulity towards Metanarratives." What "incredulity" means is that to a postmodern person, most of the world's problems are caused by people believing in big foundation stories (Grand Narratives, Metanarratives) like "original sin" and "invisible hand capitalism" or Marxist theories of economic determination. Baseline beliefs, too, like "white people are best," "men are stronger and smarter than women," and "heterosexual relationships are natural" qualify as well. Any of these "Founders Stories" ossifies into a corresponding ideology that is inherently and inescapably totalitarian and exclusive, dividing the world into a good core of people and a "necessary other," who, by not being part of the core group, are "bad," even "evil."

As postmoderns, we are skeptical about beliefs offered as "givens" or "unexamined truths" because we abhor the discriminatory prejudices and practices that come from them. We believe that the big story is as often as not a big lie that elevates a few and leaves out many more.

The key point is our shared skepticism about surety, our common belief or "shared paradigm" qua postmoderns is that, if you're certain about the world and what human beings are about or how we should behave, you're (a) stupid and (b) almost certainly dangerous, because your metanarrative is going to pigeonhole someone (and probably a lot of people as a group) as "evil." Imperialism, racism, chauvinism, unrestricted capitalism, homophobia, and ardent religious belief not tempered by individualism and a touch of hedonism are the sworn enemies of we postmoderns, at least taken as a big group.

And the world has become a much better place in important ways because of this shared "incredulity towards metanarratives." There's a reason that folks don't drag "other" people behind their cars for fun anymore or have Tailhook gauntlets at their office parties. We have learned that "the other" is not evil by necessity while the prejudice that would pigeonhole anyone certainly is.

Don't Believe What You Think – and Do 'Speak Truth to Power'!

Our core belief as postmoderns is that the 'big story,' grand myth, or cultural metanarrative that shapes our understanding of reality and guides our categorization of people and things into 'good' and 'other' pigeonholes is the source of all that is wrong with the world. Belief in core myths – white people are best, women should stay at home, poor people are lazy, businessmen are greedy, homosexuals are perverts – fosters prejudices that necessarily favor and empower one group and unfairly excludes others. The evils we show little to no tolerance for qua postmoderns, most notably, racism, sexism, classism, and homophobia, are prejudices we believe are born in mistaken metanarratives that act as tinted or distorted glasses which effectively blind us to people as they are.

That our core belief or metanarrative is "incredulity about metanarratives," of course, brings us to a contradiction. Are we also skeptical or incredulous about the *postmodern* metanarrative? Usually we aren't, just as we as a rule don't see the irony of showing no tolerance for the intolerant in the name of tolerance as a great good and virtue. Politically correct thinking has become another blinding cultural narrative, alas.

But in our belief that we need to tear down all metanarratives except the metanarrative saying all metanarratives are evil (got that?), we stumble into another belief, namely, that nothing can be known certainly. Relativism is a corollary to our core belief that our thinking is hopelessly occluded by prejudice and selfishness because we cannot know anything with certainty through this metanarrative created set of prejudices and reality filters. Nothing is what we think it is and we cannot be sure to what degree we are not understanding things as they are because nothing can be directly apprehended.

Except for the thought that we cannot know anything for sure. *That* is a sure thing.

The message we take from this Uncertainty Principle? Two things.

First, check your preconceptions at the door. Because what you think is a bunch of hooey and it hopelessly distorts your perception and understanding of what you encounter, try your best to observe with sympathy and penetration. Don't judge until you've removed those metanarrative planks from your own eye. Things are a lot more interesting and involved than your preconceptions want you to understand – and you'll never get to run with wonderful werewolves and virtuous vampires if you cannot see things with penetrating vision beyond prejudice to grasp the greater inside below the scary surface.

Last, in the absence of an ability to know anything with certainty, the only way left to act admirably is to choose correctly.

Which brings us back to choice as the standard for virtue. If we cannot know with certainty, we can only make choices as best we can. The "right choices" are those made in resistance to the myth-makers in power, the shadow-makers in the Cave, and to the shadow myths themselves. The best tests of the authenticity or freedom from prejudice and ego of any choice are if it is made sacrificially in love for the misunderstood 'other' excluded by myth and if it "speaks truth to power."[13] The metanarratives that blind us are only escaped by direct confrontation with the power holders who have their positions because of the lie inherent in the culture's defining myths.

Postmodern Literature: Stories of Sad-Sack Saviors and Sacrificial Choice

Postmodernism, then, has three defining ideas and qualities:

1. The metanarrative or defining beliefs of our culture create a society of story-empowered elites and marginalized 'others' who have no power.
2. These beliefs have so shaped and colored our vision with bias and prejudice against the 'other' that we have no direct experience or knowledge of reality, and, consequently, can know nothing with objective certainty.
3. The only freedom we can have is through choosing to champion the marginalized, deny the seeming truth of the metanarrative, and speak truth to power (confront the power holding regime and the lie of the myth giving them power).

13 Originally 'Speak Truth to Power' was the title of a 1955 Society of Friends pamphlet about Quaker beliefs and practices in the context of the Cold War. "It has become common far beyond Quaker circles, often used by people who have no idea of its origins. (One current example: Anita Hill entitled her memoir of her sensational charges of sexual harassment against Supreme Court nominee Clarence Thomas, *Speaking Truth to Power.*)" http://www2.gol.com/users/quakers/living_the_truth.htm

As noted, this set of 'anti-belief' beliefs, now that they are the defining beliefs of our culture, has its comic, confusing moments. How do you "speak truth to power" when *you* are the power holder?

Every culture's arts and letters simultaneously reflect and reinforce its beliefs in its members' hearts and minds; postmodern culture is no different. Everything from literary novels to comic books are water-bearers for the anti-prejudice, pro-choice regime of ideas that define our historical Age.

Every novel, play, poem, story, and film that expects to win an audience today carries in it the moral message of our time. It has all three features of these beliefs detailed above spelled out in story:

1. **Evil, Prejudicial Metanarrative:** The postmodern story is the tale of a marginalized 'other,' the freak dismissed or looked down on by everyone, who, though dismissed and discriminated against by the power holding authorities, turns out to have the secret power necessary to save the culture.

2. **Blindness Consequent to Prejudice:** The loser's view from the cultural margin or periphery allows our hero or heroine the necessary perspective, free as they are, relatively speaking (sic), from the delusion of the excluding myth, to see things as they are. Only the open-minded, loving seeker free of prejudice knows reality rather than myth.

3. **Choosing to Speak Truth to Power:** The defining moment of postmodern drama is when the heroic loser, call him 'David,' defies the know-it-all power-holders and slays the threat he is not equal to, call it 'Goliath.' Speaking truth to power and slaying the threat, David's choice to see past the blinders is, in postmodern language, "self-actualizing" and liberating. The entire culture is transformed and its myths re-set to "incredulity towards metarratives."

In my books about Harry Potter, I use the Rankin-Bass teevee special *Rudolph the Red-Nosed Reindeer* and a host of Hollywood movies to illustrate these steps of PoMo story-telling.[14] Here, though, Harry Potter can be the example, because as the "shared text" of our times,[15] his adventures are a collection of every postmodern belief.

14 See *Unlocking Harry Potter*, Zossima Press, 2007, and *Harry Potter's Bookshelf*, Penguin, 2009.

15 See John Granger, 'Book Binders: What I Learned About Great Books and Harry Potter,' *Touchstone*, November 2008; http://www.touchstonemag.com/archives/article.php?id=21-10-028-f

The prejudice-inducing and 'other'-creating metanarrative of Ms. Rowling's Wizarding World is the Pure Blood fantasy that wizards and witches are better than all magical creatures and Muggles – and that those from better families, meaning those that have not bred with Muggles, are consequently better people and more magical than Mud Bloods and Mixed Blood wizards. Lord Voldemort, though his father was a Muggle, incarnates this belief and his Death Eater followers work with him to take power and further ostracize those less worthy. The government resists this view nominally but secretly shares the prejudice and eventually falls to the Dark Lord.

In resistance to this metanarrative and the Dark Lord embodying it are the sad-sack saviors of the Order of the Phoenix, every one of whom is a loser in one way or another. Their ranks include a family of blood traitors with too many children and not enough money, an escaped convict, a werewolf, a half-giant, a Mud Blood witch and prodigy, a closeted homosexual, a Metamorphmagus, a petty thief, a token black man, a Squibb, and a one-eyed paranoid who has been retired because of his delusions. Not to mention the orphan boy with a scar on his forehead, mixed feelings for Muggles, and a "saving-people thing."

Lovable, certainly, but not exactly the A-Team of All-Stars you want, right? The only thing they all have in common is having suffered at the hands of discriminatory prejudice and being proud nonconformists to the Pure Blood party line held by most witches and wizards.

How do they win? As Ms. Rowling has said in interviews and the story of *Deathly Hallows* demonstrates, it is because of a choice Harry makes. In the face of the evidence that Dumbledore wasn't all Harry thought he was and despite the seemingly certain victory of the Dark Lord and the Pure Blood metanarrative of hate, Harry "chooses to believe." He chooses, specifically, to pursue Horcruxes rather than the Deathly Hallows (i.e., to do what Dumbledore told him to do) and, more importantly, to love. He chooses to walk into the Forbidden Forest and die sacrificially for his friends, which sacrificial death defeats his interior Voldemort, the scar Horcrux, and the exterior dies soon after. Harry chooses love and selflessness over power and safety at the cost of his ego existence; he transcends the metanarrative of hate and the world is saved.[16]

16 See John Granger, *The Deathly Hallows Lectures*, Zossima Press, 2008

Divisive metanarrative, a hero from the cultural periphery who has been marginalized by the pervasive mythos, and a self-actualizing and liberating choice contrary to power saves the day: *Harry Potter* is a model postmodern epic.

Literary Novels, Superhero Comic Books, and *Twilight* as Postmodern Reading

What's great about a historical period's shaping works of art is the uniformity. The concerns, beliefs, and blind-spots of an Age touch *everything* of that time, regardless of the other meaning that text may be carrying. In literary novels, books that as a rule do not advance a story with even implicit Christian or religious content, for instance, we see the same postmodern three step formula. There is an evil, prejudice-generating metanarrative, most often the beliefs of a strawman fundamentalist believer or those of either a nihilist or narcissist, which beliefs marginalize or diminish the 'other,' usually a child, a woman, a minority token figure or someone with extraordinary but misunderstood abilities or concerns (best if we have a brilliant African-American girl who doesn't fit in because of her color, gender, intelligence, or accent, or all of the above...).

Our sensitive individual struggles to escape his or her confinement or life with folks who buy into their beliefs and their choices to conform without question. But the postmodern cave mouth seems to have been closed, at least in literary novels, so rather than the escape into Eden that the stupid black hats imagine is possible, the hero or heroine seeks only self-actualizing freedom. In one way or another, even if the truth speaking is symbolic or crushed, the individual will "speak truth to power" and escape, resolve not to care, or, more likely, despair.

Great fun.

A much more popular version of the PoMo Three Step Formula comes at the opposite end of the literary taxonomy spectrum: Superhero comic books, especially those produced by Marvel Comics. Selling tens of thousands of copies each week, Marvel Comics feature usually young people with extraordinary powers they use to confront greedy or world-domination-obsessed or just psychotic super-powered bad guys. What makes these stories attractive to their many readers, old and young, besides the always full-chested women in tight elastic costumes and the inevitable fight scenes, is the conformity and confirmation of our cultural core shibboleths.

The hero or heroine, again, is almost always a misunderstood or abused young person, preferably a teen, but rarely a person in their 40s, who is blessed (or cursed, as the heroes usually see it) with a super power. Spider strength for bookworm Peter Parker comes courtesy of a radioactive spider bite. Dr. Bruce Banner, caught in a gamma ray explosion becomes Dr. Jekyll to the monster within him, The Hulk, a green giant Mr. Hyde. The Fantastic Four are four friends who are changed into freaks – the elastic Mr. Fantastic, the Invisible Girl, the Thing, and the Human Torch – after being caught in an outer space cosmic ray storm. The X-Men are teenage mutant students in Dr. Xavier's Salem Center School.

Given our age, what is the key thing all these Marvel heroes have in common beside a remarkable ability to hurt people if they want and the psychological profile "doesn't play well with others"? You got it. They all choose to use their unsought powers to protect the weak and marginalized from the Evil folks having chosen to serve only themselves. Metanarrative of power, disenfranchised losers and freaks (at least in the eyes of the world; they are heroes to us), and the sacrificial choice to forsake individual gain to beat up bad guys...

And *Twilight*? I think Mrs. Meyer really wanted to create a series for Marvel Comics but wasn't very good with drawing and inking her characters so she tried a novel instead. You think that's dismissive sarcasm?

- In Edward's first meeting with Bella, he almost loses his mind. He wrestles with the raging desires of what he repeatedly calls the "monster within" him. He imagines slaughtering the entire class so that no one will be able to tell it was the girl whose blood drove him over the edge.[17] The comic book connection? The Incredible Hulk is the "monster within" Dr. Bruce Banner, whose life is about controlling the urge to transform into the Green Giant Wrecking Crew inside him, the Id on steroids. The biology teacher in the classroom is named "Mr. Banner."
- Edward asks Bella in their first lunch date at Forks High School cafeteria what theories she has about how he was able to save her from Tyler's sliding van in the school parking lot. Her answer? "Um, well, bitten by a radioactive spider?"[18] This is the origin of Marvel Comics' most popular superhero, Peter Parker, "The Amazing Spider-Man."

17 *Midnight Sun*, chapter 1
18 *Twilight*, chapter 5, page 92

- Stephenie Meyer, when asked "Where does the mythology behind the Twilight Series come from? Do you find that you are influenced at all by the popular "vampire themed shows" like Buffy the Vampire Slayer, vampire novels and subculture, or, do you try your best to ignore this? Do you feel that your novels are a newer extension of this trend?" said:

  > It's easy to be positive that I am not influenced by *Buffy*, because I've never watched an episode of *Buffy the Vampire Slayer*. I've never been into the horror genre, so I was fairly free of preconceived notions when I began constructing the Twilight mythology. **I think the roots of my mythology are much more influenced by superheroes than by monsters.**[19]

- Mrs. Meyer has also said that the X-Men Saturday morning cartoons derived from the Marvel comic books were an "inspiration" for Twilight:

  > "This is crazy, but those Saturday-morning cartoons ... I was always fascinated with the X-Men. I love the idea of a group of people and all of them can do something really well. They're special, but they're strongest when they work together. Maybe that comes from having a big family, but I always clicked into that kind of story. And I think that really came into play when I was subconsciously forming the Cullen family. Though I certainly wasn't thinking about Cyclops when I was writing about them, I think it was there in the layers underneath."[20]

- Most writers I think would hesitate to be so open about admitting that her novels' principal characters were inspired by cartoons derived from comic books. Critics already have her pigeon-holed as a writer for Wal-Mart shoppers and Sarah Palin supporters and their disdain for comic books can't help her reputation. Comic book influence, though, doesn't make Mrs. Meyer blush probably because her favorite writer, Orson Scott Card, besides being an award-winning science fiction and fantasy writer, playwright, and LDS apologist, also has written

19 Chapters.indigo.ca online bookstore interview; emphasis added http://blogs.myspace.com/index.cfm?fuseaction=blog.view&friendId=454417681&blogId=494700862

20 Karen Valby, "Stephenie Meyer: 12 of My 'Twilight' Inspirations," *Entertainment Weekly* (EW.com), 28 September 2009. http://www.ew.com/ew/gallery/0,,20308569_20308554_3,00.html

superhero series for, that's right, Marvel Comic books.[21]

The difference between Stan Lee's Marvel Comic heroes since the early 1960's has been that they're being relatively iconoclastic and non-conformist in contrast with the Golden Age DC heroes like Batman, Wonder Woman, and Superman who are idealized, perfect human archetypes. Marvel comic books have as their brand, if you will, in contrast, that their heroes have "issues." They understand themselves, as often as not, as Edward Cullen does: they are "monsters" or just not normal and they wish they could just be human.

Marvel comic books, in being psychological drama about non-conformists who choose to do good to speak to power, are as postmodern in outlook as literary novels of relative majesty aesthetically and nihilism philosophically. Both are vehicles of PoMo anti-metanarrative morality and thinking. More to the point of our discussion, as Mrs. Meyer has said herself, her vampires were "much more influenced by superheroes" in their genesis than by vampire canon and especially as a team of super-powered teenage mutants like the X-Men.

Let's take a closer look at the Cullen family in light of this thought, because their perfect physiques and the exterior perfection of this coven made up of nigh on immortal vampires don't seem to fit the Marvel Comic "freak" model.

The Cullen Vampires: Shades of Dumbledore's Army and the Uncanny X-Men

Joanne Rowling's *Harry Potter* adventures served up two magical groups that worked in resistance to the Dark Lord's Death Eaters. We have talked about the Order of the Phoenix as a ragtag collection of brave nonconformists and those estranged from the magical core or elite because of race, sexuality, poverty, blood status, psychological issues, prior convictions, or just being a werewolf. Comic book heroes and heroines similarly are "other" both because of their funny clothes (full body spandex with cleavage?) and the super-powers that make such outfits *de rigueur*. This quality of having been excluded or marginalized is the first mark of a postmodern character.

21 My favorite? The five issue series, *Ultimate Iron Man*, Volume 1, 2005-2006, in which Card retells the Iron Man origin story so that it isn't a consequence of Tony Stark being captured in Vietnam but of his mother's work with pathogens affecting his genetic make-up so he was *all* mind from birth. Talk about a kid who is 'other'...

The Cullens all live on the periphery in several senses. In the present, they reside on the far margins of vampire culture because they do not accept the metanarrative that vampires are gods and human beings are no more than Dracula dinners. They also have difficulty mingling with non-vampires lest they reveal their secret identity or just lose control of their inner hemophage and eat their yummy friends. They cannot even enjoy time with the ostracized Native Americans – living on a reservation pretty much defines "marginalized" – because the Quileutes know their secrets and find them disgusting.

But they seem perfect, as Bella never tires of telling us. Graceful, beautiful, hypnotizing looks that bedazzle – and they all are borderline divine in terms of their physical strength, intelligence, and not needing to eat every day or sleep, breath, and move about at all. Did I mention limitless financial resources and seeming independence from the IRS? Judging from the outside, it's hard to remember that all of the Cullens are "in recovery" from traumatic events of their human and vampire existences. The members of the Olympic Coven seem to be gods from Olympus but they're more like Dumbledore's Army or Prof. Xavier's insecure adolescent X-Men.

- Carlisle Cullen – The leader of the "family" and spiritual father of the Coven, Carlisle was raised in 17th century London by a firebrand father *cum* Protestant preacher who hunted vampires. He passed this vocation on to his son, whose Christian *karma* was to be transformed from vampire hunter to vampire himself. His never forsaking his Christian faith and its commandments (i.e., Thou Shall Not Kill) to accept the foundation or metanarrative of vampire life left him alone for two centuries until Edward's green-eyed mother exacted a death bed promise from him to do all he could to keep her son alive. Carlisle still has doubts about whether vampires have souls, if his existential worries are nothing to Edward's concerns. Carlisle seems to have come to some peace about his vampire identity through his work as a physician, saving rather than taking human life. His "children" are committed to his "vision" but lack his serenity.
- Esme Anne Platt (Evenson) – Carlisle's wife and *de facto* mother to the adopted children of his coven, Esme was an abused wife who ran away from her first husband, lost her child, and attempted suicide by throwing herself from a cliff. She was "rescued" by Carlisle who discovered her still alive in

the morgue. She seems the perfect mother to the Cullens but her consciousness and empathy was won through personal suffering.

- Edward Anthony Mason – Of all the Cullens, Edward had the most normal and healthiest life before his *faux* apotheosis. He was planning to join America's WWI effort when he was left an orphan by the Spanish Influenza, a death he escaped only because of his mother's pleas to Carlisle. He has a double curse in being a vampire: he thinks his earthly immortality has been won at the cost of his soul and hope of eternal life and he is a telepath of remarkable power with the twin edged sword of being able to hear everything that everyone except Bella is thinking. For the most part, not a happy puppy!
- Rosalie Lillian Hale – Rosalie is a blonde beauty and something of a narcissist who grew up as the only child of parents who wanted to use her beauty to climb the social ladder. Alas, she was gang raped by her socialite fiancée and his friends who left her for dead. All Rosalie wants is to be human again and to have children, the two things that vampires just cannot do. Vampires as a rule despise human beings for being so far beneath them; Rosalie does not care for them (us!) because she wishes she could become one.
- Emmett Dale McCarty – Emmett is the Cullen family member about which we know the least. He was raised in the mountains of east Tennessee and Rosalie heroically rescued him after finding him badly mauled from a fight with a bear. He is coarse, even crude, though good natured and fun-loving, which suggests the simple giant was something of a hillbilly. Until Jasper arrived, Emmett was the Cullen most likely to go off the wagon and have a drink out in town (a drink, that is, from the neck of a human being).
- Alice (Mary Alice) Brandon – Alice is able to see the future but, until Bella's escape from James in *Twilight*, she had little understanding of her past. Just as well! It seems her childhood was spent with parents in Biloxi, Mississippi, who were frightened by her paranormal perception and who institutionalized her rather than deal with the differences. Her past was dark because she grew up in a darkened cell. Alice seems the most stable of her brothers and sisters, perhaps, like Esme, because she has reason to embrace the present in light of her past.

- Jasper Whitlock (Hale) – As Jasper explains to Bella in *Eclipse*, "I didn't have quite the same... upbringing as my adopted siblings here." He was "the youngest major" in the Texas division of the Confederate Army when he was made a vampire somewhere between Galveston and Houston in October, 1862. The vampire Maria, who bit him to help her raise an army of newborns for the Mexican vampire wars, was his companion for the next hundred years. Jasper killed in that time not only for food but for revenge and conquest of territory in battles with other vampires and their newborn armies. "For the first century of my life," he tells Bella, "I lived in a world of bloodthirsty vengeance. Hate was my constant companion."

  This world was especially exhausting to him, because, as an empath, he lives "every day in a climate of emotion." He escaped the vampire wars to live as a nomad with two other vampires in the North but he became increasingly depressed.

  The depression "didn't fade" and became worse after hunting and killing human beings because he "lived their emotions as I killed them." He realized that "in so many years of slaughter and mayhem, I'd lost nearly all my humanity." His depression continued until he meets Alice who takes him to the Cullens to begin a new life as a vampire that does not take human life.

Jasper is uniquely scarred, both on the surface – his skin showing the thousands of bites and venom scars of his many fights to the death with vampires – and beneath. "After a century of instant gratification, I found self-discipline... challenging." His love for Alice and his relative freedom from depression, though, helps him keep with Carlisle's "vision."[22]

At chapter's start I mentioned Edward's adolescent rebellion. He explained, as does Jasper, that the "depression" he felt after killing helped him to make the choice to deny the monster inside him. This depression in both cases is conscience, the foundation of sacrificial or aesthetic choice. This conscience, an awareness of a greater self than our desires and ego advantage, is the heart of Carlisle's vision and faith.

What do these vampires have in common that they are able to hear the voice of conscience, to connect the dots about what spurs their conscience? In a word, "humility," a humility born of their suffering.

22 Jasper's story is told in *Eclipse,* chapter 13, pages 287-309

Look at the three Cullen women. One was beaten and abused by her husband so badly that she was driven to despair and suicide. Another was raped by her husband-to-be and his pals on the street and left to die there. The third was locked up in a mental home because she was different – with the family going so far as pretending she was dead to restrict the shame of her existence. Whew.

The men aren't much better. Carlisle has to hide from his father after he is bitten because if he hadn't, daddy would have done everything possible to kill him. He lives alone for two centuries before beginning to practice medicine and another fifty years before creating a vampire companion. Edward is robbed of his parents and a human life by disease *and* by Carlisle, who transforms him on Edward's mother's request, not Edward's. Emmett is mauled by a bear, though he sees his suffering as providential and ultimately edifying, "having been rescued by an angel and brought to God." Jasper, the oldest of the Cullen adoptees but the newest to the way of life, has lived an unending century of war and fighting for survival.

In short, we have our postmodern collection of marginalized freaks – a certified rebel, an Appalachian hillbilly, and a Mason, no less! With the Cullen women, they're all damaged goods who are united only in their struggle to live their lives outside of the 'vampire first' metanarrative of the Volturi. They are the heroes of the books, ultimately, who will stare down the Black Hats in the Mountain Meadow climax.

Well, not really.

They are part of the "speaking truth to power" finale, of course, but they're not the heroes and heroines of the story. Bella Swan is the heroine of the piece because she trumps the Cullens and the La Push wolf pack in the depth of her self-actualizing choices. Her choice changes their worlds and how they understand one another.

Remember, none of the Quileute protectors or the Cullen family chose to be wolfmen or vampires. They make anti-Volturi, anti-vampire-fascism choices, certainly, but these choices are almost hard wired into them all except for Jasper, and for him it is a struggle. The Native American wolves experience their super powers as good but also with some regret despite their necessity, because becoming protectors just happened to them. It was not something they chose. The Cullens chose to be vegetarians because of Carlisle's vision rather than their independent volition. Each group, the two of which are effectively mirrored images of each other, is 100% "don't eat human" but hardly by "free agency."

Bella, though, is unique in choosing to become a vampire *and* a Cullen, anti-Volturi, protect-the-human, vegetarian vampire. She sacrifices her ego identity, embraces the difficulty, even agony of losing her humanity, out of her love for her complete opposite, Edward, with whom she longs to be joined forever.

Her seeming differences with Edward, the near God-Man, however, are superficial. Remember that, as Edward notes, she is "kind and self-effacing and unselfish and loving and brave – she was good through and through." As her name reveals, she is an ugly duckling from which a "bella" or "beautiful" swan is waiting to emerge.

The depth of her goodness and what makes her something like the Holy Virgin of Postmodernism, for which forgive me, is that her mind cannot be read or manipulated. Not by Edward, not by Jane, not by Aro. The reason her mind cannot be read is that she is almost entirely heart or cardiac intelligence, call it "conscience," rather than cranial intelligence. Brain thinking, of course, is the ego delusion and prejudices of our identification with the cultural metanarratives that separate us from experiencing reality directly or knowing it objectively. Bella isn't about that. At all.

Hence the mysterious, nigh on inexplicable attraction of true seekers Edward and Jacob (and all young human men) to the mousy girl from Phoenix. Edward three times in *Midnight Sun* describes Bella as his "opposite" and, more importantly, "entirely other." He goes so far as to think she isn't human,[23] a subject for the following chapter on allegory. Her goodness is her purity of heart, in her being only the "inner heart" of conscience; Bella's choice for vampirism to sacrifice her ego self in love transforms not only herself but the Olympic vampire and Quileute communities.

Both the Native American protectors and the Cullen family are anti-human eating vampires. They differ only in degree in this; the Quileute wolf men will hunt and kill any vampires in their territory. The Cullens simply ask nomads not to eat where they live. Neither group,

23 *Midnight Sun*, chapter 6, 'page 87': "Was she really even human? She *looked* human. She felt soft as a human. She smelled human – well, better actually. She acted human... sort of. But she didn't think like a human or act like one." See chapter three for Mrs. Meyer's comments about her being an "anti-human" writer.

though, is disturbed enough by the growing newborn vampire army in Seattle that is slaughtering humans to do anything about it.

Even more interesting, the Quileute-Cullen relationship is a function of a treaty rather than friendship. It is difficult for these paranormal Montagues and Capulets even to be near one another; quite literally as well as figuratively, each experiences the other as something that stinks. Each side has lost their perspective on why they oppose the Volturi way-of-vampire-life and taken on some part of that metanarrative which blinds them to the good in the other.

The Native American wolfmen exist to kill vampires, they think, and forget that they only kill vampires to protect their people. The Cullens as proven vampire-vegans are no threat to their people but, qua vampires, they remain 'other' and, consequently, evil.

The Cullens as a rule have forsaken taking human life. None of the Cullen children or even Esme, though, have achieved Carlisle's ability to be in a room in which there is human blood, and at least three of them still have pronounced vampire bias toward human beings as 'lesser people.' Wolfmen who hunt vampires are a notch below that. Alice and Rosalie call Jacob Black a "dog" without blushing, hesitation, or remorse; Jacob is at least as enthusiastic with "leech" and "blood sucker."

But Bella's alchemical wedding, pregnancy, childbirth, and transformation to vampire change all that. Her choice made in love for Edward has the immediate consequences of uniting the Olympic Coven and La Push Pack – Jacob's imprinting on Reneesme eliminates any chance of an attack and creates a real if unofficial alliance – which union and show of strength is responsible in large part for causing the Volturi to back down in the Mountain Meadow.

PoMo Story formula: (3) Truth is spoken to power (2) consequent to sacrificial choice (1) made by the outsider. Bella Swan, a clumsy human among shapeshifting wolfmen and vampires, is the ultimate outsider. She chooses to become a vampire at the cost of her humanity. Her life as a vampire mommy creates the alliance and power that forces the Volturi judges to retreat from their plan to destroy the Cullen family and their friends on the baseball field.

The alliance as I've noted was a big part of this, but, as important, especially in neutralizing the powers Jane and Alec have to paralyze combatants, is Bella's discovered power. Bella's pure heart or "no metanarrative mind" is her great quality as a human being which purity when ramped up by the purgatory chrysalis of a transition to vampire becomes the ability to project a force field bubble (think Sue Storm-Richards, the Invisible Girl of Marvel Comics' Fantastic Four).

But what is this force field?

It is the ability of Bella to allow others to experience her freedom from metanarrative influence or prejudice and the consequent freedom not to be manipulated by the powers of other ego-driven, advantage-focused minds. Having won the interior battle of fearing the "other" and having chosen to join herself sacrificially in love to her opposite, she becomes the means for all those she loves to transcend their restricted views and see with a pure heart (Matthew 5:8). Her exterior foes do not stand a chance, as the Volturi learn to their great frustration, hence their prudent retreat.

The Postmodern Morality of *Twilight*

If Bella is the heroine on which we are supposed to imprint to learn the lessons and the beliefs we need to have as postmoderns, there is an un-Bella in the story from whose actions and her consequent fate we are supposed to learn what happens if we don't make the heroic choice to "speak to power." What if we conform and submit to the divisive metanarrative of advantage and bias?

Ask Irina.

Irina of the Denali coven cannot transcend her mind-lock on what the regime has taught her and her own prejudices. Having loved and lost her vampire boyfriend Laurent to the La Push wolfmen and refused, consequently, to fight alongside the Cullens against Victoria's newborn army in *Eclipse*, Irina sees Reneesme in *Breaking Dawn* and makes a fatal choice. She assumes – in fear, in hope of revenging Laurent's death, and in conformity to what she had learned happened to those hiding Immortal children – that Reneesme was a child immortal like the "sister" she had that was the cause of the Volturi killing her mother.

Again, in revenge, fear, or faux fidelity to her masters, then, she reports Reneesme's existence to the Volturi who use her report as the reason they were looking for to confront and destroy the Olympic coven whose very human-serving existence challenged the foundation of their vampire order. Irina realizes, however, in the Mountain Meadow that she was mistaken and tells the Volturi to back down; Caius instead destroys her, supposedly for her false report but almost certainly for her confession of her error and exposing their mistake in believing her.

Irina's loyalty to the Volturi metanarrative and last-minute apostasy costs her her life.

The moral level of meaning in any story is pretty easy to pick up. What is good is whatever the heroes and heroines wearing White Hats believe and do – and we are supposed to leave the show sharing this belief and feeling encouraged to act as they do. The evil side of things, the foil to the good, is whatever the Black Hats are thinking and doing.

For a story to really resonate with our hearts morally, it has to do two things. First, it has to connect with the sense of right and wrong we have from living in the historical period we do. The story must simultaneously reflect *and* reinforce the core beliefs of my politically correct culture. Then it has to get past my historically isolated ideas to get to transcendent truths of truth, beauty, and virtue that are universal and which will still be relevant when we enter the post-post-postmodern period.

Twilight, as we've seen, passes the postmodern story formula checklist with flying colors. The marginalized rebels and rejects choose to transcend the prejudices they have to come together and speak to the elites who have been empowered by a divisive, false, and cruel myth. The key heroine is "entirely other" and sacrifices herself, by which death to ego and false identity and obedience to heart and conscience she is divinized and saves those around her. The ugly duckling-become-"beautiful swan" unites Montague vampires and wolfpack Capulet to free them the Olympic Peninsula of their historic prejudices and the shadow of the Volturi in their own hearts.

Which makes our politically correct hearts swell and eyes water.

But what about those larger meanings of truth, goodness, and beauty? Is there anything spiritual, something hinting of the Absolute or God in these romances? Once this historical period's fascination with the evils of prejudice, our inability to know, and with the inevitable marginalizing of those not celebrated in a culture's myth. Is there still any story here to enjoy?

Yes, there is. For the allegorical layer of meaning and the greater "wow" of *Twilight,* just turn the page.

Chapter 3

The Allegorial Layer of Meaning:

The Satirical Stories and God-Man 'Everyman' Drama within the Bella-Edward Love Story

I explained in the Preface how the four senses of any text, its layers of meaning, correspond to the four types of human knowing. The surface meaning of the story, its plot and narrative drive, is what we know directly from it, the way we get information about our world from sense perception. The moral layer of meaning is imbedded in the surface, the Good Guys and Bad Guys and what kind of behavior and thinking the author gives us as models. This 'right and wrong' corresponds to the kind of knowledge we call opinion, that is, 'information filtered through our beliefs about good and bad.'

That was worth the effort, but I don't think we found more there than a story told well enough to fully engage us and one confirming the beliefs we all share. Nothing especially mythic or profound in that, as much as a challenge as it can be to look at our own postmodern eyeballs. To get at the meanings of a text, though, that explain the depth of reader attachment to the *Twilight* novels and the number of books sold, we have to go deeper. We need to get into the allegorical and anagogical meanings of Mrs. Meyer's work for that, the artistry that corresponds to sure knowledge and wisdom.

The first two layers are pretty straightforward because they are both in the story plot we read and understand consciously. The next two layers, in contrast, are experienced largely beneath our thinking consciousness. They are not less real experiences, however, but more real and more important for penetrating beyond the surface of our understanding and beliefs. The power and meat of story is in its allegorical and anagogical layers that touch and shape our hearts.

To see the surface artistry and meaning we had to look at the narrative line diagonally, something like those cut-away diagrams in our school geology and biology texts that reveal the various strata of earth and the 57 varieties of dermal layers in our skin. To get at the morality of the novels we x-rayed the surface layer which revealed the skeletal scaffolding of right and wrong, good guys and bad guys that holds the story structure up like bones do our bodies.

For allegory and the sublime anagogical meaning, we will look at story symbolism and structures as if they were windows. Allegorical meaning is found in seeing through story content as if it were a *transparency* whose inside is a greater reality. It has us looking in. The anagogical experience is less us looking in than our being illumined imaginatively by the light of something more real shining on us through the story content as if it were a *translucency.*

Why bother with these windows into the text? To figure out how they do what they do.

In a nutshell, the reason we and millions of other readers around the world respond to these stories is that their allegorical and anagogical meanings are about the central drama and relationship of human existence – our life with God – told in compelling, engaging fashion.

Remember the Eliade thesis about why we love to read? Entertainments serve a mythic or religious function in secular culture. We live in a country whose *de facto* state religion is atheistic naturalism, meaning the core truth we learn in school is that only matter and energy quantities are real, with side cults of relativism, individualism and narcissism. These are all the zombie existence of life without God that Mrs. Meyer satirizes in *New Moon.* The *Twilight* novels in their allegorical and sublime content give us imaginative experience of spiritual, transcendent reality and foster our cardiac intelligence.

We'll start with *Twilight's* allegories, the story transparencies or windows for looking through the content to see something greater. An allegory or "alieniloquium," literally, "one thing saying another thing," is the story behind or within the story that the author tells us in the shadow of the surface narrative. Think *Pilgrim's Progress, Animal Farm, Gulliver's Travels* and *Canterbury Tales* - stories with messages beneath the story being told. The goal of this figurative "double-talk" is transcending our fallen human state.

Is Bella "Anti-Human"? Mrs. Meyer Sure Is

I think the text makes it pretty clear that this is a story about being *truly* human, which is to say, being *beyond* or even *anti-human* , but here we have Mrs. Meyer's testimony as well on the human and anti-human allegorical content of her work.

When asked if her books were vampire novels, she balked, insisting that insomuch as they are stories about "monsters" they are about monsters trying to be truly human:

> "I don't know what that comes under, what the genre title is for that so it is hard to classify it. As regards horror, I was inspired to write about vampires because I had a dream about vampires which was odd for me because I'd had no interest in vampires before I started to write about them so why I was dreaming about them, I don't know. But it was a great dream and it wasn't about this character being a monster. **It was about this character trying to be human and that was what fascinated me and that's what made me want to write it down."**[1]

When accused of being anti-feminist because Bella is insufficiently strident in standing up to the men in her life, Mrs. Meyer has written on her website that she isn't anti-women but *anti-human*:

> There are those who think Bella is a wuss. There are those who think my stories are misogynistic—the damsel in distress must be rescued by strong hero. ...
>
> I emphatically reject the [accusation of misogyny]. I am all about girl power—look at Alice and Jane if you doubt that. I am not anti-female, **I am anti-human**. [highlighting in original] I wrote this story from the perspective of a female human because that came most naturally, as you might imagine. But if the narrator had been a male human, it would not have changed the events. When a human being is totally surrounded by creatures with supernatural strength, speed, senses, and various other uncanny powers, he or she is not going to be able to hold his or her own. Sorry. That's just the way it is. We can't all be slayers. Bella does pretty well I think, all things considered. She saves Edward, after all.[2]

1 Emphasis added; http://www.rte.ie/arts/2008/1212/stephaniemeyer.html

2 http://stepheniemeyer.com/nm_thestory.html

As we discussed last chapter, Edward in *Midnight Sun* is flummoxed by Bella's reaction to blood, most especially by her ability to *smell* it.

> Was she really even human? She *looked* human. She felt soft as a human. She smelled human – well, better actually. She acted human ... sort of. But she didn't think like a human or act like one.
>
> What other option was there, though?[3]

How about a human doing her best to live beyond her human, psychological limits? In brief, Bella is a seeker, the spiritually focused anti-human human wanting to transcend normal life and become divine.

But before we unwrap the big *kahuna* allegory, let's open up with the more obvious correspondences, where single characters represent groups of people we know, and work our way up to the more profound spiritual references. First stop, the coalition of friends gathered to testify for the Cullens in the Mountain Meadow finale.

The Allegory of Obvious Stick-Figure Stand-Ins

Breaking Dawn's finale in the Mountain Meadow was a huge event toward which the drama of the Saga had been heading for the better part of three books. It's an allegorical play land with almost everyone involved as a witness for the Cullen Coven and Renesmee standing in for a type of person or as a token for a group of people. The actual historical event that took place in a Mountain Meadow which inspired Mrs. Meyer's original dream will have to wait until Chapter 6, along with the real-world referents for the Volturi, the Cullen Coven, and the La Push Wolf Pack. But their witnesses for the Cullens are fair game for tit-for-tat translation; who or what are the referents for these allegorical stick figures?

- Garrett, whom we met in the last chapter, is an American patriot who sings out a Thomas Paine philippic celebrating Revolutionary virtues of freedom and individualism contra group-think to the Volturi. He is the best of American independent thinking and character.[4]

3 *Midnight Sun*, chapter 6, 'page 87'

4 *Breaking Dawn*, page 610

- Zafrina, Senna, and Kachiri are, as is natural I suppose for women appropriately called "Amazons," wild women that, of all the witness covens, frighten Bella. She says "everything about them" from their animal hide clothes and appearance to their way of moving seemed "wild;" "I'd never met any vampires less civilized." After experiencing indirectly Zafrina's power to project compelling illusions into other people's minds and sparring with her, Bella notes: "In truth, though I liked Zafrina very much and I knew she wouldn't really hurt me, the wild woman scared me to death." The Amazons, I suggest for your consideration, are feminists, the "wild women" without men in their midst who are simultaneously attractive and repulsive to the married and relatively domestic Bella.[5]
- The Egyptian Coven has four members but the two women are shadows of their partners. Amun with silent wife Kebi are cartoon stereotypes of old guard Middle Eastern Arabs with exaggerated sense of family obligation, of being insulted, and paranoia about the designs of other people. Benjamin with his mate Tia are nominally the "children" of Amun because he made them vampires, but Benjamin's abilities to manipulate the elements are so remarkable that everything in the coven turns on his views. Edward likes Benjamin because of this independence and his unwillingness to be used by Amun: "He has a very clear sense of right and wrong. I like his attitude."[6] The Egyptian coven are allegorical back-lot stick figures for 21st century Muslims and the generational divide in the Arabic world.
- The Irish Clan are led by Siobhan and include Maggie and Siobhan's mate Liam. The women here are the power holders; Maggie is a truth-or-lie litmus strip able to detect the veracity of any spoken word and Siobhan, though she denies it, has the "subtle but powerful gift to make things go her way."[7] Just a guess here, but I suspect the Irish vampires are place-holders in the story for real world 'Celtic' pagans and druid wanna-bes, the traditional Gaelic foundation that New Age mind masters like to claim as their own.

5 Op.cit., pages 612-613, 617
6 Op.cit, page 610
7 Op.cit., page 608, 660

- The Romanian Coven, Stefan and Vladimir, at first seem to be included just for comic relief. They are the most Hollywood-Dracula like of any of Mrs. Meyer's vampires (think of Rowling's similarly funny Legosi-look-alike 'Sanguini' in *Half-Blood Prince*), about whom Jacob Black observes to Bella "Dracula One and Dracula Two are creep-tacular."[8] Their Balkan heritage, ancient lineage, and, most of all, their obsessive vendetta with the Volturi, though, mark them as Orthodox Christian cut-outs.

If that seems a laughable stretch to you, I can only beg for your patience. All of these allegorical characters and covens align themselves with the Cullens and against the Volturi because of the allegorical referents of those White and Black Hat wearing groups. That is the subject of chapter 6, alas, in which I will gladly explain why it is important that such an unlikely group of non-conformists and 'family-style' vampires, if not "vegetarians" would risk all against the hated Volturi. Don't miss it.

My favorite Allegorical note that Mrs. Meyer strikes, though, is satirical and comes in the beginning of Bella's re-awakening from the shock of Edward's departure in *New Moon.*

Remember Bella's response to Edward's fare-thee-well in the backyard forest?

> He was gone.
>
> With shaky legs, ignoring the fact that my action was useless, I followed him into the forest. The evidence of his path had disappeared instantly. There were no footprints, the leaves were still again, but I walked forward without thinking. I could not do anything else. I had to keep moving. If I stopped looking for him, it was over.
>
> Love, life, meaning... over.[9]

The agony of *New Moon* – and with Edward absent and Bella longing for him constantly, it is easily the most difficult of the four books to enjoy – is Bella's struggle to find a meaningful life without him. Her "love, life, and meaning" are "over." We readers get the blank-

8 Op.cit., page 631

9 *New Moon,* Chapter 3, page 73

pages-as-chapters trip through the next four months[10] until Bella wakes up in a new year and begins a zombie-in-recovery existence.

The allegorical element here is most evident in what Bella is reading for school and watching at the movies: *Animal Farm* by George Orwell in the classroom and *Dead End,* a zombie slasher flick at the theatre in Port Angeles. Mrs. Meyer is writing a story about human life without the presence of the divine Beloved; her lead character, appropriately, is reading a satire of the human condition in an atheist culture and watching a horror movie about mindless, worse-than-dead human beings.

Dead End is a pointer to the six *Living Dead* movies of director George Romero. These movies are satirical depictions of life in America, in which country the mindless consumers are taking over both by sheer force of numbers and by eating the few remaining people who can still think for themselves or who have the remnants of a conscience. Mrs. Meyer echoes this message in her depiction of Bella's friends, whose petty concerns and cluelessness reflect something like Romero's zombie-land of shopping malls and mechanical, materialist living.

Bella, having lived with the Cullens, however, gets Orwell's and Romero's message and looks for a greater life than she can have as a zombie. Bella, a character responding to satire within a satire, deciphers the satire all around her – from her reading, from the movie, and self-reflection on her experience – and changes her life. This self-awareness, perhaps, is the effect all satirists or just the naïve ones must hope their works have on readers. To really understand how knowing the Cullens helped Bella with *Animal Farm,* we have to unwrap the allegorical meaning of the Olympic Coven.

The Cullen Family as Holy Trinity and Edward as Word of God

Mrs. Meyer has pointed to the different qualities reflected in the Cullen coven or "family" couples as the meaning that their characters reflect. In answer to a *Twilight Lexicon* question about which couple is the "closest," she said:

> **Q.** Ok, so we know that Alice and Jasper are very close, so I was wondering how close are Emmett and Rosalie, and Carlisle and Esme? Out of the three couples which one has the closest relationship?

---

10 Op.cit., pages 85-94

> **A.** This is an apples to oranges question, because their relationships are so different. Rosalie and Emmett's might be seen as the most superficial in a way, because their relationship is so intensely physical. But they are entirely committed to each other, so that's hardly superficial... Esme and Carlisle have the most spiritual relationship, for lack of a better word. Their relationship is on another plane from Rosalie and Emmett's. And then Alice and Jasper's is the most...mystical. They just ARE together, and have been from before they even met. They are not complete without each other–and never were. That's what makes them different from the other couples, the "never were." They were already not-whole before they met, waiting for each other.[11]

The first thing to see here is what is fairly obvious; the couples are distinct and their differences reflect the qualities of the powers or characteristics they embody. Emmett the strong man and Rosalie the bombshell are about their bodies. Alice the prophetess and Jasper the empath are both damaged goods but are attuned to the psychic sphere of relative intangibles like emotion and future possibilities. Esme and Carlisle are loving and at peace; they live entirely for others, especially their adopted children, in light of Carlisle's "vision" and "principle."

Looking at these three couples as a whole or as units, which is to say, as if they were each one person, then, we can see the three pairs as pictures of body, soul, and spirit. They work together, when harmonious, in obedience and deference to spirit, and with body taking direction as well from the insights of soul aligned to spirit. The Cullens are a story snapshot of the human being with its three aspects or faculties working in harmony for the greater spiritual life.

Mrs. Meyer isn't inventing this on her own, if the couples variation is a wonderful twist. The idea of three persons representing the faculties of soul can be seen in Plato's Charioteer in the *Phaedrus* and in Hume's *Dialogue Concerning Human Understanding.* The "soul triptych" or three person representation of one human soul in story is a *topos* of modern literature beginning with Dmitri, Ivan, and Alyosha in *The Brothers Karamazov,* arguably the greatest novel ever written. We know it best in our day from its use in teevee shows like *Star Trek,* in which 'Bones' is body, 'Spock' is mind, and Kirk is Captain and spirit, and movies like *Star Wars,* with Han Solo as body, Leia as will, and Luke "Use the Force" Skywalker as spirit.

11 Personal correspondence 9 http://www.twilightlexicon.com/?p=81

It is in our favorite books, too, with the three hobbits on Mt. Doom in *Return of the King* being Tolkien's picture of the body (Gollum), will (Sam), and selfless spirit (Frodo). The triptych of the Hogwarts Adventures, too, Ron the Body, Hermione the Brainiac, and Harry the Eye of the Heart, conform to traditional formula.

Mrs. Meyer, of course, isn't saying these couples embody these ideas to the exclusion of the others. Emmett and Rosalie aren't just bodies but predominantly physical, hence their being believable allegorical figures of the body, which doesn't exist without soul or spirit, either.[12] But that they represent increasingly spiritual aspects of the person – body to soul to spirit – is hard to miss. Their role in the story as divine immortals beyond temporal human concerns suggests an even larger allegorical use than the formulaic one of the three aspects of a human person. The Cullens are also a story symbol of the Holy Trinity of Father, Son, and Holy Spirit.

That may seem a great leap to you, but hang with me. Traditionally, human beings are understood as having been created "in the image of God" and our task as creations is to grow "in His likeness." Exegetes of this *Genesis* idea have uniformly said it is not in man's body that we find God's image or reflection but in the faculties of the human soul; God is a Trinity and the human soul's faculties align themselves body and soul in hierarchal relation with spirit as Son and Holy Spirit act as the "two hands" [13] of the Father from which one is "begotten" and the other "proceeds."

---

12 Twilight Lexicon.com, Personal Correspondence 10, http://www.twilightlexicon.com/?p=198

Q. *On one thread you said that Carlisle & Esme have a spiritual relationship, Rosalie & Emmett were physical, and Alice & Jasper were mythical. I was wondering about Bella's and Edward's relationship, what is theirs?*

A. Before I answer this, I want to say that the traits I assigned to the Cullen couples were not to be understood as totally definitive; these characteristics, spiritual, physical and mythical, were merely the most prominent facet of each relationship—other facets are still quite strong with each. For example, though Carlisle and Esme have a very strong spiritual and intellectual link, they also are quite attracted to each other physically. The same goes for the others.

13 St. Irenaeus, *Against Heresies*, Book V, Chapter 17, Point 4; cited in Kallistos Ware, *The Orthodox Way*, pages 35-36; for man as Trinity, see chapters 6-8 of James Cutsinger, *That Man Might Become God*, http://www.cutsinger.net/pdf/that_man_might_become_god.pdf

From this traditional view, as a divine Body-Soul-Spirit triptych, the Cullens are story-incarnations of the 'Father,' Carlisle and Esme together, the 'Holy Spirit,' the "mystical" Alice and Jasper, and the 'Incarnate Son,' the relatively carnal Emmett and Rosalie. The other-worldly house of light, brilliant white walls, beautiful music, and wall sized windows in which no one sleeps or eats is their heavenly home.

I confess this would strike me as so much forced-meaning-into-text nonsense except for how it opens up the core allegory of the story, the love of Edward and Bella.

Edward as Word of God:
Bella's Means to Joining Holy Family

As noted above, Bella is our archetypal "seeker," the spiritually focused 'anti-human' human wanting to transcend normal life and become divine. The *Twilight* Saga is, consequently, the story of her transition from living in Charlie's house in Forks to the Cullen heavenly mansion outside town. Her means to make this remarkable trip, of course, is her relationship with Edward. Their romance and union is Bella's ticket to life with the three immortal couples living in something like paradise.

The reason I think the three Cullens pairs are best understood as story reflections of the Holy Trinity or God rather than just as a soul triptych is because of what Edward does in the story. He is Bella's means to a life with God and the story-equivalent of immortality or eternal life. Though he is described many times as an "angel" and is portrayed as the vampire-immortal struggling with his human aspect, Edward is more than messenger and paranormal Peter Parker. As the First Son of the Cullen Father and Bella's only means to joining this Holy Family and Trinity, Edward is the Christ figure of the story.

This interpretation is problematic on at least two levels. One that I'll get into (in Part 2) is because he has a more down-to-earth historical human referent than the God-Man. Another is just that Christ as 'Son of God' is already part of the Trinity and it's sloppy, to say the least, to have a Holy Trinity triptych and an independent Christ figure in the same story. I see that and grant that it is not as neat as we all like our tit-for-tat story correspondences to work. The White Whale shouldn't represent God if there is another compelling God image in *Moby Dick.*

Edward as Christ, however, works not only in his being the only avenue Bella the Seeker has at hand to move from her fallen human condition to life as a principle-observing immortal but also because of his singular gift. Edward is the giant among the Cullens, if everyone also defers to Carlisle and Esme and to Alice's visions, because he is a mind reader.

So what?

Well, you don't just walk on with this ability, at least not in stories. The ability to see all thoughts speaks to there being a unity of thought, a common ground. If everyone were thinking on different frequencies or if our thinking were entirely individual, not somehow joined, then Edward could not read and understand everyone's thinking regardless of language as he does.

This "common ground," however, is a distinctly Christian thought. The *Logos* or Word in Christian belief is the uncreated aspect of our minds and the pre-existent "cohesion of all things" (Col 1:17), the Creative Principle, "without Which was not anything made that was made" (John 1:3). This *Logos* is the "inside bigger than the outside" of all things, both the fabric of existent reality *and* of thought. Hence C. S. Lewis' belief after Owen Barfield and S. T. Coleridge that the "universe was mental" and our lives and thinking a "participation in a cosmic *Logos*."[14]

Edward's signature ability to enter into all minds except Bella's is something that is possible of the *Logos*. How do we know this *Logos* in Itself? We know It by listening to that *logos* in us that is the uncreated aspect of our minds – usually called "conscience" – and by fostering this *logos* faculty within us in its ability to recognize its reflection in the inner principles (*logoi*) of everything and everyone else. Christian natural theology teaches that this *logos* recognition is the only way we know anything at all.[15]

14 "I was therefore compelled [via Barfield's argument] to give up realism. . . . I must admit that mind was no late-come epiphenomenon; that the whole universe was, in the last resort, mental; that our logic was participation in a cosmic *Logos*. C. S. Lewis, *Surprised by Joy: The Shape of My Early Life* (New York: Harcourt, Brace, Jovanovich, 1955), pp 208-209

15 Hence Coleridge's famous assertion that all knowledge is the "coincidence of subject and object," the logos recognizing itself in others, eliding knowing subject and known object as does a mirror.

And we know the *Logos* or Son of God in the Word's historical Incarnation as Jesus of Nazareth, also known as the Christ. Christians worship Jesus the Christ because they believe He is the Man-God through Whom they can have Communion with God and achieve *theosis* or divinization. They know Him as the Word of God Who is the *Logos* foundation of everything existent and of all thought.

This is what Edward the immortal mind-reader is to Bella. Again, Edward is the Christ figure of *Twilight*.

Man-God Love Story: Garden of Eden Fall Re-told as Romance

We will have to come back to the subject of a common mind in the conclusion to Part 1 and again in chapters 6 and 7, because there is a lot more to be said about the idea of the "universe being mental" and shared thinking in *Twilight*. The La Push Pack and their one mind, for instance, and Bella's perceiving each person inside her force field as light reflect Mrs. Meyer's artistry with the idea of *logos* epistemology extending beyond just Edward.

For now, though, it is sufficient to see Edward as *somehow* divine and as a story stand-in for God. Bella is the actress playing 'Human Seeker' in this drama and Edward is an actor playing 'God.' The principal and most powerful allegorical meaning of the *Twilight* Saga, not too surprisingly, is the story of God's love for man, man's longing for God, human relationship and communion with Him, and the drama of this relationship.

Twilight is largely a retelling of the Adam and Eve narrative we have in *Genesis*, the first book of the Bible.

You know that story, right? God creates Adam in His image and Eve to be Adam's helpmate. The only rules in Eden are not to eat the fruit from the tree at the Center of the Garden, the Tree of the Knowledge of Good and Evil. The Serpent seduces Eve into eating the apple and Adam follows her lead. Man's fall, his disobedience, results in God expelling them from the Garden. Just like *Twilight*.

As my daughters say, "Not."

Well, there **are** quite a few pointers from *Twilight* to Eden, sufficient, in fact, that suggesting the author wants us to be thinking about the one while reading her story is reasonable.

Start with the cover of the first book in the series. It features a woman's arms and hands holding out an apple. The author has said that "The apple on the cover of *Twilight* represents 'forbidden fruit'" and "I love the beautiful simplicity of the picture. To me it says: *choice*."[16]

Not good enough? How about the epigraph that starts the book:

> But of the tree of the knowledge of good and evil, thou shalt not eat of it: for in the day that thou eatest thereof thou shalt surely die. (Genesis 2:37)

Mrs. Meyer links the cover and the epigraph in her answer to the question about the apple:

> The apple on the cover of *Twilight* represents "forbidden fruit." I used the scripture from *Genesis* (located just after the table of contents) because I loved the phrase "the fruit of the knowledge of good and evil." Isn't this exactly what Bella ends up with?

So, add that up. The front cover of the first book and the first words in the series are about Adam and Eve in the Garden of Eden. The author confirms this was intentional and that the heroine in the story learns the Eden lesson in the book.

There's more.

When Bella first sits down next to Edward in Mr. Banner's biology classroom, he tightens up strangely, his hands balled up into fists and sitting "so still he seemed not to be breathing." Bella thinks the guy has problems. "It couldn't have anything to do with me. He didn't know me from Eve."[17]

Even before this, when she first sees the Cullens, her 'First Sight' of the first chapter's title, Alice gets up to leave the cafeteria and the only food on her tray is an "unbitten apple."[18] Much better, Bella and Edward's first significant, wide open conversation at school takes place in the cafeteria the day after their adventure in Port Angeles. Edward goes through the cafeteria line with her and "filled a tray with food." The food she chooses to picks up from the full tray first, of course, is an apple.[19]

---

16 http://www.stepheniemeyer.com/twilight_faq.html#apple
17 *Twilight*, page 24
18 Op.cit., page 19
19 Op.cit., page 207

I'm not sure, beyond citing the Bible story in an epigraph in the "this is what the story is about" place, having Bella call herself Eve in relation to an angry Edward, and the apples on the cover and in the story between Bella and Edward, what more Mrs. Meyer could do to make this connection with the Garden of Eden. Maybe have them wear fig leaves?

Actually, she does something better. She states and repeats endlessly that there is a Grand Canyon of difference between these two. As Bella explains to Edward when he asserts she cannot know she cares for him more than he does for her, they're obviously not equally matched:

> "Well, look at me," I said, unnecessarily as he was already staring. "I'm absolutely ordinary – well, except for bad things like all the near-death experiences and being so clumsy that I'm almost disabled. And look at you." I waved my hand toward him and all his bewildering perfection.[20]

Of course, Edward in his version of this story, *Midnight Sun*, marvels repeatedly at her being "entirely other." This becomes something like their conversational story loop until they are married and she makes the leap into vampire-hood. She marvels at his perfect beauty, his grace, his angelic features, etc. He coos at her beauty and tells her how far from meaningless plainness and from the ordinary she really is.

That could be just Love Story formula infatuation, I suppose, except that Edward really **is** an example of "bewildering perfection" and other-worldly excellence. It is no stretch to think of him as human story-stand-in for God because he is essentially unkillable, never eats or sleeps as a human does, doesn't need to breathe, and, no matter how long he lives, he won't age. Did I mention superhuman strength, sensitivity, and speed? Sacrificial love? He has it all. The guy is a natural for God's part in the Garden drama.

Bella is a fit for the leading role in the "Fall of Man" play largely because she falls down a lot. I'm not joking. Think of *New Moon*. Almost every major plot shift in the second *Twilight* novel is initiated by Bella falling down. Quite literally.

The major allegorical question to be explored in *New Moon* as I'll explain in a second is "How do we live without God in our lives?" The answer to "What if God leaves?" is presented quite literally as a "fall" to represent our "fall from grace" at birth. On Bella's birthday, then,

---

20 *Twilight*, page 210

appropriately enough, she cuts her finger when opening presents at the party Alice throws for her. Jasper attacks, and, in Edwards haste to protect her, he hits her hard enough into a table stacked with gifts and crystal that "it fell, as I did." She cuts her arm from wrist to elbow. Bella's fall causes Edward's departure and prompts Carlisle's explanation of why Edward would leave.

The other two "falls" in *New Moon* that serve as markers for story shifts are (1) Bella's fall from the Cliff on the Quileute reservation, which jump, because of Alice's misunderstanding it as meaning Bella is dead, brings on Edward's attempted suicide in Volterra, and (2) the descent through the grate and underground sewers to enter the Volturi castle. The "fall" at the Cullens' house causes the separation of Edward and Bella, the jump from the cliffs, inspired as it was by Bella's desire to hear Edward's voice, is the cause of their reconciliation, and the descent into Volterra's slice of hell is the passage Edward and Bella take together to the crucible in which their union is sealed.

The God-Man Love Story: Limits and Responsibilities of each one's love

What makes this Garden of Eden love story work for me, though, isn't the artful touches and clues with which Mrs. Meyer litters her story. What seals the deal on *Twilight* as a God-Man love story with Edward as God and Bella as the Human Seeker are the specific qualities of their love for one another, loves that are really quite different. Think about it.

Edward's love is constant, unchanging, respectful and extremely *careful*; Bella's love is selfless, total, and sacrificial. Their romance, cosmically disproportionate, is a parable or transparency of the inequalities and responsibilities of the divine-human synergy. God, like Edward his Bella, cannot love man fully or He would destroy the human free capacity to love and the virtue in the human choice of obedience to God. Man, like Bella seeking her beloved Edward, must die to the "flesh" identity of body and soul and risk all to love God truly.

Hence Edward-God's looking over Bella every night as she sleeps but not daring to get too close lest he destroy her. These overnights, especially in light of Bella's father's being clueless about them, would be a moral disaster except that we've stepped into the world of parable and Mystery Play and out of day-to-day conventions. Edward's need as God is, first, always to respect the boundaries dividing God and Man;

lest he destroy her, he must wait for her choice for their union to have any meaning.

Even acknowledging their communion or love is a problem for God-Edward because loving God means death to mundane human life; the life of the spirit means forsaking even the soul aspects of "flesh." Edward is always troubled by her understanding of the choice she is making and if he can be sure she understands what she is forsaking. Without this understanding, divinization is not really desirable or will require the Purgatory of life as an uncontrollable newborn.

From her side, Bella as Human Seeker really has no choice, as we see in the *Twilight* pivotal scene in which she realizes that she loves God-Edward, cannot imagine any other life but with Him, and that she must live her life accordingly whatever the cost. God-Edward's love is constant and careful; Bella the spiritual Seeker's synergistic responsibility is selfless, sacrificial love.

A brief book-by-book look reveals the Saga's God-Man love story plays out this way:

- In *Twilight*, the curtain goes up and we meet all the principal players in our Medieval play: Bella, the Human Seeker, Edward the Divine, and the Cullen trio of couples as the Holy Trinity. Bella's goal is to love Edward totally and eternally, which she understands will mean her eventually becoming a vampire-goddess shorn of her fallen (and falling down) humanity. Edward is preoccupied with not destroying her, either by his carelessness or by her being taken into her family before she understands what she is giving up. The crisis of the play has Bella sacrificing her life to save a human being and Edward demonstrating, in his rescue, that he is capable of loving her without destroying her. Bella remains human but begins her absorption into the Holy Family

- In *New Moon*, we take a big detour. Instead of the "How can Man and God love another?" struggle, the story is "How do human beings live without God?" The answer is pretty much "like a zombie." Bella's heart and the hole where her heart should be cause her agony throughout the story as her spiritual faculty longs for the divine Edward. She does anything to hear his voice speak within her, usually something remarkably reckless. The drama ends with the reunion and the revelation that the Edward driven separation was as agonizing for God as for Man. Bella sacrificially offers her life to do the right thing and is rewarded with God's greater attention and devotion.

- In *Eclipse*, Edward-God must respect the attachment his beloved has made with his human mirror image in his absence. Though it drives him crazy with jealousy, he shares Bella's attention with the equally jealous and seemingly as devoted Jacob Black. Again in the story finale, Bella the Seeker offers herself as sacrificial distraction a la the Quileute legendary third wife to show her worthiness and selflessness in love. The wedding date for God-and-Seeker is set.
- In *Breaking Dawn*, Edward and Bella are married and each retains their identity as sacred "other" to their spouse. In consummating the marriage, however, the unexpected happens and the Human Seeker becomes pregnant. This confirms all the divine Edward's worries that he would destroy his fragile human beloved and he suffers through the pregnancy. The divine-human androgyne, of course, costs Bella her human life in delivery but her sacrifice results in apotheosis. More wonderfully, the child born of God and Human is the cause of peace between vampires and wolfmen, the revelation of the evil Volturi's power lust and their eventual defeat before a crowd of witnesses testifying to her reality.

Close curtain. The God-Man love story has moved from the discovery (revelation?) of an incredible mystery by the worthy Seeker through repeated demonstrations of sacrificial and restrained love until the Human Seeker is brought into the Holy Family and life of the Trinity. The world is redeemed and renewed via the fruits of her divinization and life in Christ. *Omnes Exeunt.*

The heart of the allegorical reading of the *Twilight Saga* is that we have the Garden of Eden metanarrative re-written in *Twilight*, so that God and Man are played by Edward and Bella, and the play is re-imagined as a gothic romance. *New Moon*, similarly, is the Morality Play *cum* Harlequin romance version of the agony experienced by God and Man after Man has been expelled from the Garden and no longer walks and talks with God. *Eclipse* and *Breaking Dawn* finish the Eden Everyman re-telling by relating in story form the competing demands of world and the divine for the human heart in a fallen world and, ultimately, of the sacrifices, agony, and rewards to be expected in union with God.

It's a winner.

But What is a 'Romance' Really?

When we talk about the genre of literature devoted to love stories we talk about 'Romance Fiction' and we use the word "romance" as a synonym for "love." In literary criticism, though, the word has a different usage, which explains, I think, why allegorical meaning is the power of the best storytelling, and, more specifically, why the allegorical God-Man love story as we have in *Twilight* is so engaging.

This gets a little dense but hang on. The payoff is worth it, believe me.

Northrop Frye, arguably the seminal literary critic of the past hundred years (the best because so different from his deconstructive contemporaries and critical progeny), in his *Anatomy of Criticism* describes the spectrum of literary modes or design as a continuum stretching from pure, idealized myth through romance to just describing things as we experience them (what Frye calls "naturalism").[21] The middle ground between fairy tales and gritty realism is the relatively idealized fiction called "romance," which may or may not involve a love story. As Frye explains, a romance is a world apart from experience and "romantic" is a word for describing the *tendency* towards idealizing a story's subject matter:

> The mode of romance presents an idealized world: in romance, heroes are brave, heroines beautiful, villains villainous, and the frustrations, ambiguities, and embarrassments of ordinary life are made little of.[22]
>
> The words "romantic" and "realistic," for instance, as ordinarily used, are relative or comparative terms; they illustrate tendencies in fiction, and cannot be used as simply descriptive adjectives with any sort of exactness...[23]

---

21 Northrop Frye, *The Anatomy of Criticism*, Princeton University Press: Princeton, NJ, 1957; pages 136-137 "Myth, then, is one extreme of literary design; naturalism is the other, and in between lies the whole area of romance, using that term to mean..the tendency... to displace myth in a human direction and yet, in contrast to "realism," to conventionalize content in an idealized direction. The central principle of displacement is that what can be metaphorically identified in a myth can only be linked in a romance by some form of simile: analogy, significant association, incidental accompanying imagery, and the like. In a myth we can have a sun-god or a tree-god; in a romance we may have a person who is significantly associated with the sun or the trees. In more realistic modes the association becomes less significant and more a matter of incidental, even coincidental or accidental, imagery."

22 Frye, op.cit., page 151

23 Frye, op.cit., page 49; the contrary tendency to romantic is "naturalist" or "realistic"

In myth, the characters of story are so far abstracted from the human that they are not recognizable as such; gods and goddesses, heroes, and supernatural figures are the protagonists and antagonists. In realistic fiction, say as in a conventional detective novel, the reader's skepticism and expectations for a "believable" story are such that the writer would be making a great mistake to introduce even a ghost, something normal in myth and acceptable in romance.[24]

An Agatha Christie mystery, then, would be considered relatively "romantic" or idealized compared to a newspaper, concerned as Poirot and Marple are more with character types than description of specific people or historical events. Mrs. Meyer's Forks novels, compared with the Christie fictions, are even more "romantic," what Frye calls "high mimetic."[25]

"On the other hand, the term "naturalism" shows up in its proper perspective as a phase of fiction which... begins as an intensification of low mimetic, an attempt to describe life exactly as it is, and ends, by the very logic of that attempt, in pure irony." See also the definitions of 'romance' given online at 'Frye studies' web sites like http://artsweb.uwaterloo.ca/~mr2campb/Learning%20Object/terminology.html#romance:

ROMANCE: The mythos of literature concerned primarily with an idealized world.

ROMANTIC: (1) A fictional mode in which the chief characters live in a world of marvels (naïve romance) or in which the mood is elegiac or idyllic and hence less subject to social criticism than in the mimetic modes. (2) The general tendency to present myth and metaphor in an idealized human form, midway between undisplaced myth and "realism".

24 Frye, op.cit., page 50 "Let us take, as a random example, the use of ghosts in fiction. In a true myth there can obviously be no consistent distinction between ghosts and living beings. In romance we have real human beings, and, consequently, ghosts are in a separate category, but in a romance a ghost as a rule is merely one more character: he causes little surprise because his appearance is no more marvelous than many other events. In high mimetic, where we are within the order of nature, a ghost is relatively easy to introduce because the plane of experience is above our own, but when he appears he is an awful and mysterious being from what is perceptibly another world. In low mimetic, ghosts have been, ever since Defoe, almost entirely confined to a separate category of "ghost stories." In ordinary low mimetic fiction they are inadmissible, "in compliance to the Skepticism of the reader," as Fielding puts it, a skepticism which extends only to low mimetic conventions."

25 Frye, op.cit, page 113; (on Aristotelian ideas of *mimesis* and mythos, see pages 82-84) "We are interpreting mimesis, however, not as a Platonic "recollection," but as an emancipation of externality into image, nature into art." [Hence, 'high mimetic' in Frye is greater emancipation, more idealized; 'low mimetic' is less released, more realistic, historical, or natural.]. cf., also Frye, op.cit., page 154 "In the low mimetic area we enter a world that we may call the *analogy of experience,*

> Romance peoples the world with fantastic, normally invisible personalities or powers: angels, demons, fairies, ghosts, enchanted animals, elemental spirits like those in *The Tempest* and *Comus.* Dante wrote in this mode... [26]

The vampires, wolfmen shape-changers, allegorical figures, and larger than life adventures in the four *Twilight* books are "romances" both in being love-stories and in being fantastic, which is to say, more fantasy fiction than realistic but still believably human rather than overtly mythic or religious.

Has anybody left yet? Good. Here is the payoff I mentioned.

The "romances" of literary criticism, the idealized stories in which we recognize abstracted and heroic qualities rather than "analogies of our experience," which is to say "life and people as we know them," are by nature allegorical. Allegories are those story elements that act as a kind of transparency through which we can see greater realities. Romantic heroes are best for this kind of work because they are still sufficiently human to be believable and engaging, however incredible the story events may be. The more incredible, in fact, that these story elements are in a Romance, the easier it is to see or experience in them the virtues, beauty, and principles or truth we miss in mundane reality.

The best type of Romances for experiencing the goal of our most basic longings for 'other,' for love, namely God, then, would be those stories that are idealized representations of heroic, allegorical male-female relationships, call them "love stories" or "romances" with a little 'r.' In these boy-meets-girl tales, both literary Romances and love-story romances, are the clearest transparencies through which we can imaginatively enter into the Human Seeker-God *agape* love.

---

and which bears a relation to the demonic world corresponding to the relation of the romantic innocent world to the apocalyptic one....[T]he images are the ordinary images of experience... Divine and spiritual beings have little functional place in low mimetic fiction..."

26 Frye, op.cit., page 64 "Similarly, each mode of literature develops its own existential projection. Mythology projects itself as theology: that is, a mythopoeic poet usually accepts some myths as "true" and shapes his poetic structure accordingly. Romance peoples the world with fantastic, normally invisible personalities or powers: angels, demons, fairies, ghosts, enchanted animals, elemental spirits like those in *The Tempest* and *Comus.* Dante wrote in this mode, but not speculatively: he accepted the spiritual beings recognized by Christian doctrine, and concerns himself with no others."

We all know what it is like to love a person. As Socrates teaches in *The Symposium*, though, this erotic love is only the beginning of or a shadow of the greater loves of friendship, fellowship, and family. These, too, are just shades of Love Itself, love of the Good, divine love, in which there is no 'other.'

But how can we express that kind of love so everyone can understand it or enter it, whatever their spiritual maturity? By telling love stories. Especially those love stories that are allegorical and offer representations not only of one person fascinated with another person but which also point, however obliquely, to the greatest love relationship, that of Man and God. In scripture, we have this in the *Song of Songs*. In literature, we see it in Dante's Romance, *The Divine Comedy*, in which his idealized love for Beatrice is his means to the Beatific Vision and union with God in Paradise.

Irony of Ironies: The Reason Critics Despise *Twilight* is Why Readers Love It

Twilight, as I hope we've made clear, isn't especially subtle in its allegorical content. The cover, the epigraph, the apples exchanged Edward to Bella, and the wildly different responsibilities and concerns they have in their mutually consuming love all point to the series being an allegorical Romance, capital 'R,' about how Man loves God as a spiritual seeker and how God loves Man, as totally, but with care lest He destroy the fragile human capacity for authentic free choice.

Here's the part I like the most about this. *Twilight* has as its core genre among several story types the one that is probably taken the least seriously by "serious readers" and the critical establishment: Young Adult Romance (love story). Love stories for "mass market" publication – can you say "Harlequin"? – are bad enough, but those marketed to teen girls? This is the bottom of the literary totem pole, the part below the ground that no one can see.

But how do Young Adult Romances differ from literary love stories that critics review with great attention and seriousness? The biggest difference is that the despised genre of love stories is *less* realistic and *more* idealized because it is written for supposedly less sophisticated readers. Young Adult Romance, then, is *more* Romantic, a *more* suitable vehicle for allegory, and a *more* likely means for the reader to experience greater truths, beauty, and virtues that resonate within their hearts.

Twilight, with its paranormal cast of characters with vampires and wolfmen at times all but taking over the west coast of the Olympic Peninsula, features an impossible love. Edward and Bella as vampire and human cannot, we are told for the greater part of three books, consummate their love safely; Bella's body will be destroyed by Edward's passion or her soul (at best) will be consumed if he loses his self-control. Their desire for one another, consequently, is relatively restricted in its carnality and free in its spiritual quality, especially in light of Edward's just-short-of-divine powers.

However Romantic, capital 'R,' the stories are, though, they remain realistic and romantic, little 'r,' enough to fully engage the whole of the reader's person through his or her imagination. Mrs. Meyer hits the mean between myth and realism so cleanly that the categories almost elide. Young Adult Romance may be a teen girl genre according to book marketers but *Twilight* sales in stores, the testimony of librarians I know, and the fact that Amazon sales records are being broken more than a year after the release of the series' final book all point to Mrs. Meyer's reading audience being men and women of all ages. Her 'anti-human' allegory of the God-Man love story appeals to readers, young and old, who are able to get over the genre revulsion hurdle, because it makes them feel more human.

Again, it comes back to Eliade. Readers in a secular culture love their novels because they serve a mythic or religious function in a world from which God and the Transcendent have been marginalized if not denied. Mrs. Meyer in these paranormal Romances, big 'R' and little 'r,' engages us with a blockbuster plot and voice, hooks us deep by confirming our postmodern beliefs about right and wrong, and then offers us a look into a greater reality, perhaps the greatest reality, through the allegorical transparency of Edward and Bella's love.

You cannot do much better than that. The only thing left is artistry that creates story elements that are translucent or sublime, which subtly transform us as we read them. For the anagogical meaning of *Twilight*, Mrs. Meyer's best work, turn the page.

Chapter 4

The Anagogical Layer of Meaning:

The Circle and Alchemical Symbolism of the Twilight Novels

There are few words in the English language that receive the same response as "Anagogical." The first three layers of meaning have names, after all, that most folks have heard or even used. But the last one, anagogical, is a head-shaker. In my experience using it, the person I'm speaking with almost inevitably turns his or her eyes and face in a peculiar direction to ask non-verbally "What does *that* mean?" and "Do you really think that's a word?"

It *is* a word, which literally means "driving back," if it is one word I often switch out for near synonyms like "hermetic," "sublime," or "metaphysical" as often as not because those words don't get the same negative reaction ("hermetic," though, to many means "living like a hermit" or "taking drugs to throw up" rather than "esoteric;" there's no winning here). Like the layer or depth of meaning it describes, the anagogical word needs more than a bit of up-front explanation.

Mrs. Meyer once said about the Cullen coven and Quileute Wolf Pack that the vampires to her were more science than magic, but the wolfmen were magic more than science.[1] That is not a bad analogy for the difference between allegorical and anagogical meaning. If allegory is a function of straightforward correspondence between story item 'a' and real world or even spiritual referent 'b' it is a relatively mechanical

1 "The sun does not damage [vampire] skin regardless of the reflecting. My reasoning was, why should the sun burn them? That seemed like a very mystical kind of thing, and my vampires are more science than magic to me (whereas my werewolves are more magic than science)." http://www.twilightmoms.com/interviews/stephenie-meyer/stephenie-meyer-answers-questions-from-twilightmoms-members-2/

science, especially to interpret it. Anagogical artistry, in contrast, is a much more subtle work, something like literary magic.

The nearest thing to anagogical experience we have in school is the "aha" moment of suddenly understanding a geometry proof. Remember the flash of insight you had after "seeing" the connection of what is known, the given principles, and what was to be proven? And the insight didn't just go away. Once we saw it demonstrated that complementary angles were 180 degrees, we could add that to our pile of 'known things' for our next proofs. The "aha" gave us both a knowledge changing perspective on angles and an understanding of geometric objects we could use later. We were transformed.

But Anagogical meaning isn't out just to add to your knowledge and it almost certainly won't make you more aware of the change with a "Eureka!" moment of discovery as a geometry proof will. There's no "boy, am I clever for seeing that!" satisfaction here. Most of this kind of artistry works on our unconscious mind and is invisible except to the most patient and careful reader.

How invisible? I think of C. S. Lewis' *Chronicles of Narnia.* Few books that aren't considered revelations from God have been read as closely and interpreted from as many angles as these children's stories by the 20th century's most famous Christian apologist. But it was more than 50 years after they were written and the critics had all but exhausted their moral and allegorical content before Michael Ward discovered and unpacked these books' astrological scaffolding and profound, unifying Christological meaning in his *Planet Narnia.* The anagogical, if not discussed or even overtly suggested by the author, can be subtle to the point of undetectable, like an edifying increase in the amount of oxygen in the air we're breathing.

Joanne Rowling worked a similar magic in her *Harry Potter* novels, albeit with alchemical symbolism rather than stars and planets. She wasn't as subtle as Lewis – I mean, c'mon, the title of the first book includes the alchemical goal, a Philosopher's Stone, and Dumbledore is introduced via his Frog Card as a master alchemist – but most readers missed this esoteric story scaffolding. And many of them were remarkably resistant to my exegesis of this artistry, to say the least, until a 1998 interview with the author (which confirmed that alchemy sets "the magical parameters" of the Hogwarts Saga) was found in early 2007.

The Alchemy of a Good Book

And perhaps alchemy is a better way of thinking about this sense of a text; the effect of anagogical artistry, after all, is something like the magic of alchemy. Reading a text built on a hermetic lattice of symbols and plot elements corresponds to what happens to an object coming into contact with a Philosopher's Stone.

That object, we're told by tradition, is turned into gold. The hard thing for us to get about this transformation is that the change to the alchemist and for traditional people in general isn't one from lead, a metal of no value, to gold, bullion worth a bundle, but from "hard darkness" to "solid light." Alchemy takes stillborn metal that lives in shadow and brings out its inner principle or greater reality of light. We call this restored and perfected metal "gold."

The reason poets and writers from Shakespeare, the Alchemical Bard, to C. S. Lewis, whose *Ransom Trilogy* of science fiction novels are built on alchemical principles the way the *Narniad* is on astrology, weave the symbols and stages of the 'Great Work' into their novels, poems, and plays is to do to the reader something like what the Philosopher's Stone does to lead. Their hope is that the reader will be similarly made into light; call it spiritual transformation, or, better, "illumination." The archetypal symbolism and storytelling of this hermetic artistry acts as a translucency, with the "light" of greater truths emanating from the surface text "enlightening" the engrossed reader.

Allegories are story-transparencies through which you can see greater realities. Anagogical or sublime meaning in stories are story-*translucencies* through which greater realities of truth, beauty, and goodness shine through to illumine our hearts. It is, I believe, exactly this transforming touch of the Transcendent that brings readers back for repeated readings, the experience that makes us "love a book."

This fourth sense or dimension obviously requires both significant artistry and knowledge of the rules, elements, and tradition of such work in English letters. As I said, I saw evidence of this conscious artistry in Ms. Rowling's work and had to argue from text that she couldn't be doing this "by accident"(!); the critical audience was very skeptical that this single mum on the dole was using Shakespearean tools that most of them were not familiar with.

I was similarly skeptical, though, when friends told me that Mrs. Meyer was "obviously" writing hermetic fiction because the colors on her *Twilight* covers were all black, white, and red. These are the primary colors used to describe the three stages of alchemy. And Edward's eyes are "golden!" That seemed a pretty thin basis for arguing there was great depth and merit in a Young Adult Romance series featuring vampires and werewolves.

Imagine my surprise (embarrassment, really, after years of confronting similar misogyny and genre bias in others) to find that, as simple and direct as her narrative prose is, the hermetic elements of anagogical artistry were in the books and almost certainly a big part of what causes her readers to love and return to the experience.

The usual objection to literary alchemy and anagogical meaning in general in either *Harry Potter* or *Twilight* I've learned is that, as a rule of thumb, the poets, playwrights and novelists engaged in this work are writers with big reputations rather than writing hacks. Herbert, Blake, Yeats, Shakespeare, T. S. Eliot, C. S. Lewis, Charles Williams, George MacDonald, and company are not a match with Rowling and Meyer. The literary alchemist's work involves, as a rule, magisterial prose and poesy and accomplished use of symbols and archetypal metaphors.

It doesn't diminish Mrs. Meyer's achievement, though, as a writer working on the anagogical layer of meaning as well as the other three, to point out the obvious lack of anything approaching "magisterial" or even "elevated" in her writing. If anything, this absence highlights the heavy freight her story symbols have to carry and succeed in carrying themselves.

I mentioned above that "anagogical" literally means "driving back" and I hope in this chapter to share two points of *Twilight's* anagogical meaning that "drive us back" into the "metaphysical inside" that is greater than the mundane or narrative outside. The allegorical layer is one of correspondence, this stands for that, which provides a bridge to the anagogical, in which the correspondences are not with worldly or religious referents but with spiritual or metaphysical reality. At this depth we are "driven back" into the mythic layer of meaning for an immersion in transcendent truth.

Let's look at the circles in the *Twilight* novels and the literary alchemy in them. If you or someone you know became enchanted by Mrs. Meyer's Forks Saga, I'm pretty sure it was because of its anagogical heft, which is the greater artistry of storytelling and the real magic and transforming power of story.

The Romance of a Hero's Journey: The Metaphysics of the Circle

If you were living in Bella's world and you *really* wanted to find a vampire, I'm thinking your best bet, based on the *Twilight* novels, is to spend time in mountain meadows, especially those well off the beaten track. Think about it.

- It's where they play baseball and football;
- They seem to run into each other in meadows as often as not (think of James, Victoria, and Laurent just happening by the Cullen Coven's game in the Olympic meadow);
- Meadows seem to be the venue of choice for vampire battles, as the *Eclipse* showdown with Victoria's newborns has its main arena in one and the Volturi come *en masse* to the same spot in *Breaking Dawn* to deliver their ultimatum about Renesmee;
- Carlisle has a painting in his office that catches Edward's interest on Bella's first visit when he tells her about Carlisle's new attempts as a newborn vampire to destroy himself. The painting is of "an empty, shadowed meadow in a forest, with a craggy peak in the distance;"[2]
- Bella happens upon Laurent in *New Moon* in a mountain meadow and she is saved from becoming his lunch only by the appearance of the Quileute Protectors. She sees Jacob Black in his wolf form here for the first time.

Mountain meadows play a huge part in the *Twilight* saga, obviously, and Chapter 6 is largely about why they are so important in Mrs. Meyer's fiction. The reason Bella happened to be in that meadow when Laurent appeared in *New Moon* was because she was desperate to find the meadow where Edward had taken her soon after they met to reveal why vampires avoid sunlight when human beings are present. Chapter 13 in *Twilight*, 'Confessions,' according to Mrs. Meyer, is the record of the dream she had on 2 June 2003 of a vampire and young woman in a mountain meadow, the dream that inspired her to write the first book.

This is a curious meadow. It's not very big for one thing, which, as Bella learns, makes it hard to find. On the day Edward and Bella first visit, it is sunny, filled with wild flowers, and, Bella thinks, "the loveliest place I had ever seen." The oddest thing about it is its shape; the

---

2 *Twilight*, page 336

meadow is a sunlit circle in the darkness of the forest, not just circular but "perfectly round."

In *New Moon* Bella says she'd "never seen another clearing so symmetrical. It was perfectly round as if someone had intentionally created the flawless circle."[3] Edward and Bella have their "lion fell in love with the lamb" moments here, most of which they spend in the circle center, him telling her to "Be very still," her telling him "Don't move" ("No one could be still like Edward. He closed his eyes and became as immobile as a stone…").[4]

The heart of *Twilight* is a place of light in darkness, a "flawless circle" "perfectly round" whose unmoving center is love.

I might not make too much of this, peculiar as the perfection certainly is, except Mrs. Meyer doesn't leave it at that. Circles are the predominant shape of people, places, and items in big events in the Forks saga. From the top of my head:

- There is the stone circular room in which Bella, Edward, and Alice have a heart to heart with the Volturi in *New Moon* (the center of this circle is a drain for human remains);
- The magical "fairy tale" love cottage the Cullen family create for Edward and his newborn bride in *Breaking Dawn* has a "rounded door" and a "small round pond, smooth as a mirror;"[5]
- The locket that Bella buys for 'Nessie as a keepsake of the love of her parents in anticipation of a Volturi victory in the *Breaking Dawn* finale is, of course, a circle;
- The Cullens all would be perfect albinos except for "the circles" around their eyes;
- Leah, Jacob, and Seth run in near endless patrol circles around the Cullen home in *Breaking Dawn*;
- In the *Twilight* conversion scene in which Bella makes her defining choice to love Edward though he is a vampire, Bella's "head spun around in answerless circles;"[6] and
- After Edward's departure in *New Moon* – a good-bye set in the same grove in the forest behind her house in which Bella chose

3 *New Moon*, page 234
4 Op.cit., pages 275, 277
5 *Breaking Dawn*, page 481
6 *Twilight*, page 139

> to love Edward, whatever the cost – Bella's response is to walk in circles; "I started to worry that I was traveling in a circle, a very small circle at that, but I kept going." She eventually curls herself into a fetal position, which Mrs. Meyer invariably calls a "ball" of suffering. We see the Bella Ball ten times in *New Moon;*

Edward, too, spends *New Moon* as a sphere. As he puts it, "I more or less curled into a ball and let the misery have me."[7] But Bella Ball is a constant from Edward's goodbye until his return at book's end. Only the "hole in the chest" image, also something round, occurs more often in *New Moon* than the Bella Ball, checking in at a heart stopping (forgive me that) 37 times.

And the stories themselves are circles. They start one place, circle out, and cycle back as return in the monomyth-hero's journey formula of escape-transformation-and-return. Bella's trips in *Twilight* to Phoenix, to Volterra in *New Moon,* to the aerie above the *Eclipse* battlefield, and to Isle Esme in *Breaking Dawn* are occasions in which Bella faces a crisis or situation she has long anticipated, with dread or excitement, and is transformed there by her choices and experience.

Trace these story circles in each book. In *Twilight's* trip to Phoenix, her sacrificial near-death in the mirrored room catalyzes Edward's decision to leave her for her own good, her meeting with the Volturi in *New Moon* all but cinches her fate to become a vampire, her kiss with Jacob and Third Wife imitation in *Eclipse* decide her for Edward and marriage, and in *Breaking Dawn* she comes home from Isle Esme pregnant and on the conveyor belt to her three day transformation and resurrection.

Northrop Frye in *Anatomy of Criticism* talks about Romance both as a mode between myth and mundane fiction of relatively idealized but believable stories (see Chapter 3). He also talks about Romance as one of the four archetypal myths of literature.

> The complete form of the romance is clearly the successful quest, and such a completed form has three main stages: the stage of the perilous journey and the preliminary minor adventures; the crucial struggle, usually some kind of battle in which the hero or his foe, or both, must die; and the exaltation of the hero.[8]

---

7 *New Moon,* page 528

8 Frye, *Anatomy,* op.cit., page 187; cf., 'The Mythos of Summer: Romance' discussion in same, pages 186-206

This Romantic Hero's Quest is "the structural core of all fiction"[9] because of its Christian and hermetic content:

> The typical structure of romance includes apotheosis, sacred marriage, and the gaining of Paradise. In addition to the presence of characters with magical powers, the faithful companion and the bride commonly appear as subordinate characters to a central hero, who is usually semi-divine and always succeeds in his quest by the end, even if this results in his own death....
>
> Adventure is the essential element in romance, and it is a lot easier to represent adventure in fiction than in drama. If the culture of the ancient Greeks largely centred upon the tragic vision of the *Iliad* and the works of the Athenian dramatists, the modern West has been predominantly romantic in its vision, having at its centre the myth of the man-god Christ who ultimately triumphs over death itself.[10]

This salutary Adventure as Quest takes the shape of a Going-Out and Coming-Back-Again circle because of the metaphysical content of the circle or sphere as a story symbol. To understand this, we have to talk about sacred geometry and unwrap the metaphysical symbolism of the Circle and the Center, a symbolism Mircea Eliade discusses in *Myth of the Eternal Return.*[11]

So we're all on the same page, here is a little Euclid to define what it is we mean by 'circle' and 'center:' *A circle is the uniform radiation of a spaceless point, the center, into space.*

All points of a circle are equidistant from a center point, right? This center, then, really *defines* the circle, of which point the circle is only a radiation or extension. Think of a ripple moving away from a rock dropped in the pond. The rock at the center both causes and defines the circle rippling away from it. A circle, which is visible, is only intelligible and understandable because of the defining and spaceless center that is usually invisible and unknowable in itself.

So far, so good, I hope. Now for the harder part. The reason Bella and Edward are motionless in the "perfectly" circular mountain meadow

---

9 Frye, *Secular Scripture* 15, cited in the summation of Frye's thoughts on Romance at 'Archetypal Pursuit:' http://artsweb.uwaterloo.ca/~mr2campb/Learning%20Object "This site was created by Meaghan Campbell, Kyle Fredenburg and Craig Love as part of English 701 at the University of Waterloo."

10 'Archetypal Pursuit, see note 7 above, in summary of Frye, *Anatomy of Criticism*, pages 186-296

11 Mircea Eliade, *Myth of the Eternal Return*, Princeton University Press, 1971, 'The Symbolism of the Center,' pages 12-16

is to invoke in the reader's mind the power of the center. As its radiation or visible aspect, the circle is *essentially* the same thing as its defining center or origin. If the Transcendent and Immanent God or Absolute has a shape, it is a circle and it is the circle's unplottable and defining center that is the heart and power of the mystery.

In Christian art and literature, the circle is a traditional and a profound representation of God as Trinity. God the Father is the Center, the Word or *Logos* is the visible Circle or sphere, and the Holy Spirit is the radiation proceeding from the Center. The Father is only knowable through His Word and because of the Holy Spirit; each is distinct and the center is logically, but not temporally, prior. St. Bonaventure, echoing a neo-platonic text, describes God as a sphere whose center is everywhere and whose periphery is nowhere.

The Hero's Journey isn't a story formula, ultimately, or just a mechanical structure to hang a plot on. It's really about this symbolism of the Circle and the Center.

Every hero's journey is a figurative, completed circle, if not a geometric one, and the circle is a symbol of God and Creation, specifically of the unknown center defining and creating the visible circle.

A hero completing a circular journey has ritually arrived by his circumnavigation at the defining center because the circle he or she has completed is one with the center. To repeat myself, as its radiation or visible aspect, the circle is *essentially* the same thing as its defining center or origin. If God as He can be known has a geometric or story shape, it is a circle and it is the circle's unplottable and defining center that is the heart and power of the story-magic.

To understand why Bella and Edward are the unmoved Mover center of the Edenic field in which Edward reveals he is Light incarnate to Bella, draw a cross in your hero's journey circle or meadow to divide that circle into four pie pieces. That cross, like the circle, is defined by the center point at which a horizontal and vertical line meet. This point which defines the cross, the circle and the end (*telos* in Greek; the goal or purpose) of the journey brings the hero into the "sacred space" or point creating the world.

The hero's journey is a circle for much the same reason that the events of Calvary have their meaning and why Christ died on a geometric cross. In achieving the symbolic Center, Bella and Edward have become, if not one, then "not two" with the transcendent Absolute.

Riding the Circle: Experiencing the Hero's Journey

Mircea Eliade in *Myth of the Eternal Return* explains the difference between archaic, primitive man and modern people.[12] The primitives are those who understand reality as cosmos, myth, and cycles in which they can participate ritually to transcend themselves and enter the center of sacred space and time. In this, the primitive person becomes more real and has more being because, to use spatial terms in metaphor, he is closer to the fount of Being, the Supreme Reality. Modern people, in contrast, live in an ontologically flat world of time, space, matter, and linear, sequential history. We cannot, as Moderns at least, "approach the center" anymore than we can become alchemists or druids.

In myth and story, however, as well as religious ritual, we can reenter an ontologically rich or "more real" non-local "place" in which we can transcend ourselves and "have" more being. As I hope you recall by now, this is exactly Eliade's point in *The Sacred and the Profane* about modern people's preoccupation with entertainments, movies, story, and novels. In a secular culture, he says, entertainment serves a mythic or religious function. These are the activities in which even the atheist and ideologically secular person can have mythic, even religious experience of a world other than that defined by the ego-self of the individual.[13]

The Hero's Journey in *Twilight* is grounded in the dream image of the meadow that is a perfect circle and Edward and Bella coming together at its motionless center; the repeated story images of the circles are echoes and extensions of this mythic image and point. As the genesis of the series in Mrs. Meyer's original inspiration, it also explains in large part why we love the books and why they end as they do. As the Lion and Lamb have achieved the Absolute and Transcendent unity and whole, the origin of life, they cannot be defeated by the Volturi who are consumed by such mundane concerns as their power relative to other vampire groups.

And we, meeting Bella and Edward in this circle origin or center, have had some imaginative experience of our own hope of defeating death. No wonder we read and reread these books! Bella's adventure from Meadow Center to apotheosis in childbirth to vanquisher of the Volturi is the journey from a "private" or ego-driven conception of self to the illuminating experience of the point defining the circle, the Cross, and everything in existence. "Except for the point, the still point,/ There

12 Op.cit., page 14

13 Mircea Eliade, *The Sacred and the Profane* , Harcourt, 2007, pages 204-5

would be no dance, and there is only the dance."[14] Sacrificing ourselves in love for our friends alongside Bella, we perceive and experience the eternal verities as much as our spiritual capacity allows.

Too much? Try thinking of the Bella-Edward in Meadow-Circle center in Christian terms.

The essence of the Christian historical event, the Incarnation of the *Logos* as Man in Jesus of Nazareth, according to St. Athanasios and echoed by the Church Fathers everywhere, is that "God became man so that man might become god."[15] We can see in this patristic formula the two complementary and synergistic movements necessary in God and Man for human divinization or Communion with the Godhead. Opposites, in brief, move toward their contraries and in their conjunction or resolution the ephemeral touches and in some fashion becomes what is eternal.

That's not an easy image to share in story, right? But think about what we have in the heart of *Twilight's* defining image, the still players at the center of the Meadow circle.

There is Edward, the all-but-immortal Adonis and picture of unknowable and unreachable perfection. His journey in *Twilight*, though, is about his longing to become or recall his *humanity*. As he says to Bella in the Meadow and repeatedly thoughout *Twilight*: "I'm not used to feeling so human" and "I have human instincts – they may be buried deep, but they're there." Bella notes after they leave the Meadow, "how human he seemed" and that "he was a different Edward than the one I had known."[16]

And Bella, of course, is human but she is joined with Edward by her love for and longing to be with him "forever." In this meeting of mortal and immortal, male and female, in the Meadow center, we have the Christian Tao of the human-divine conjunction in Christ, the God-Man; it is in the resolution of these contraries in which our hope of transcending our ego selves, of our apotheosis, rests.

In the story, Bella and Edward's meeting is the perumbration of their alchemical marriage in *Breaking Dawn* and the life that comes from their union, Renesmee, the philosophical orphan and story savior

14 T. S. Eliot, *Four Quartets: Burnt Norton*; cf., Tillyard, *Elizabethan World Picture*, Chapter 8, "The Cosmic Dance"

15 St. Athanasios, *De Incarnatione*, 54:3, PG 25:192B

16 *Twilight*, pages 278, 283

that unites all opposites and reveals and resolves all contraries. Which brings us to alchemy and the reason the Meadow in *Twilight* is sunlit and Edward a creature of light.

Literary Alchemy: The Transformative Power of Story

The power of the Hero's Journey, which as "monomyth," literary critics and anthropologists acknowledge as the foundation of human story, is largely a function of the circle symbolism. The hero or heroine in completing circle of journey becomes the transcendent and defining center, call it the "Divine Unknown" or "Absolute," in which non-local place the reader, having identified with the story lead, has an experience transcending self, the world, even the sense of subject and object. 'Self' and 'Other,' with all contraries, elide in the mythic center, defining point, and creative principle.

If readers recall anything, though, about Mrs. Meyer's story circle, the "perfectly round" mountain meadow in her dream and *Twilight,* what they recall doesn't have anything to do with this mythic meaning. What happens in the circle-meadow that we all remember is that Edward reveals to Bella there the fact that he sparkles in the sunshine.

> Edward in the sunlight was shocking. I couldn't get used to it, though I'd been staring at him all afternoon. His skin, white despite the faint flush from yesterday's hunting trip, literally sparkled, like thousands of tiny diamonds were embedded in the surface. He lay perfectly still in the grass, his shirt open over his sculpted, incandescent chest, his scintillating arms bare. His glistening, pale lavender lids were shut, though of course he didn't sleep. A perfect statue, carved in some unknown stone, smooth like marble, glittering like crystal.[17]

We talked above about his stillness in the center being a reflection of his being a symbol of the Absolute, the God of the Eden allegory (Bella: "I was wishing that I could believe that you were real. And I was wishing that I wasn't afraid"[18]). Edward being quite literally a *reflection* of light means much the same thing.

The Meadow circle is sunlit, remember: "The sun was directly overhead, filling the circle with a haze of buttery sunshine." Because light along with the sun are universal symbols or story ciphers for

17 *Twilight,* page 260
18 Op.cit., page 262

eternal verities and reality (in contrast to darkness meaning error, ephemerality, sin, and death), vampires in Mrs. Meyer's conception, contra tradition and Stoker canon, are all-but-immortal creatures of light points to their divinity.

And the subject of light brings us to alchemy.

Alchemy today is a dead subject the remains of which historians of science and Jungian analysts like to pick through in search of "early chemistry" and "archetypes of the collective unconscious." Most of us only know three things about this Medieval science: (1) it was the precursor to modern chemistry, (2) its goal was creating a Philosopher's Stone from which an 'Elixir of Life' would spring, giving the alchemist immortality and gold, and (3) it was a sham.

That's pretty much all wrong. In order to understand *literary alchemy*, the only surviving alchemy and the heart of *Twilight's* anagogical meaning and power, we need to get this right, so here is a quick course in what alchemy is and how it shapes much of the best plays, poems, and novels in English literature.

The first thing to get clear is that alchemy wasn't "stupid chemistry" or a "precursor" to the modern science in any way except in having come before it. The aim of modern chemistry is manipulation of molecular bonds and states of matter; the chemist, barring accidents in the laboratory, is entirely unaffected by changes in the matter and energy quantities in play.

Alchemy, in strong contrast, was about the sanctification or illumination of the alchemist, a change in his soul and inner heart from "fallen" or "darkened" to an Edenic perfection or enlightenment. The metallurgical component of this change was necessary because the alchemist was transformed *in sympathy with* the change in a physical object moving from lead to gold, or, as mentioned at this chapter's beginning, its illumination and restoration from "hard darkness" to "solid light."

Alchemy was about gold, then, but not in the sense of creating quick monetary gain but to purify and illumine an object to foster a similar change in the knowing subject. Titus Burckhardt, the Swiss art historian and expert on the traditional and spiritual aspects of alchemy, explains in terms of light why gold is the key product of alchemy:

> Gold itself, which outwardly represents the fruit of the work, appears as an opaque body become luminous, or as a light become solid. Transposed into the human and spiritual order, gold is bodily consciousness transmuted into spirit or spirit fixed in the body.[19]

Gold is "light become solid" and the alchemist is "spirit become human" via his purification and enlightenment. If your high school science teachers were like mine, that's not what you were told about alchemy.

Alchemy and English Literature: The Play's the Thing

Alchemy went into precipitous decline and corruption at the time of the Renaissance through the Enlightenment when it was eclipsed by the materialist view and priorities of modern chemistry. Though there was a glut of publication of alchemical treatises as it declined, this is evidence of its corruption. The "great work" was only passed in person from master to apprentice; books contain only the most arcane and hidden guides to the work, metallurgical and spiritual.

American readers, consequently, are unaware of alchemy except as the chemists, the illegitimate and disowned children of the alchemists, want us to remember them. This is perhaps no great loss, except for its reinforcement of our naturalist state religion, but it does have one consequence that touches on *Twilight* fans.

Alchemy infected the religious understanding of Reformation England and is, consequently, near to the heart of all subsequent great English fiction. The religious history we will have to come back to in the next chapter. It's the literature that matters here.

English Literature is rich in alchemical language, references, themes, and symbols from Chaucer to Rowling; to be ignorant of this language and imagery is to miss out on the depths and heights of Shakespeare, Blake, Donne, Milton, even C. S. Lewis and James Joyce. Mrs. Meyer is no stranger to this tradition, because its symbols, stages, and structures are evident in her *Twilight* novels.

I discuss the tradition of literary alchemy at much greater length in my other books in which I explain why the serious reader requires at least a grounding in alchemy to understand many of the best and more difficult writers in our tradition. Even if the alchemy-literature connection is all news to you and you go to the grave believing alchemy

19 Titus Burckhardt, *Mirror of the Intellect*, Quinta Essentia, 1987, p. 132

is just for New Age nits or Historians of Science, please play along with me. Pretend as if you accept it as gospel truth that English Literature from beginning to *Twilight* is frontloaded with alchemical devices and images.

Why, if this is the case, should this be so? What is the connection between alchemy and literature that makes these images the preferred tools of the best writers for centuries?

I think the connection is probably most clear in drama. Eliade even suggests that the alchemical work grew out of initiatory dramas of the Greek Mystery religions.[20] Shakespeare doesn't just make asides to alchemy in his plays; many if not most of them are written on alchemical skeletons and themes. *The Tempest, Romeo and Juliet, Anthony and Cleopatra, Two Gentlemen of Verona, The Comedy of Errors, Love's Labours Lost,* and *The Merchant of Venice* come to mind.[21] Frances Yates argues persuasively that Shakespeare built the Globe Theatre on Hermetic principles for the proper staging of his alchemical dramas.[22] Why?

If you recall your Aristotle on what happens in a proper tragedy, the audience identifies with the hero in his agony and shares in his passion. This identification and shared passion is effectively the same as the experience of the event; the audience experiences catharsis or 'purification' in correspondence. Shakespeare and Jonson among others use alchemical imagery and themes because they understood that the work of theatre in human transformation was parallel if not identical to the alchemical work. The alchemical work, of course, claimed to be greater than an imaginative experience, but the idea of purification by identification or correspondence with an object and its transformations is 'spot on' with the purpose of theatre.

Alchemical language and themes are the shorthand, consequently, of many great English novels, drama, poetry and prose. The success of an artist following this tradition is measured by the edification of their audience. By means of traditional methods and symbols, the alchemical artist provides delight and dramatic release for our souls through archetypal and purifying experiences.

---

20 Eliade, *Forge*, p. 149

21 see Jean Paris' 'The Alchemistic Theatre' (*Shakespeare*, Grove Press, 1960, pp. 87-116), and Martin Lings, *The Secret of Shakespeare* (Aquarian Press, 1984)

22 Frances Yates, *The Art of Memory,* University of Chicago Press, 1974, p. 365

That may be harder for some of us than the whole idea of alchemy as a sacred science. If you're like me, you grew up with the idea that entertainment was just-for-fun diversion and anything but lifechanging. It turns out this 'diversion' idea, really only in currency for the last seventy or eighty years, is a gross misconception. Anthropologists, historians of religion, and professors of literature will tell you that the rule in traditional as well as profane cultures such as ours is that Story, in whatever form, has an instructional or initiatory purpose.

You may be tired of me saying it, but, again, Eliade makes just this point in his *The Sacred and the Profane*. Especially in a profane culture, entertainments such as reading fiction serve a religious function; they remove us from our ego-bound consciousness for an experience or immersion in another world or subcreation. C. S. Lewis in *Preface to Paradise Lost* asserts that this is the traditional understanding of the best writers, namely, that their role in culture is "to instruct while delighting."

Alchemy and literature are such a powerful and enduring match because they both endeavor in their undegenerate or orthodox state to transform the human person. Literary alchemy, the use of alchemical images and structures, has, consequently, been a constant in English poems, plays, and novels for six centuries.

Harry Potter, Twilight, and Literary Alchemy

Forgive me, but I have to imagine that at least some readers going over this are saying to themselves (and to me), "Okay, I accept that *Twilight* may be better than the junk I've been told it is, but I know it's not written at the level of Shakespeare, Blake, or Joyce. You're asking way too much of me, Granger. I'm at my limit."

Would it help if I pointed out that Mrs. Meyer isn't the only best selling 21st Century writer to work the alchemical vein of English literature? Joanne Rowling is a confessed literary alchemist, believe it or not. She said in a 1998 interview, point blank, that her books are suffused by alchemy, which sets both "the parameters of magic" and "internal logic of the series:"

> "I've never wanted to be a witch, but an alchemist, now that's a different matter. To invent this wizard world, I've learned a ridiculous amount about alchemy. Perhaps much of it I'll never use in the books, but I have to know

> in detail what magic can and cannot do in order to set the parameters and establish the stories' internal logic."[23]

And even if she didn't admit it, the stories themselves scream it out. The *Harry Potter* books individually and as a series are built on alchemical structures, written in alchemical language, and have alchemical themes at their core.[24]

The reason that readers pressed me to give *Twilight* a chance was because I had explained how each *Harry Potter* novel and the series as a whole was written as a story-version of the alchemical 'Great Work.' Several astute *Twilight* fans wrote me to say that Mrs. Meyer was doing something similar. Just as Ms. Rowling hadn't been especially subtle about the alchemy in Harry's adventures – the title of the first book is *Harry Potter and the Philosopher's Stone*, after all – they thought Mrs. Meyer's book covers, of all things, were alchemical pointers because they were black, white, and red.

They thought that was meaningful because literary alchemy, like spiritual alchemy, is described in three stages, each of which stages has a signature color. Those colors are black, white, and red.

Alchemy as a spiritual work follows the revealed traditions in being a three-part task. The *nigredo* or "black" dissolution stage is the work of "renunciation" or "repentance." It is preparatory to the work of "purification" and "illumination" that in alchemy is done in the second so-called "white" stage," the *albedo*. Alchemy represents spiritual accomplishment or perfection in its *rubedo* or "red stage."

"The *albedo* occurs after the blackened matter, the putrefied body of the Stone has been washed to whiteness by the mercurial waters or fire."[25] This is the stage of purification and the transformation of the subject, already broken down into *prima materia*, into the *rebis* or Philosopher's Stone. This work, though, is hidden; the accomplishments of the white stage are revealed in the drama of the red finale.

---

23 Anne Simpson, 'Face to Face with J K Rowling: Casting a spell over young minds,' *The Herald*, 7 December 1998; though the interview was given in 1998, it was lost to readers until February 2007 when it was posted at www.accio-quote.org/articles/1998/1298-herald-simpson.htm

24 Again, see the alchemy chapters in *The New Unlocking Harry Potter* (Zossima, 2010) and *The Deathly Hallows Lectures* (Zossima, 2008)

25 Lyndy Abraham, *Dictionary of Alchemical Imagery*, Cambridge University Press, page 4.

To understand the *albedo,* it helps to know that the Latin root of "*albedo*" is 'albus,' meaning both "white" and "resplendent." There's a hint of "luminescent" or "brilliant;" "purification unto illumination" perhaps best describes the "albification" process.

The three colors can be seen as metallurgical steps: dissolution or "blackening," distillation and purification or "bleaching," and recongealing or "reddening." I remember these steps by thinking of the sun at day's end. As the sun sets, the sky darkens and I become less focused; my ego self dissolves into sleep. In the night, there is reflected light, sun on the moon, which illumines my supraconscious self in secret. At dawn, in the light of day, I am re-membered and different because of my purifying rest in the lunar light.

Waking up is important but I am re-born, in a way, every morning because of my rest in the darkness. Which is not a bad summary of the alchemical work. The recongealing or perfection of the human person in the *rubedo* or red stage is really only a revelation of the renewing, purifying transformation that took place in the dark. Throw in a full moon and a long bath in that white stage at night, and you have a snapshot of the predominant white stage imagery and meaning.

This second step, the *albedo,* is represented in literature with the color white, the silver element or color, with light, especially the light at night (the moon or 'Luna' frequently plays a part), and with water. These elements are used as backdrops and props to story events of purification, illumination, and reconciliation or healing. Again, think of a prophetic dream or insight while lying in bed under the moon after a long bath when recovering from a shattering day; that's an *albedo.* No one will know about it until it is revealed in the light and through the events of the coming day, but that change in the moonlight is the greater part of the Great Work.

The *rubedo* or third step is "the reddening of the white matter of the stone at the final stage of the opus alchymicum."[26] In the *nigredo,* all form, color, and light are taken from the substance to reduce it to blackened "prime matter." In the *albedo,* a light like the moon's reflected colorless light is evident in the white stone produced. In the *rubedo,* the contraries are resolved, the white stage's accomplishments are revealed, and the Stone becomes red.

26 Op.cit., page 174

As important as the idea of light as a symbol is in understanding alchemical gold, perhaps it's best if the three stages of the work are understood in terms of light as well as color. As Burckhardt writes: "Black is the absence of color and light. White is purity; it is undivided light – light not broken down into colors. Red is the epitome of colors, its zenith and its point of greatest intensity."[27] Imagine the lunar light in the darkness of night shining through a prism to reveal all colors and especially their epitome, red.

In *Harry Potter,* the last three books are the black, white, and red novels of the series, if each book also has its *nigredo, albedo,* and *rubedo.*

- *Order of the Phoenix,* Harry's very long fifth year nightmare begins with Sirius Black in the House of Black and things get a lot darker faster as the year progresses. He is stripped of every idea and positive scrap of identity to be reduced at the death of Godfather Black to just the Prophecy.
- *Half-Blood Prince*, the series' penultimate adventure, is Harry's tutorial preparation time with Albus Dumbledore, whose "white" name and death in this book, like Black's in *Phoenix,* reflect the alchemical stage we are in. Harry learns in the series *albedo* what he must know about the Dark Lord to defeat him in the finale.
- *Deathly Hallows,* the *rubedo,* opens with the alchemical wedding of the Red King and White Queen, Bill Weasley and Fleur Delacour, but the action begins and ends with two "red" deaths; Rufus Scrimgeour and Fred Weasley both have names meaning red or with "red" in them. Harry, the story equivalent of the Philosophical Orphan or "Chosen One," sacrifices himself in love for his friends and defeats Lord Voldemort by choosing death to self.

Twilight, a four part series, also has its black, white, and red books, not to mention an Alchemical Wedding. Before I lay this out, though, it's helpful to understand how the series was conceived and the sequence in which the books were written. It isn't the progression that the reader experiences by starting with *Twilight* and plowing through the four books to the end of *Breaking Dawn.*

27 Burckhardt, *Alchemy,* page 182

You know that the series began with a dream in June, 2003. Mrs. Meyer woke the morning after having this story come into her head and ran to her computer to write the circular meadow scene that became chapter 13 of *Twilight*. She wrote the book to the finish from the meadow and then completed the first draft by writing from what is now the first chapter to this scene (making the meadow the real first chapter and "origin" as well as the center of the first book). Two important things to note here:

First, *Twilight* was not started as a series but as a single novel. The story as first conceived and written wasn't a four book set.

Second, Mrs. Meyer has said repeatedly that the first draft of *Twilight* was not conceived or completed with the expectation that she would publish it. It was written for an audience of one, herself, which audience grew to two, her sister, which reader, given their near genetic and circumstantial identity, amounted to a mirror that talks.

The good news is that Mrs. Meyer's first reader loved the story and encouraged her to find a publisher. Here is where the story gets interesting.

Mrs. Meyer finds an agent who loves *Twilight.* Because of the strength of series fiction, no doubt (think *Harry Potter*), and the open ending of *Twilight,* the agent decides to pitch the book to publishers as a three-book deal. Mrs. Meyer gathers her *Twilight* "appendices," ideas she had about where the first book's story threads would lead, into two more books to complete the hoped-for three book deal. She calls these books *Forever Dawn.*

Incredibly, Mrs. Meyer's agent finds a publisher that wants *Twilight* and a three-book deal. They pay her a *Potter*-esque advance – $750,000 for a first time author! – and begin editing *Twilight* and asking where the books are headed. They expect the series to end with three books and make this clear to Mrs. Meyer.

The problem starts when she discusses the two books that she has in mind, *Forever Dawn,* which we know as the two halves of *Breaking Dawn*: Edward and Bella's wedding with Renesmee's birth and Bella's apotheosis and the climactic confrontation in the Olympic Mountain Meadow with the Volturi.[28] The publisher nixes the idea. It simply isn't

28 Q: How different is *Breaking Dawn* from *Forever Dawn*? What changed, what stayed the same, and why? Will you ever post extras from *Forever Dawn*?
Meyer: The basic story is the same. Bella and Edward get married and go to

"Young Adult" or a conventional romance in content.

So Mrs. Meyer is sent back to the drawing board. She likes to say she had "to fight for Renesmee" and for the fourth book because everything she wrote in *New Moon* and *Eclipse* was written "with the knowledge that it was all going to end up with the events in *Breaking Dawn*."[29]

The publisher wants two more books with Edward and Bella in high school to fulfill the contract. Mrs. Meyer is determined to write two books that set the stage for the wedding, birth, transformation, and final near-battle in *Dawn*. She inserts *New Moon* and *Eclipse* as steps, first, to bridge the publisher-created gap between *Twilight* and the original three-book series ending *Forever Dawn*, and, then, to create the proper set-up for that ending.[30]

Isle Esme for their honeymoon. Bella gets pregnant with Renesmee. The birth just about kills Bella, but Edward makes her a vampire in time. Jacob imprints on Renesmee. Alice has a vision of the Volturi coming to destroy the Cullens with the "immortal child" as their excuse. Alice bails. Bella's shielding abilities turn the tide in the Cullen's favor, along with Alice bringing home another half-vampire to prove that Nessie isn't a danger. http://www.stepheniemeyer.com/bd_faq.html

29 "When my editor and I decided to go back and really develop Bella's last year of high school, I did so with the knowledge that it was all going to end up with the events in *Breaking Dawn*. Everything I wrote was pointed in that direction. " http://www.stepheniemeyer.com/bd_faq.html

Electra: Now how long have you had Renesmee in your mind? Jacqueline _____ says Bella getting pregnant just threw her for a loop. I loved it, don't get me wrong, I still had the 'what?' (reading from Jacqueline's question)

S: Um, actually, Nessie was one of the reasons that *Breaking Dawn* exists. When I first started working with an editor, I had *Twilight* and I showed them what I was working on for *Forever Dawn* and they said 'you know, we'd really like to keep Bella in high school for a little bit longer, develop that more, keep it more YA.' And I said 'Ok, there are some interesting stories to do in there. I first started working on it and they said 'we'd just really just like it to be three books, and end with *Eclipse*. Can you make an ending that you're happy with?' And I said 'no, I can't make an ending that I'm happy with.' This was a very hard fought battle and I was fighting for Nessie the whole time. She was a character that I was not going to allow to be destroyed. She had to exist. So, she was in my *Forever Dawn*. http://twilighttabloid.wordpress.com/the-books/personal-correspondence/qa-breaking-dawn-concert-tour-chicago/

30 For obvious reasons, Mrs. Meyer doesn't discuss her disagreements with her publisher in great detail but it is in her comments about how she wrote the books. See this comment from her *Breaking Dawn* tour as an example:

Q: What made you decide to do the pregnancy story line because it seems kind of far from where the characters seem to be heading.

A: I have heard that and let me tell you in *New Moon* and *Eclipse*, with one exception, every plot line, every moment is heading towards what happens in

As you can imagine, these changes weren't easy and the decisions Mrs. Meyer makes gives the series its much greater depth. She was forced to write *New Moon* the way the publisher wanted it, that is, Bella still at Forks High School, but this inspired her to expand on the Jacob Black character. As she wrote in her description of writing *New Moon*: "Ah, and then there is my favorite gift that *New Moon* gave to me: Jacob Black."[31]

Black was just a plot device in *Twilight*, a minor character invented to spill the Cullens' vampire secret to Bella. But, with the *rubedo* finish already in place complete with alchemical wedding and "philosophical orphan," *New Moon* becomes the series *nigredo* featuring the appropriately named Jacob *Black.*

I am not asserting that Mrs. Meyer conceived of the story at this point deliberately and intentionally as an alchemical work. She denies anything like this kind of crafting and planning in her artistry.[32] She insists, though, in the same breath almost, that *New Moon* is based on *Romeo and Juliet* and that *Breaking Dawn* was inspired by both *Midsummer Night's Dream* and *Merchant of Venice*, all Shakespearean alchemical dramas.

Whether by intention or by unconscious inspiration, however, the books in the series work as alchemical set pieces. We need the following elements in addition to identifiable 'black,' 'white,' and 'red' stages for

breaking dawn. I knew exactly where it was going and all the hints are actually in there. You kind of have to dig for them but everything that happens happens for this reason. The one exception is actually the back story of the Quileutes. That was something I that wrote when there was this possibility that I was going to be forced into this 3 book thing which I didn't see how I could do an ending I liked. I came up with an alternate ending that, I had, I kind of get a kick out of it. It was a little different. I don't think anyone else would have liked it; my mom hates it. But the Quileute backstory indirectly leads into that. So that's really the only part that wasn't focused on this ending. (emphasis added) http://twilighttabloid.wordpress.com/the-books/personal-correspondence/qa-breaking-dawn-concert-tour-la/

31 http://www.stepheniemeyer.com/nm_thestory.html

32 See for example her comments at Twilight Moms: http://www.twilightmoms.net/viewtopic.php?f=99&t=3309

TM:As an author do you really consider the things like theme, archetypes, foreshadowing, symbolism, etc. or are you just writing a good story?

Steph: As an author, I consider NOTHING, ha ha ha. I just tell a story. All the symbolism and themes and archetypes are things I discover after the fact. All that stuff in the above paragraph–I didn't think of any of those things until after the story was done. Then I would read through it and think, "Hey, the pack kind of reminds me of those Ammonite kids. Wonder if that's where I got it from?"

Twilight to be obviously alchemical:

- **Contraries to be Resolved:** the drama isn't just a protagonist-antagonist conflict but a set of larger bands or ideas that are at war and which need resolution. Think Capulets and Montagues, or Dickens' 'Two Cities,' or Rowling's Gryffindor and Slytherin.
- **Catalysts to the Reaction:** the stages of alchemy are powered by the play of two complementary and antagonistic forces usually called "alchemical Mercury" and "alchemical Sulphur," who together are the "Quarreling Couple." Mercury is intelligent and feminine while Sulphur is passionate or hot-headed and masculine. Think of Shakespeare's Mercutio and Tybalt in *Romeo and Juliet* or Ron and Hermione in *Harry Potter*. Hermione is even more obviously alchemical and mercurial than Mercutio because her name is the feminine version of Hermes for 'Mercury' and she is a girl brainiac – not to mention that her initials are 'Hg' and her parents are dentists!
- **Character Seeking Transformation:** literary alchemy, like its metallurgical origin, is about change in general and spiritual perfection in particular. The lead character or couple in an alchemical drama have to be seeking heroic transcendence of their mundane existence for a greater life or in sacrifice for those they love. Romeo and Juliet, Dickens' Sydney Carton, and Harry Potter fill this role.

Twilight delivers on all of these points.

The drama begins in the first book with the introduction of the two seekers who become star-crossed lovers. Edward Cullen, the near god who wants to recover his humanity, meets Bella Swan, who upon learning Edward's true nature wants nothing as much as she desires to be with him forever. The contraries here are the Cullens, enlightened and misunderstood vampires, and human beings. There seems to be no way for Bella and Edward to cross the divide. In Bella's sacrifice in Phoenix to save her mother's life from James, she transcends all her ego concerns and begins in this act of renunciation the Great Work of her transformation.

The *nigredo* or "black" work of her soul's dissolution begins, appropriately enough, on her birthday. Edward decides after her fall and Jasper's attack that she will never be safe as long as he is in her life. He leaves – and Bella becomes a soulless person or zombie, the alchemical *prima materia*. She is only saved from this life-like-death (death-like-life?) by who else? Jacob *Black*, her "earthborn sun." He is the light of her darkness, having fallen from celestial love down to earth, her "love, life, meaning… over" at Edward's departure.[33] She risks her life repeatedly in *New Moon* to hear Edward's voice in her head and, indirectly through these self-sacrifices, she is united with him in the end.

New Moon is all about darkness and dissolution until this reunion with Edward, a darkness intentionally played on in the title. As Mrs. Meyer says: "To follow after *Twilight*, I needed a time of day to reflect the mood of the sequel. As **this is the blackest period of Bella's life**, I thought it appropriate to name the book after the darkest kind of night, a night with no moon" (my emphasis).[34] She has become just the love of Edward and prepared for the cost of the changes necessary to be with him always.

But with the introduction of the La Push Wolf Pack and Jacob Black, we now have a set of Contraries to vie with Shakespeare's Capulet and Montague's and a "Quarreling Couple" as ardent and antagonistic as Mercutio and Tybalt. The story during *New Moon* expands from the God-Man allegory a la *Genesis* in the first book to a drama about the conflicts between the Quileute Wolfmen protectors and the Cullens – not to mention the Volturi!

And *Eclipse*, the intersection of sun and moon, is largely about the hermetic rivalry of *Twilight's* "Quarreling Couple," Edward and Jacob. Could these guys be more different?

- The One is pale white, all mind, ice cold, and self-denying or asthetic by principle, eating animal food rather than human beings.
- The Other is named "black," embodies passion and impulsiveness, radiates heat, and eats meat by nature in his paranormal state to defend humans.

Edward sparkles in the light as a creature of the sun; Jacob and the Quileute Pack run by night and are lunar if not exactly werewolves.

---

33 *New Moon*, pages 145, 73

34 http://www.stepheniemeyer.com/nm_thestory.html; see also *http://www.stepheniemeyer.com/nm_faq.html*
Q: What does the title refer to? Is it a werewolf reference?
Meyer: Nope. The term "new moon" refers to the phase of the moon opposite a full moon. It is when the sun is on the opposite side of the moon from us and thus the bright side of the moon is not visible from earth. This is the darkest kind of night. *New Moon* is the darkest period of Bella's life.

Category	Edward and Cullens	Jacob and Quileutes
Temperature	Cold	Hot
Color	White	'Black' (Jacob's name)
Approach	Reason, Conscience	Passion, Intuition

They're ancient enemies and complementary antagonists, yin and yang, form and matter, Mercury and Sulphur. In the alchemical drama of the Forks Saga, Edward and Jacob are the reagents whose explosive interactions act as catalysts to Bella's transfiguration and divinization in *Breaking Dawn.*

Alchemical Formula	Romeo and Juliet	New Moon
'Lead' being transformed	Romeo and Juliet	Bella Swan
Polarity being resolved	Capulets and Montagues	Cullens and Quileutes
Quarreling Couple	Mercutio and Tybalt	Edward and Jacob
Sepulcher-Crucible	Capulet Tomb	Volturi Death Chamber
Illumination	Golden Statues	Bella's Heart, Epiphany

It is the friction of their antagonism in *Eclipse* and the divine and human love of each that she feels in the third book that do the purification and preparatory work necessary for her transformation in *Breaking Dawn.* Bella spends most of her "black" stage with Jacob Black in *New Moon* while Edward is away; her *albedo* in *Eclipse* is spent principally with her albino love.

The *nigredo* of *New Moon* and the *albedo* of *Eclipse,* though, only make sense if they are leads to the *rubedo* of *Breaking Dawn,* which is the ending Mrs. Meyer envisioned for the Forks Saga as soon as she began writing a series rather than a single novel.[35]

---

35 I first started working on it and they said 'we'd just really just like it to be three books, and end with *Eclipse.* Can you make an ending that you're happy with?' And I said 'no, I can't make an ending that I'm happy with.' This was a very hard fought battle and I was fighting for Nessie the whole time. She was a character that I was not going to allow her to be destroyed. She had to exist. So, she was in my *Forever Dawn.* http://twilighttabloid.wordpress.com/the-books/personal-correspondence/qa-breaking-dawn-concert-tour-chicago/

That this is her original ending is significant because it is hard to imagine, since she cites both *Midsummer Night's Dream* and *Merchant of Venice* as her inspiration, that she didn't see the alchemical symbolism of the book, and, working backward, to the black and white elements of *New Moon* and *Eclipse*. There's not much you could add to *Breaking Dawn* to make it more a *rubedo* or a better alchemical finish.

It starts off, for example, with the wedding of Edward and Bella. The *rubedo* has to begin with the Alchemical wedding of the Red King and the White Queen. The cover has red pawn and white queen chess pieces that Mrs. Meyer says represent Bella's transition from weakling to Wonder Woman[36] and Edward and Bella are, after a fashion, the *White* King and *Red* Queen.[37] How important is this wedding to alchemical drama?

Burckhart calls it "the central symbol of alchemy"[38] because this marriage reveals both the action and the end of the Great Work. Just as in a wedding, two people "die" to themselves, a "married" or "blended" couple is born, and life is conceived in this "deadly" union of contraries. The alchemical wedding, by the "marriage" or "quarrel" of sulphur and quicksilver, creates both an alchemist, that is a "*rebis*" or double-natured person, and the Philosopher's Stone (sometimes called the Philosophical Orphan). The wedding occurs in the *albedo* or before the *rubedo*, the last stage of the seven-cycle work.

Lyndy Abraham, whose *Dictionary of Alchemical Imagery* is such a boon to understanding both alchemy itself and the use of its images in English Literature, writes that:

> Metaphysically, the chemical wedding is the perfect union of creative will or power (male) with wisdom (female) to produce pure love (the child, the Stone). The creation of this Stone always involves some kind of sacrifice or death. Thus emblems of the chemical wedding almost always include emblems of death which overshadow the *conjunctio*....

---

36 http://www.stepheniemeyer.com/bd_faq.html
Q: What does the cover mean?
Meyer: *Breaking Dawn*'s cover is a metaphor for Bella's progression throughout the entire saga. She began as the weakest (at least physically, when compared to vampires and werewolves) player on the board: the pawn. She ended as the strongest: the queen. In the end, it's Bella that brings about the win for the Cullens.

37 You'll recall that Bella's hair looks red, albeit "only in the sun." *Twilight*, page 143

38 Titus Burckhardt, *Alchemy*, Penguin, 1971, page 149

> The death at the wedding symbolizes the extinction of the earlier differentiated state before union, and also powerfully conveys the alacrity with which the festive moment of the *coagula* or wedding is transformed into the lamentation of the *solve* or death.[39]

In *Harry Potter,* I think the alchemical wedding of Bill and Fleur was a nice touch and the "philosophical orphan" of Teddy Lupin completed the circle of the story that began with orphan Harry being left on the Dursley's Privet Drive porch. But the Potter story could have worked without these specific alchemical notes.

Try to imagine, though, *Romeo and Juliet* without the wedding in Brother Lawrence's cell or *Tale of Two Cities* without the marriage of Charles Darnay and Lucie Manette or C. S. Lewis' *Perelandra* without the mythic wedding of King and Queen at the end of this *albedo* novel. They just wouldn't work.

Twilight the series is like that. The crisis novel must begin with the alchemical wedding if the Philosopher's Stone, also called the Philosophical Orphan or 'The Child,' is to be born. Meyer says she fought with her publishers for 'Nessie because this character "had to exist."[40] She "had to exist" because she is the end of the all the alchemical work.

She is the "resolution of contraries" and the embodiment of peace in three significant ways:

- She is an androgyne of the Human and Vampire antagonism. None of the Volturi had imagined such a person in thousands of years of existence because to them human beings were only food, like cattle. The birth of Renesmee resets all conceptions of human-vampire relations.
- Nessie is also the cause of Cullen-Quileute conflict resolution. Once Jacob imprints on Renesmee, Sam cannot attack and the alliance is set for the confrontation with the Volturi. The Quarreling Couple of Edward and Jacob, too, are united as father and son soon after her birth.
- Perhaps most importantly, the birth of the human-vampire hermaphrodite causes the Volturi-Cullen conflict to come to a head so that all hidden enmities and differences are brought

39 Abraham, *Dictionary of Alchemical Imagery,* pages 36-37

40 http://twilighttabloid.wordpress.com/the-books/personal-correspondence/qa-breaking-dawn-concert-tour-chicago/

into the open. The Volturi are exposed as power mongers in the Mountain Meadow rather than the agents of justice and order they were thought to be.

Little wonder, then, that Renesmee is treated by all those who meet her as something like a savior or Christ, the God-Man androgen who came into the world as Prince of Peace and Deliverer.

> "Renesmee is healthy and well," [Edward] promised, a gleam I'd never seen before in his eyes. He said her name with an understated fervor. A reverence. The way devout people talked about their gods....
>
> "She's like nothing else in the world, [Edward] told me, and the sound of an almost religious devotion was there again in his voice....
>
> Renesmee was irresistible. What was it about her that drew everyone to her, that made them willing even to pledge their lives in her defense?[41]

Of course, she is no ordinary child, beyond the seeming miracle of her conception. She develops at a supernatural rate and is intelligently conversant at an age when most babies are making their first meaningful eye contact. In light of the God-Man allegory of the series, I think it not too much of a stretch to see her conception and arrival as a fantasy Annunciation and Nativity. Bella's middle name, after all, is 'Marie.'

This leads to the more obvious story point consequent to Nessie's delivery, one that we have been waiting on for the better part of four books: Bella's death and resurrection. Having died sacrificially, albeit only figuratively, however near her real physical deaths had been in Phoenix, in Volterra, and on the bluff above the Olympic Meadow, Bella decides to take her unexpected pregnancy to term in *Breaking Dawn*, though the vampire-fetus is breaking her bones.

This leads to Renesmee, the story's Philosophical Orphan or Child, but equally important, it finally gives us the "beautiful swan" Bella the ugly duckling was named for. She dies in agony on the delivery table but refuses to leave her body. Edward's inserting vampire venom into her heart and no little CPR keep her human body alive just long enough for the venom to do its purgatory work.

Bella experiences the flames of the *rubedo* as if she were in the alchemical crucible. After three days of silence and stillness at the center of her circle, she rises from her chrysalis tomb and is all-but-divine.

41 *Breaking Dawn*, page 396; 428, 593

Having died to herself in love for her baby and husband, she experiences resurrection in a glorified body. She also, to everyone's surprise and delight except Jasper's, experiences very little of the uncontrollable newborn destructive impulses to kill.

Her remarkable self-control, though, isn't her super-power. It turns out she is able to project her mind's shield out from her own thoughts to protect others as well. This ability to open her mind and embrace others, literally and figuratively, is the difference that saves the Cullen Coven alliance and Renesmee's witnesses in the showdown with the Volturi. Having transcended the limitations of her personal understanding by sacrificing herself in love for others, like Renesmee, Bella has become a story savior or 'little Christ.'

Why Literary Alchemy Works: Seeing the Light Outside the Cave

Why is it that literary alchemy, stories, poems, and plays about the resolution of contraries, with bizarre symbols and color sequences an author couldn't make up have such power over readers' hearts and minds, even with prose as pedestrian as Mrs. Meyer's?

I think our best bet is to go back with Plato and Eliade to the Cave Allegory discussed in the Preface to Part 1. If they're right, reading gives us some experience, maybe only imaginative, of a Self greater than our egos, the 'I' that Lewis said is a "sacred name." Those books that describe the experience of slipping our bonds and stepping into the light, naturally, will be the books we respond to the most fervently.

Literary alchemy is the story of the apotheosis of a hero or heroine. We experience this transformation if we have succeeded in suspending our disbelief and identifying ourselves with this character. Through the golden eyes and re-birth of these characters, we gain a glimpse of glory, the God who is Light outside the postmodern Cave we live in.

If you ask the man on the street what alchemy is all about, most folks will say "changing lead into gold" or just "gold." That's not quite right. The alchemist is trying to create the Philosopher's Stone, from which he can draw the Elixir of Life or Dragon's Blood. This effluent, if drunk, keeps the alchemist alive for as long as he keeps drinking it, and, if poured on any other substance, turns that material into gold. The most visible end product, of course, is gold, which if understood correctly as "solid light" is explanation in itself of why the alchemical work is about "resolving contraries."

In the traditional view of the alchemist, remember, the created world is an image of its Unknowable Creator in being a balance or imbalance of contrary tendencies, call them "male" and "female" or "yin" and "yang." Our polarized existence reflects God's being simultaneously and as a unicity both within and outside creation (panentheism). Those things that are "most like" this Reality are a fixed balance or resolution of the contrary masculine and feminine principles, which resolution is a unity and peace that reflects in time and space God's unicity.

We don't see things this way for a variety for reasons. Our response to literary alchemy, however, say, in Shakespeare, *Harry Potter,* and *Twilight,* suggests that there is a resonance between our cardiac intelligence and the nature of things, even God. The Cullens see the world through golden, luminous eyes, and, as the story stand-ins for the Holy Trinity and God's Word or *Logos,* I think it fair to say that we are being called in these books to adopt a similar golden view or alchemical understanding of the world we live in.

In the conclusion to part 1 that follows, we'll see how Mrs. Meyer makes this idea of "light" and "mind" being the unity of existence, even the fabric of reality, the backdrop of her heroes' super-powers and her story finale. A tale of the heart love-story turns out in the end to be a tale about the "inner heart" and how we know God.

Out of the Alchemical Laboratory and Up to the Mountain Meadow

Too many hours in the alchemical laboratory makes Jack a dull boy! Get out of here, boy, and run up to the Olympic Mountain Meadow where the Volturi and the Cullens are having their great confrontation. You can use all the tools and ideas you've practiced in these first four chapters to figure out the several meanings of Mrs. Meyer's series finale.

I'm going to hang back here and air out the lab. Wow, that sulfur stinks, doesn't it?

Alchemy	***Romeo & Juliet***	***Tale of Two Cities***	***Harry Potter***	***Twilight***
Nigredo The Black Stage 'Dissolution'	Act 1	Book 1	*Order of the Phoenix*	*New Moon*
Albedo The White Stage Purification	The Love Story	Book 2	*Half-Blood Prince*	*Eclipse*
Red King Alchemical Wedding White Queen	Br. Lawrence	Charles/Lucie	Weasley/ Delacour	Edward/Bella *Breaking Dawn* wedding
Rubedo The Red Stage Resolution, Perfection	Acts 4 & 5	Book 3	*Deathly Hallows*	*Breaking Dawn* Volturi
Alchemical Sulfur Quarreling Couple Alchemical Mercury	Mercutio/ Tybalt	Darnay/ Evremonde	Ron/Hermione	Jacob/Edward
Core Contraries	Capulet/ Montague	The Two Cities	Gryffindor/ Slytherin	Volturi/ Cullen Cullen/ Quilleute Vampire/ Human
Doppelgangers		Darnay/Carton	Harry/Draco Harry/ Voldemort	Carlisle/Sam Edward/Bella
Metanarrative Enemy	Clan Pride	Aristocracy Class Hatred Revolution	Economic Prejudice Racism	Veggie Vampires Prejudice Human Other
Androgyne Philosophical Orphan *Rebis*	Joined in Death The Prince	Sydney Carton Darnay	Rubeus Hagrid Harry Potter Teddy Lupin	Renesmee
Resolution	Peace in Verona	Epilogue Peace	Marriages Voldemort Defeat Ministry Reform	Marriages Volturi Defeat Alliance(s)
Death Apotheosis Resurrection	Shared Death, Golden Statues	Sydney's Resurrection Immortality	Into the Forest Harry's Sacrifice King's Cross	Renesmee Birth Bella Swan Opening of Mind

Conclusion to Part 1

The Meanings of Breaking Dawn

Reading the Twilight's Series Finale with the Four Senses

"No Way the Author Meant That or Any Reader Gets It"

After a few hours in the alchemical laboratory with story translucencies and the occasional 'Eureka' insight, a time like we've just had, I sometimes hear voices of skeptical readers in my head, voices saying, "Oh, c'mon, John. Get real. These books don't have all this meaning. If they do, the readers aren't getting it. And I just cannot believe that the author, a stay-at-home Sarah Palin look-alike, put the meaning you're finding into the books." As we exit the anagogical and, with it, the iconological four-layered discussion of *Twilight*, I want to answer those voices.

To the objection that the books don't have, in addition to their surface meaning, an implicit morality and an allegorical, even a sublime meaning, I can only ask the skeptical reader to let me know the specific places in the last four chapters where I have left the rails. The observation or, more likely, the assumption that readers aren't 'getting it' or that the author didn't plan it is not a valid argument against multivalent and profound meaning in a book.

As I tried to explain in the preface to these chapters, the four senses of a text are less about deliberate planning and mechanical artistry than they are a function of how we as human beings know things, meaning "everything," to include fiction. We have sense perception for data, a moral filter that yields opinions after straining this data, a capacity to "see through" that specific data for greater, abstract truths we call "knowledge" per se or "science," and we have a relatively spiritual capacity to know the true, good, and beautiful shining through what we sense. This last knowing we call "wisdom."

All four knowings come through or are confirmed by sense perception; very little of any of our knowing is what we could call conscious or self-aware knowledge. I don't think about my thinking while I'm thinking, though it's obvious I'm thinking. It is an edifying exercise when I do think about thinking, but, like looking at your own eyeballs or way of seeing, it's not something you can do while driving or talking with a friend. Life happens in the great blocks of time between self-conscious reflection.

And our thinking and knowing on multi-levels doesn't stop in those blocks of life. I see something and immediately it passes through my opinion-generating filters of "good" and "bad" which produces my opinion on the matter. If I see a trend in the data, that observation yields an abstracted or generalized truth which is more sure and valuable than any point of data. And, when the beauty of what I am seeing or its evident truth or virtue, say, in a sunset or a heroic act, the fourth dimension of knowing comes through my sense perception or in reflection on it as well.

I don't experience the senses or layers of meaning or various "knowings" independently of the sense perception or reflection on same. I am not conscious of it, either, as a separate, distinct knowledge, though, when discussing how I know anything, that I am talking about data, opinion, science, or wisdom is fairly obvious.

Something very similar happens when reading a book. As I enter into a story's narrative I cannot follow consciously more meaning than the story-line or plot gives me at the surface without exiting the experience of the story to think about it. This stepping out of the reading experience is the equivalent of closing my eyes in the forest in order to appreciate the sublime quality of a cataract or waterfall whose beauty has stunned me. Once my eyes are closed, the feeling of the sublime may remain fleetingly but I can no longer sense or experience it directly.

All of the story's meaning and power in similar fashion come through its surface elements. Very little of that meaning is grasped consciously, if, I believe, almost all of it is experienced immediately and directly. As C. S. Lewis wrote about the beauty of translations, "an influence which cannot evade our consciousness will not go very deep."[1] That readers do not consciously understand or that they cannot explain with ease what

1 C. S. Lewis, *The Literary Impact of The Authorised Version*. The Ethel M. Wood Lecture delivered before the University of London on 20 March 1950. London: The Athlone Press, 1950. http://www.biblicalstudies.org.uk/pdf/kjv_lewis.pdf

they love about a story does not mean they have not experienced it. If they love a book or just want to re-read it to repeat their experience or deepen their appreciation of it, they almost certainly have.

That an author was inspired to write a multivalent text and is unaware of greater meaning or denies there is any (perhaps for other reasons) tells us less about a story than a reader's conscious comprehension of its depths. Since the time of Socrates' talks with Athenian poets about the meaning of their work, it has been the rule rather than the exception of literary criticism that artists understand their work imperfectly, to say the least.

This is only logical because writing is a function of inspiration for the most part rather than deliberation, though certainly there is greater and lesser artistry and majesty of language in written work. The artist's Muse, however generous, is not a Rhetoric Instructor and rarely glosses or provides footnotes alongside inspiration.

I confess to finding objections to interpretation of text that are based on audience comprehension or auctorial understanding bizarre. Whatever the author intended and whatever most people 'get' consciously, the text itself is there to be interpreted and only this text, ultimately, does or does not communicate coherent meaning. Looking at it and knowing its four senses through the four human ways of knowing anything reveals the meaning which should in turn explain why readers love it.

To finish off the discussion, then, of the anagogical or translucent meaning of *Twilight* and the four chapters of iconological interpretation, let's look at the multivalent text within the *Breaking Dawn* finale.

The Four Senses of *Breaking Dawn's* Last Battle

True confessions time. When I was a lot younger and had disposable income, I was a comic book junkie. I read every *Batman* and *Captain America* comic book I could get my hands on and even read books about comic book history and artistry. A super-hero trivia geek. Pathetic, I know.

Anyway, one of my favorite comic books was Marvel Comics' *X-Men*. Not the Golden Age originals written by Stan Lee and drawn by Jack Kirby, but the revival series in the 70's written by Chris Claremont and drawn by John Byrne. I remember buying the few issues I was missing to complete my *X-Men* collection with the first paycheck I earned after graduating from college.

The problem that *X-Men* writers had, I think, was coming up with bad guys with sufficient power and intelligence to fight the over-the-top abilities of Professor Xavier's mutants, especially after Jean Grey became the Phoenix. Claremont eventually had to invent extra-terrestrial and Cosmic evil-doers to make any kind of confrontation with the *X-Men* a decent fight.

Mrs. Meyer, as I mentioned, has said that the cartoon versions of Marvel's *X-Men* influenced her work and that she thinks of her characters as having been shaped more by super-hero fiction than vampire canon. Anyone who has read the *X-Men* story who hears this and has read *Twilight* will see Edward as Cyclops, Bella as Marvel Girl/Phoenix, and Jacob as Wolverine, pining after Marvel Girl, Cyclops' true love.

The place in *Twilight* where I was struck by the comic book influence, though, wasn't in the love triangle between the lead characters. It was in the lead up to the confrontation with the Volturi in the *Breaking Dawn* finale. Carlisle here plays the part of Professor Xavier by gathering as many "witnesses" as he can in his mansion, almost all of whom feature some kind of superpower in addition to normal vampire invincibility.

For one thing, that there are the four element powers of Benjamin in the Egyptian coven is a direct take from the *X-Men's* Storm character. The zapping on touch ability that the Denali Coven's Kate has, too, is a lot like the Marvel bad guy; Electro, if it has another, more likely origin I'll talk about in the coming chapter.

It is the gathering and battle preparations, though, that have all the touches of *X-Men* studies with Professor X, especially Bella's learning combat skills. When Kate grabs Renesmee to try to inspire Bella to use her mind shield, the scene could have been taken from any *X-Men* workout scenario dreamed up by the Professor.

The face-off with the Volturi, of course, is all comic book melodrama. It is essentially the X-Men standing up against Magneto and the Brotherhood of Evil Mutants. The principal players, good and bad, are all vampires/mutants or paranormal/superpowered humans. Aro/Magneto insists he is only doing what is best for vampires/mutants, who deserve to be the dominant race; Carlisle/Professor X with the werewolves/human super-heroes argue for the coexistence and rights of human beings. And the story is largely about the two sides pairing off for the climactic battle.

We get the pairing off in *Breaking Dawn,* even an exploring of the Cullen perimeter and mind-shield by Jane and Alec, a brother-sister duo reminiscent of the original Evil Mutant family act of Quicksilver and the Scarlet Witch. Bella becomes Sue Storm-Richards of *The Fantastic Four,* aka 'The Invisible Girl,' with her marvelous mind force-field powers. We don't, alas, get the take-down comic book 'fight to the finish.'

No loss, really, because the surface story does everything we want the narrative line to do without it. For readers to experience the three senses beneath the plot, they have to be sufficiently drawn into it that they can suspend disbelief and identify with their favorite characters. *Breaking Dawn's* finale is engaging in several ways.

- **The Cullen characters are fighting for their lives,** and, if we've read this far into the series, we definitely are determined to know the fates of Bella, Edward, Jacob, and Renesmee;
- **The Bad Guys are really bad.** The injustice of the Volturi position and the transparency of their power grab puts into gear the reader's sense of and hope for justice;
- **The Superpowers are fascinating**. Hey, comic books are as popular as they are for a reason, but more on that in a minute; And
- **The Outcome is Very Much in Doubt**. The Volturi seem to be a sure thing and our heroes seem doomed. *They* think they're doomed.

Totally wrapped up in this high powered drama, it's time for the moral content of the play to be smuggled into the reader's heart and mind. Not too surprisingly, we get a big dose of postmodern fundamentals.

Postmodern Victory: An Open Mind Revealing the Cultural Blind Spot

The good guys win because Bella is able to shield all the White Hats standing with the Cullen Coven and because Alice appears with Nahuel, the half-vampire, whose existence explodes the Volturi's pretense for wanting to destroy Renesmee. Both these events are laden with moral meaning of the postmodern, politically correct variety.

We need to note first that almost all of the "action" in the Olympic Mountain Meadow is mental or about the mind. The power the Volturi have is essentially Jane's ability to cause mental anguish and Alec's capacity for inducing paralysis through mind control. The good guys have some big guns on the physical plain with the Quileute Wolf Pack and Benjamin's 'Earth-Wind-and Fire' act, but even Edward's mental telepathy has nothing useful in response to the Jane and Alec one-two punch. "Their powers were the cornerstone of the Volturi offensive."[2]

Enter Bella.

In the run-up to the confrontation, we learned that Bella could project her mind shield outwards to protect others. It doesn't seem to be of much use, though, because, when the Volturi arrive, she hasn't learned to reach very far with it or for any period of time. She is safe from Alec and Jane, but she cannot help her friends and family.

Until she gets really pissed.

The first thing that sets her off is the appearance of the Quileute Pack. There are a lot more wolfmen than there had been before; the presence of the many Cullen witnesses had caused the tribe's children to make the transformation in response to the need for protectors. Bella feels rage over the almost certain death of these children at the hands of the Volturi.

She keeps her act together, though, until Edward steps forward to "consult with" Aro and Jane smiles because she knows she can turn him into mental silly putty. Bella's response changes everything, as she notes, so it's worth quoting at length:

> That smug little smile did it. My fury peaked, higher even than the raging bloodlust I'd felt the moment the wolves had committed to this doomed fight. I could taste madness on my tongue – I felt it flow through me like a tidal wave of pure power. My muscles tightened, and I acted automatically. I threw my shield with all the force in my mind, flung it across the impossible expanse of the field – ten times my best distance – like a javelin. My breath rushed out in a huff with the exertion.
>
> The shield blew out from me in a bubble of sheer energy, a mushroom cloud of liquid steel. It pulsed like a living thing – I could *feel* it, from the apex to the edges.
>
> There was no recoil to the elastic fabric now; in that instant of raw force, I saw that the backlash I'd felt before was of my own making – I had been clinging to that invisible part of me in self-defense, subconsciously unwilling to let it go. Now I set

---

2 *Breaking Dawn,* page 684

> it free, and my shield exploded a good fifty yards out from me effortlessly, taking only a fraction of my concentration. I could feel it flex like just another muscle, obedient to my will. I pushed it, shaped it to a long, pointed oval. Everything underneath the flexible iron shield was suddenly a part of me – I could feel the life force of everything it covered like points of bright heat, dazzling sparks of light surrounding me. I thrust the shield forward the length of the clearing, and exhaled in relief when I felt Edward's brilliant light within my protection. I held there, contracting this new muscle so that it closely surrounded Edward, a thin but unbreakable sheet between his body and our enemies.
>
> Barely a second had passed. Edward was still walking to Aro. Everything had changed absolutely, but no one had noticed the explosion except for me. A startled laugh bursts through my lips. I felt the others glancing at me and saw Jacob's big black eye roll down to stare at me like I'd lost my mind.[3]

Bella's ability to open her mind shield at this point means "everything has changed" because she can blunt the offensive weapons of the bad guys. As long as Bella is okay, the fight with the Volturi is a straight-up bit of vampire fisticuffs.

The Volturi struggle with the decision to fight or to depart from the Mountain Meadow because they will lose face with the many vampire witnesses they had assembled to see the Cullen Coven destroyed. The Volturi learn that Renesmee is a half-vampire rather than an immortal, that is, a child made into a vampire, the existence of which was forbidden by vampire law. Despite knowing this, they still insist she must be destroyed as an immortal would be because they cannot know if the half-vampire will *eventually* compromise their collective invisibility to humans.

That at least is their face-saving argument for an attack to eliminate the Cullen Coven as a rival power center among vampires.

Enter Alice and Nahuel.

Alice and Jasper had seemingly abandoned their adoptive family in the face of the Volturi's arrival. Because of Alice's ability to see the future, the Cullens assumed she left them because their cause was hopeless. Nope.

---

3 *Breaking Dawn.* Pages 690-691

They had left without telling anyone why lest Aro discover what they were up to inadvertently. Alice and Jasper arrive in the Mountain Meadow *ex machina* to throw light in the blind spot of the Volturi. They have found a mature half-vampire and he is no threat to vampire security because he is stable and rational (unlike an immortal). The Volturi depart.

The morality lessons in this are the postmodernist's greatest hits.

- **Power and reality are all about the mind:** You'll recall from the moral layer chapter that the core idea of postmodernism is "incredulity about metanarratives," i.e., we're skeptical about all big ideas (except skepticism) because cultural myths divide the world into power-haves and have-nots and create the blinders or mind-filters of prejudice keeping us from seeing things as they are. The power holders, the Cave's shadow casters, keep us enslaved through the delusions in our heads.
- **Only the 'Other' can understand:** The 'haves' who are empowered by the metanarrative cannot see outside it. Only the ostracized and marginalized outsiders can see the injustice of things.
- **Freedom Means 'Speaking Truth to Power:'** The only freedom for those in the Caves chains requires crying out against the shadow-casters creating their delusions. Throw off the metanarrative! The relative truth will make you free! Identifying with and feeling the injustice of the oppressed, loving them, will lead to the expansion of your mind and your liberating rage against the oppressor.
- **Truth is Found in the Metanarrative Blind-Spot:** Our prejudices act as super-glued colored glasses that effectively blind us to things as they are because we cannot see things except indirectly through the distorting lenses of our core beliefs. The place to look for truth, consequently, is not head on but in our peripheral vision, the blind-spot outside our line of sight, where the distortion is minimal.
- **Choice is the Summum Bonum:** In postmodern morality, prejudice is the core evil. Self-actualizing choice, because it means stepping outside what the culture or family binding narrative says we are, is the chief good and the hallmark of the free person. Free choice is a greater good even than life (hence its use currently as a euphemism for abortion).

The expansion of Bella's power and Alice's reappearance with Nahuel, then, the two events that spell defeat for the Volturi, are both laden with postmodern ideas of what is right and wrong.

The key battle between the sides is the invisible one about mind control. The metanarrative empowered Volturi have the ability to paralyze and crush the thinking of even the most thoughtful. Garrett's philippic in the Meadow to the Volturi and company is a passionate plea for freedom of thought.[4] Edward's plea to the witnesses is "throw away your preconceived notions."[5] The only freedom from this mind-lock, though, will come from a powerful shield against this prejudicial intrusion.

Where does such a shield come from? Bella's shielding power had been strictly personal because she had been "subconsciously unwilling to let it go." She says later her shield is the part of her "that fought against separation from me, the automatic instinct to preserve self above all else."[6] But it explodes at Jane's smirk and the idea of the dead Quileute wolf children because she feels rage with the power-holding, vicious Volturi. She feels the injustice of arbitrarily used force by those who wield it against the weak and innocent for their own advantage.

Identifying with those suffering injustice, her mind literally expands to include under its umbrella-like protection the people she loves. Love and rage open Bella's mind and the power of the metanarrative holders is broken.

The core or defining belief of the world dominated by the Volturi is that vampires are gods and the rightful power holders, human beings are no more than cows to feed on, and there can be no conjunction between vampires and the 'other.' Renesmee must be destroyed because her very existence, if not eradicated, will be a demonstration that vampires and human beings are capable of inter-marriage (miscegenation!) and reproduction – a proof of the error of the metanarrative justifying Volturi rule and 'justice.'[7]

Alice's appearance with Nahuel is light thrown in just this Volturi blind-spot.[8] The truth that Renesmee is no threat, that a human-vampire

4 *Breaking Dawn*, page 717
5 *Breaking Dawn*, page 585
6 *Breaking Dawn*, page 752
7 Hence Bella's noting that her daughter is the ultimate outsider, the 'other' of vampiric metanarrative, who "fits nowhere" (*Breaking Dawn*, page 582).
8 Alice describes her search for Nahuel as "searching for a blind spot," her own,

androgen is possible and no danger, is demonstrated. The Volturi power is effectively broken and they retreat.

What has won the day? Our sacrificial choices, of course. Jasper and Alice choose to leave hearth and home in the hope of finding proof of the liberating truth they know exists. Bella chooses to feel love for the vulnerable and oppressed and the consequent rage against the powerful and their injustice masquerading as 'good.' This choice leads to the opening of her mind and the freedom of everyone around her from slavery to their controlling idea. It's something of a postmodern morality play, no?

Seeing the Light:
The Allegorical Meaning of *Breaking Dawn's* Finale

Much of the allegory or story transparency in the Showdown at Mountain Meadows is in the archetypal referents in the various witnesses and the Cullens. The Holy Family, especially Alice and Jasper (Oh, come Holy Spirit!), perform according to Trinitarian and triptych qualities discussed in the chapter above on allegory. The gathered witnesses, too, from Garrett the Revolutionary Patriot to the Amazon coven feminists all say their lines appropriately as representative types "speaking truth to power."

All the characters in *Twilight,* the human ones as well as the vampires, of course, are relatively idealized stock-role players who have been scrubbed clean of anything but stereotypical problems and concerns. No one is constipated or obese in the books and only the token rape-murderer has drinking issues. Sheesh, the kids at the un-chaperoned beach party on the reservation are all drinking soda. Just like real life!

This isn't a failing, though, but effective Romance, as Frye defines it, the mode of fiction whose ideal qualities are more like myth than realist, newspaper depiction. The power here of the story mode featuring human-like characters who embody archetypal qualities and perform idealized heroics is that we identify with them and experience the referents for which they are caricatures more easily than we do with finely-drawn, detailed character portraits.

---

of course, not the Volturi's, but as a vampire it means much the same thing: deliverance from the vampire metanarrative; *Breaking Dawn,* page 747

Trash *Twilight* all you want for being a Young Adult comic book retelling of the "ugly duckling" fairy tale in which the awkward wall flower, after making the heroic, sacrificial choices to love, becomes post-chrysalis and story crisis the "beautiful swan." I mean, it is what it is and it's not as if the author didn't telegraph the "ugly duckling" story ending and meaning by giving the heroine a name meaning "beautiful swan." This ain't A. S. Byatt.

It is exactly in this fairy tale quality, though, that the *Twilight* novels especially resonate with readers the way Byatt's artistry never will. Reading is a religious experience in which the reader suspends disbelief and has a transpersonal existence and experience in identification with the characters found therein. The more idealized and less realistic these characters are while remaining sufficiently humanesque to be believable, the more profoundly the reader can enter into them, experience and embrace the heroic qualities they embody and reject the bad choices and failings of the cartoon Black Hats.

The mythic or unrealistic cartoon quality of *Twilight,* call it what you want, is the allegorical sense of these novels and the reason readers love them. It allows reading to do – serve that mythic or religious function in their lives the secular culture has forbidden elsewhere – what readers want it to do.

But Mrs. Meyer goes beyond this. She gives the *Breaking Dawn* finale specific allegorical meaning that is religious in nature, beyond the 3 day resurrection our ugly duckling experiences to become the all-new, glorified Bella Swan.

Roll back to the mind-opening scene in which Bella throws out her shield to protect Edward.

> I pushed [the mind shield], shaped it to a long pointed oval. Everything underneath the flexible iron shield was suddenly a part of me – I could feel the life force of everything it covered like points of bright heat, dazzling sparks of light surrounding me....[9]

Bella experiences the minds of people under her projected mind-shield as "life-force" and "light." She details this a few pages later:

> I could still feel the sharp plumes of light where my family and friends stood – each one an individual flavor that I thought I

9 *Breaking Dawn.* Pages 690-691

> would be able to recognize with practice. I already knew Edward's – his was the brightest of them all.[10]

Bella's mind shield is "drawn to [the] spark"[11] of any individual she wanted to protect, suggesting a correspondence between her outstretched mind and the mental "plume of light" in each person. It is no surprise that Edward's plume is the "brightest of them all." As we talked about in the allegory chapter, Edward's mind is what makes him the Christ figure of the book. He is, through his signature ability to know all thoughts, the story cipher for the *Logos*-Man, the "Light of the world."[12]

But, though Edward as allegorical Christ is the "brightest light" he isn't the only light and he isn't the only one with the capacity for shared mind.

Everyone has this "sharp plume of light," right? This is because this *Logos* that is the "light of the world" is the "light of men," "the true Light, which lighteth every man that cometh into the world." This is not esoteric spirituality; it's Christianity 101.

> 1 In the beginning was the Word [*Logos*], and the Word was with God, and the Word was God.
> 2 The same was in the beginning with God.
> 3 All things were made by him; and without him was not any thing made that was made.
> 4 In him was life; and **the life was the light of men.**
> 5 And the light shineth in darkness; and the darkness comprehended it not.
> 6 There was a man sent from God, whose name was John.
> 7 The same came for a witness, to bear witness of the Light, that all men through him might believe.
> 8 He was not that Light, but was sent to bear witness of that Light.
> 9 That was the true Light, **which lighteth every man that cometh into the world.**[13]

Every person in existence, good or evil, smart or stupid, just in being human, comes into the world with this light of Christ in them.

10 *Breaking Dawn.* Page 703

11 Op.cit., page 703

12 "Then spake Jesus again unto them, saying, I am the light of the world: he that followeth me shall not walk in darkness, but shall have the light of life." (John 8:12)

13 John 1: 1-9

This intelligence or mind is not individual but the shared conscience of every human being. "Conscience" means "shared knowing" and, in Greek, "shared vision." The paranormal or supernatural players in Mrs. Meyer's archetypal drama, consequently, good and evil, all have powers involving mind. As Owen Barfield taught C. S. Lewis, the "universe is mental" and reality and our experience of it is just our "participation in a cosmic *Logos*."

We get a story picture of our identity or unicity in mind not only in the Christ figure Edward but in the shared mind of the La Push Wolf Pack. The werewolves, too, have a group mind by which their thoughts are all shared.

Bella, not surprisingly, finds that the Quileute wolves are different than the vampire mind-lights she is protecting. She can only feel or sense the vampire minds if they are under her shield. If her shield is covering the Alpha wolf of a pack, however, the whole pack is protected and she can sense their lights.

> I edged [the mind shield] outward again, and as soon as Sam [Uley, Alpha wolf of the La Push pack] was under cover, all the wolves were brilliant sparks again.
>
> Their minds must have been more interconnected than I'd imagined. If the Alpha was inside my shield, the rest of their minds were every bit as protected as his.[14]

All minds are joined in the *Logos* fabric or light that is their common substance. Bella's opened mind is "drawn to the [spark]" of light in any mind because it recognizes its reflection or likeness in Christ, the foundation of all reality and thought, "in Whom we live and move and have our being."[15]

The Anagogical Meaning of the Big Finish: Heart and Mind

The word "sublime" is from two Latin words "sub" and "limen." Sub-limen means, literally, "under-the-threshold" and the English words 'sublime' and 'subliminal' both take their meaning from the suggestion of "under-the-threshold" that the subject in question cannot be directly perceived. Being at the entrance way, too, suggests that grasping the sublime point of the matter means gaining entry into a different space and, symbolically, a greater understanding.

---

14 *Breaking Dawn*, pages 703-704

15 Acts 17:28

The core allegory of the *Twilight* books is the God-Man love story from Eden retold and recast in a Romance, meant in both the sense of idealized story and tale of courtship and love. Bella is the ugly duckling human seeker, Edward is the Word and Light become flesh, and their love for each – hers sacrificial and total, his reserved lest he destroy or consume her – are story-ciphers for the synergistic love between God and Man.

Bella is the narrator, appropriately, because we are meant to identify with her human love for the Christ of the story. If Edward is the incarnate *Logos* and Light, the Divine Mind, Bella is the human "inner heart" designed to receive this Mind.[16] *Twilight*'s anagogical meaning is the translucency of their union and our experience in it imaginatively of communion with the Absolute and our self-transcendence.

Did you miss Bella as "heart"? Go back to *New Moon.*

In every book, Bella's heart speeds and flutters in reaction to every move or glance that Edward makes. I have a good friend who works in a cardiology lab and he told me this part of *Twilight* drove him half-bonkers. "The girl needs some beta blockers or something" was his thought. I get that. In *New Moon,* though, we really discover how much Bella's heart lives for Edward because of his absence through most of that book.

Mrs. Meyer uses a host of similes and uses them repeatedly to drive home Bella's emotional barrenness in *New Moon* after Edward departs. Two of the bigger ones I'm sure you recall are the darkness of a 'new moon' and the void of an 'empty house.' The workhorse metaphor, though, is a chest without a beating heart; as I mentioned in chapter 3, I counted 37 different passages leaning on this "painfully empty" chest image. *Thirty-seven.*

That kind of repetition is a cue we should be paying attention.

The heart here is not a Hallmark valentine but a story-stand-in for the *lebh* and *kardia* of scripture, the faculty of soul which serves as the interface between God as He can be known and Man (cf., Psalm 51:10, Matthew 5:8). When Edward-God is gone, "a huge hole had been punched through my chest;" when Edward-God returns, "my heart inflated like it was going to crack right through my ribs. It filled my

---

16 Mrs. Meyer says Edward and Bella are "perfectly designed for Each other" and "their pairing feels very fated." Personal Correspondence 10, Twilight Lexicon; http://www.twilightlexicon.com/?p=198

chest and blocked my throat so that I could not speak." She describes her realization that Edward-God loves her as an "epiphany," religious-speak less for "revelation" than for a "theophany" or appearing of God.[17]

New Moon, as we have discussed above, is an allegory about the zombie-like existence of human life without belief in God's presence and His love; it serves as Bella's alchemical *nigredo.* Fast forward through the *Eclipse albedo* to the very end of *Breaking Dawn,* and our farewell to Edward and Bella.

By this point, they've been married, consummated their love, God and Mary (Bella's middle name is 'Marie,' of course), and the Holy Mother has delivered the God-Man androgen who is the world savior. Renesmee's presence in the world has brought peace between Quileutes and Cullens and revealed the Volturi for the evil they are. What's left for the drama?

The absolute and total communion of human Heart and divine Mind.

And this, of course, is what we get in the final scene of the *Twilighti* Saga when Bella and Edward retreat to their cabin from Casa Cullen for the usual night of endless vampire sex. Bella tonight, though, has a special surprise for *Logos* on legs. She will at last open her mind to him:

> "I want to try something," I informed him, smiling slightly at his bewildered expression.
>
> I put my hands on both sides of his face and closed my eyes in concentration.
>
> I hadn't done very well with this when Zafrina had tried to teach me before, but I knew my shield better now. I understood the part that fought against separation from me, the automatic instinct to preserve self above all else.
>
> It still wasn't anything near as easy as shielding other people along with myself. I felt the elastic recoil again as my shield fought to protect me. I had to strain to push it entirely away from me; it took all of my focus.
>
> "Bella!" Edward whispered in shock.
>
> I knew it was working then, so I concentrated even harder, dredging up the specific memories I'd saved for this moment, letting them flood my mind, and hopefully his as well.[18]

---

17 *New Moon,* pages 526-527

18 *Breaking Dawn,* page 752-53

She summons up a few suitably erotic moments from their past. He gives her a big kiss which breaks her concentration and the opening to her mind.

> "Oops, lost it!" I sighed.
>
> "I *heard* you," he breathed. "How? How did you do that?"
>
> "Zafrina's idea. We practiced with it a few times."
>
> He was dazed. He blinked twice and shook his head.
>
> "Now you know," I said lightly and shrugged. "No one's ever loved anyone as much as I love you."
>
> "You're almost right." He smiled, his eyes still a little wider than usual. "I know of just one exception."
>
> "Liar."

She shows him a few more erotic scenes by pulling back her mental movie curtain and he interrupts her again.

> "Damn it," he growled, kissing hungrily down the edge of my jaw.
>
> "We have plenty of time to work on it," I reminded him.
>
> "Forever and forever and forever," he murmured.
>
> "That sounds exactly right to me."
>
> And then we continued blissfully into this small but perfect piece of our forever.[19]

The anagogical heart of *Twilight* is alchemical, as detailed in the previous chapter, and the bumper sticker definition of alchemy is "the resolution of contraries in Christ" or just "divinization." In this coital finish of *Breaking Dawn*, we get the conjunction of opposites, human seeker heart and the Divine Mind, in which the human heart finally opens up completely to the God who would never force His way there. The result is a love that is "forever" or eternal and a bliss that is continuous in the ultimate communion of Creator and Created-image.

We find in this Harlequin edition of the *Song of Songs* the God-Man love story that is the key to unlocking *Twilight* mania. Eliade is right; in a secular culture, entertainments serve a religious function – and this most fundamental spiritual drama is as popular as it is because it smuggles the core religious message of the Western tradition, the Fall

19 *Breaking Dawn*, page 754

of man and his return to union with God through His Word. *Twilight* mania is largely a function of the success Mrs. Meyer has in delivering her hermetic punch. In each reader's identification with Bella, the story figure of our "inner heart," and her love and longing for its union with Edward as Word or Christ, that reader transcends his or her individual ego persona's concerns for an imaginative experience of what is much more real and lasting.

"So Where did Mrs. Meyer Learn How to Do This?"

I hope this look at the *Breaking Dawn* finish -- the battle with the Volturi and the bedroom finale – clarifies the four senses of the text and how the subliminal three all come simultaneously and subconsciously through the surface narrative.

- The great plot and blockbuster storyline lures us in,
- the postmodern morality we all agree with hooks us hard,
- the story transparencies working as allegory give us the imaginative room we need for religious experience inside the story, and
- the alchemical artistry of the story gives us the final 'wow' experience of transcending our ego identities and feeling the unity of all things in the *Logos.*

And that's why *Twilight* has sold a gazillion copies and why the movies are so important to people. The story is engaging, edifying, even ennobling (and, yes, not just a little erotic!).

But maybe you're wondering: "How did Mrs. Meyer pull off this kind of story telling in her first attempt?" That is a fair question, if it somehow assumes that artistry is solely the product of craftsmanship skills honed with years of practice. This is to discount too heavily the weight of inspiration in the balance of fine writing.

But even allowing that Mrs. Meyer has a generous Muse, the alchemical wedding stuff and God-Man allegory – this isn't stuff they're teaching in the public schools or even the better private schools any more (if they ever did!). She is an avid reader, averaging two or three books a week, she says, before *Twilight* fame and obligations came and swallowed her life. Shakespeare, the alchemical dramatist, too, is also a big favorite of hers. Maybe she picked it up there?

It's possible, certainly. She might have just had a brilliant English teacher at BYU who initiated her into the hermetic mysteries of Shakespeare and literary alchemy. Bella's English teacher in *Twilight* is Mr. Mason and maybe that is a tip of the occult hat to her unnamed mentor.

I doubt it, but only because there's a much more obvious explanation.

Mrs. Meyer is a Latter-day Saint, born and bred, and Mormon belief and practices, to include the ideas of divinization, alchemical apotheosis, and human beings as "intelligences" are the great backdrop to the *Twilight* novels. Let's shift gears here from the literary and sublime down to something like the dreaded "Personal Heresy"[20] to explore three ways Mormonism suffuses Mrs. Meyer's artistry.

---

20 *The Personal Heresy: A Controversy* (1939) was a written debate by E. M. W. Tillyard and C. S. Lewis. The authors each wrote alternating chapters. Lewis' position can be summed up in the following selection:

> Let it be granted that I do approach the poet; at least I do it by sharing his consciousness, not by studying it. I look with his eyes, not at him ... To see things as the poet sees them I must share his consciousness and not attend to it; I must look where he looks and not turn round to face him.; I must make of him not a spectacle but a pair of spectacles; in fine, as Professor Alexander would say, I must *enjoy* him and not *contemplate* him. (page 12)

Part Two: Twilight as an LDS Midsummer Night's Dream

Reading as Dream Interpretation

Chapter 5

Twilight as the Work of a Mormon Artist

How Mrs. Meyer's LDS Faith Shapes Her Twilight Novels

If I had my 'druthers,' as my mother used to say, I'd rather not get into Mrs. Meyer's Mormon faith. Some football coaches who live and die by the running game explain their aversion to the forward pass by saying, correctly, that when the football is thrown only three things can happen and two of these possibilities – interception and incompletion – are bad. My thought on writing about Mormonism in the *Twilight* novels is that, however necessary it may be, it has a steep and inevitable downside much worse than a football turnover or loss of down.

- Most obviously, some Latter-day Saints will be offended because any representation of their faith here will be considered a *mis*representation.
- As regrettably, some non-Mormons will read this discussion as if it were a proper or substantive introduction to LDS history, beliefs, and practices from which they might make informed opinions on those subjects.
- Worse, for me at least, I have to suspect that many readers will neglect the longer and more important part of *Spotlight*, the chapters on the artistry and meaning of the *Twilight* novels you've just finished, and remember only this chapter on Mormonism and its influence on said artistry and meaning.

That would be a real shame.

So why talk about the LDS content of Mrs. Meyer's work? Are the *Twilight* books a second *Book of Mormon* rewritten as an Ugly Duckling becomes Goddess Vampire fairy tale?

No, they are not.

I regret, consequently, that my discussion of the author's faith might foster the idea that Mrs. Meyer's novels can justifiably be pigeon-holed (and neglected) by readers as "just Mormon fiction" or "Mormon entertainment." She is an important and excellent writer who is a Mormon, not a Mormon writer crafting books as proselytizing tracts or as vessels in which to "smuggle the Gospel" of Joseph Smith, Jr., the Mormon prophet.

But I am obliged in a book on the "artistry and meaning of Stephenie Meyer's *Twilight* novels" to write at length about how her faith informs the story. As we'll learn in this chapter, (1) common sense, (2) the genesis of the story in Mrs. Meyer's June 2003 dream, and (3) the part the LDS content plays in explaining the popularity of her books make the author's Mormon faith the elephant in the room that cannot be denied or neglected by serious readers. We'll see that the *Twilight* novels can be read as a prolonged allegory of conversion to LDS faith, a sort of Mormon *Pilgrim's Progress*, albeit one with both a wish-fulfillment apology for the faith and implicit criticism of its failings.

In brief, the Mormon content in the *Twilight* series is huge.

A Portrait of the Artist as a Young Mormon

Let's start with some common sense. The author of the *Twilight* books is a Latter-day Saint. The *Twilight* story meaning, consequently, will to one degree or another necessarily reflect Mormon beliefs and perspectives.

That seems pretty straightforward to me, but, as the chapters that follow rest on this "given," it deserves some discussion.

C. S. Lewis wrote in his essay *On Stories* that "To construct plausible and moving 'other worlds' you must draw upon the only real 'other world' we know, that of the spirit."[1] Simply put, writers of fantasy fiction (and all fiction is to one degree or another fantastic or imaginary) necessarily create their sub-creations in the image of how they understand the world. Whether a writer is an atheist or piously faithful, an author's beliefs are the template from which his or her work's implicit cosmology is drawn.[2]

---

1 C. S. Lewis, *On Stories and Other Essays on Literature*, Harvest Books, 2002, pages 12.

2 See, for instance, Orson Scott Card's discussion of 'Religion in Science Fiction

There is a veritable industry consequent to this truism in which serious readers "unpack" the Catholic baggage of Tolkien, the "Ulsterior motives" of Lewis, and Joanne Rowling's nonconformist Christian beliefs.[3] Examination of Mrs. Meyer's *Twilight* Saga, coming as it does from the heart of a faithful Latter-day Saint (LDS), begins most fruitfully with attention to those spiritual beliefs and their reflection in her books.

I should add that this is especially true in Mrs. Meyer's case because her method of composition is almost entirely a function of her reception to inspiration rather than deliberate planning or design of her work. As she explains:

> I know that a lot of the people who read my books would like to write their own books, and I want to be as helpful to those writers as possibly. This is one of those areas where I can't be super helpful, because I don't have a process to be learned from or imitated. The original inspiration I had, the dream that spawned *Twilight*, was hardly something I invited or controlled. After that unconscious beginning, pretty much everything just came to me in a very effortless and natural way. Characters, particularly, seem to spring to life for me, fully rounded and completely intriguing (to me, anyway) from conception.[4]

Her writing, in effect, comes from her unconscious or super-conscious mind. What has shaped that mind or fills it are the predominant ideas of her education or spirituality, just like everyone else. Mrs. Meyer's world-view, though, the sum of her family's beliefs, those of the schools she attended, and the faith she believes is true and salvific, is entirely Mormon.

On her Mormon bona fides, I am obliged to note:

- that the author grew up in Phoenix, Arizona, whose county has the largest number of LDS communities outside of Utah,[5]
- that she kept her faith's Word of Wisdom and Law of Chastity faithfully as a single woman and still avoids R-rated movies and the like today,

---

and Fantasy' at writing-world.com for his critique of how the invisibility of religion in most fiction today reflects the atheism of the intellectual class: http://www.writing-world.com/sf/card.shtml

3 http://hogwartsprofessor.com/?p=1113

4 TwilightLexicon.com, Personal Correspondence 10, http://www.twilightlexicon.com/?p=198

5 http://www.adherents.com/largecom/com_lds.html

- that she attended Brigham Young University, the Mormon academic Mecca, where she studied English literature,
- that she teaches Sunday School classes for teen-agers at her local LDS meeting-house,[6]
- that she married while still a student, has had three sons, and, outside of writing the *Twilight* series, is a conventional LDS wife and stay-at-home mom,
- that the most influential book in her life is *The Book of Mormon* and the book that most influenced her as a writer is fellow LDS author Orson Scott Card's *Speaker for the Dead*,[7] and
- that she has admitted to interviewers that her books have a "Mormon message" that she hopes "comes through"[8] and that *Twilight*'s Native Americans were lifted in large part from a specific passage of *The Book of Mormon* she has always loved.[9]

In sum, Mrs. Meyer grew up in a largely LDS community and her personal life – from what she eats and the clothes she wears (can you say "Mormon underwear Temple garments"?) to the movies she watches and the boys she dated and the one she married – was shaped by and continues to conform with Mormon standard practice. Her higher education, her regular reading, and her religious observances *per se* were shaped by and are subject to church direction.

This may not seem like a very big deal to you because, like many gentiles, you may imagine that being a Latter-day Saint is something like being Presbyterian, Baptist, or Lutheran.

---

6 Page 2: http://www.twilightmoms.net/viewtopic.php?f=99&t=3228
TM: So do the 14-18 year olds your teach at church love you as a teacher? Have they all read your books? Do you get lots of visitors to your class?
Steph: I think I'm kind of a boring teacher. Mostly I just stick to the scriptures, so a lot of them sneak over to the 12-13 year old class, where the teacher is a nice looking newly returned missionary who brings homemade cinnamon rolls and plays hangman all hour. I've gotten a few visitors, who are also no doubt bored. Some of the girls have read my books, but none of the boys.

7 http://www.amazon.com/Twilight-Book-1-Stephenie-Meyer/dp/0316160172

8 http://www.meridianmagazine.com/books/080806vampire.html

9 Growing up, Meyer's favorite *Book of Mormon* story was the one about the 2,000 stripling warriors, from the book of Alma. In the story, the parents of a small group of boys are under attack but have taken a blood oath never to fight again after their conversion to Christianity. They consider breaking the oath but are persuaded not to by a prophet. Their sons, who never took the oath, go to fight instead, and because of their faith, not a single one is harmed. Meyer sees her werewolves as her stripling warriors.
http://www.phoenixnewtimes.com/content/printVersion/481142

It isn't.

Not to diminish the large part that congregational life in the Protestant sects I mentioned may make in shaping an individual believer's understanding of the world, but it just isn't comparable to Mormonism. LDS faith *totally* shapes that view. A closer religious analogy for Mormonism than Main Line Christianity, if the word comes with the same unfortunate connotations as "cult," would be fundamentalism.

Mormonism is a religious culture that consumes its adherents, for better or worse.

This isn't just John the Gentile talking. Orson Scott Card, a Mormon apologist as well as Mrs. Meyer's favorite living author,[10] whose fifty books she claims to have read twice[11] and whom she ranks with Jane Austen and William Shakespeare,[12] has said:

> The LDS Church is an exceptionally involving organization. It is as impossible for a raised-in-the-Church Mormon to escape his Mormon-ness as it is for a Jew to escape his Jewishness. Being a Mormon has shaped my experiences, and since my attitudes and experiences are the stuff of my fiction and plays, everything I have done is colored by them.[13]

Common sense suggests this is as true for Mr. Card's disciple, Mrs. Meyer, as it is for him, so that focusing on her Mormon beliefs as a starting point in the effort to understand the popularity of her books is only logical. Reading Isaac Bashevis Singer without a thought about Judaism or Tolstoy and Dostoevsky without Orthodox Christianity is covering one eye; ignoring the Mormon content of *Twilight* is a similar dodge of the elephant in the room.

Does Mrs. Meyer set out to write an LDS allegory of an ugly duckling's conversion and divinization with characters from the Utah back-lot a la Bunyan's *Pilgrim's Progress*? Frankly, I would be astonished if that was the case. She has said "All the symbolism and themes and archetypes are things I discover after the fact.... I didn't think of any

10 http://www.ew.com/ew/article/0,,20049578,00.html

11 http://www.coldtwilight.com/crew/stephenie-meyer/stephanie-meyer-reflects-on-bright-twilight-as-dvd-looms/5399

12 http://www.motleyvision.org/2005/interview-twilight-author-stephanie-meyer/

13 cited in Michael R. Collings, *In the Image of God: Theme Characterization, and Landscape in the Fiction of Orson Scott Card,* Michael R. Collings, Greenwood Press, 1990, pp 9-10

of those things until after the story was done."[14] Note that she is saying there *is* substantial meaning in the stories – "symbolism and themes and archetypes" – but that she doesn't plan them. They come from her sub- or supra-conscious mind as inspiration and she "discovers" them "after the fact" of writing.

It's just that the substance, orientation, and focus of her thinking, experience, and faith are essentially and almost exclusively Mormon. With that as our base-line, is it any surprise that when Mrs. Meyer writes a love story, the romance turns out to be about human striving for immortality? That it is about the relationship of Man and God as it can be perfected through marriage and childbirth? That it is filled with Mormon beliefs and practices, not to mention the only loosely disguised heroes and demons from LDS history?

It would be much more of a surprise if this weren't the case. If the cook is Japanese and the food available in the cook's kitchen is rice, sea vegetables, and tofu, don't be looking for your favorite French dishes or for hamburgers and fries. The artist and cook work with the media at hand; the writer draws from the substance of the imagination, namely, his or her experience, education, and beliefs. Mrs. Meyer's imagination draws almost exclusively from the deep well of Mormon scripture, culture, and ideas.

Lest you think this is only the case of a mad-eyed gentile forcing these meanings onto and into a nice story that could be interpreted in many other ways, Mrs. Meyer says her books have Mormon meaning[15] and at least one Mormon critic has spelled out the LDS content of *Twilight* with references to Mormon scripture and doctrinal authorities.

Edwin Arnaudin, in his *Mormon Vampires: The Twilight Saga and Religious Literacy*,[16] details the "bleed" between Mrs. Meyer's beliefs from LDS scripture (especially *Doctrines and* Covenants and the Word of Wisdom) and Bella Swan's adventures. Arnaudin, in laborious but convincing fashion, connects the dots between *Twilight* plot points and

14 TwilightMoms.com, Page 3: http://www.twilightmoms.net/viewtopic.php?f=99&t=3309

15 ""Mormon themes do come through in Twilight. Free agency – I see that in the Cullens. The vampires made the choice to be something more – that's my belief, the importance of free will to being human." http://www.bookpage.com/books-12904-Twilight

16 Edwin B. Arnaudin. "Mormon Vampires: The Twilight Saga and Religious Literacy." A Master's Paper for the M.S. in L.S degree. April, 2008. http://www.ils.unc.edu/MSpapers/3348.pdf

their background in LDS teachings on nine subjects. To give you a taste of his exegesis, here are snippets from the headers of those discussions (page references are all to *Mormon Vampires*):

- **"Milk Before Meat:"** Arnaudin explains that LDS missionaries work in strict adherence to the principle of "progressive truth," which gentiles might call "deceptive advertising." Simply put, they are not to spill the beans of the more difficult Mormon teachings or practices until the potential convert has been exposed to the more conventional elements of the faith. Talk about "strong families" before "baptizing the dead," for instance. Arnaudin argues persuasively that this is exactly the policy practiced by the secretive Cullens and by the Quileute wolfmen, whose secrets Bella learns progressively and in digestible "milk before meat" sequence lest she be overwhelmed or alarmed. (pages 19-26)
- **Free Agency – Mormon Choice:** Mormon life is all about choosing to obey God's revealed path to life with Him. Arnaudin cites *Doctrine and Covenants*, the LDS record of the Prophet's revelations about this path: "Practicing agency is a spiritual matter (D&C 29:35) which in its most basic form is the choice to accept God's enlightenment and commandments or to resist and reject them by yielding to the temptations of the devil (D&C 93:13)." He quotes Bella's "motto on agency,"[17] the *Twilight* cover, and the original title of the first book – *Forks* – and the series of choices Bella makes in the book as evidence of Mrs. Meyer's conformity to LDS beliefs about the centrality of "agency" to a fully human life (pages 27-36).
- **Sexuality and the Law of Chastity:** Arnaudin baldly states that "sexual purity is one of the most important aspects of LDS life. Church members are required to refrain from any sexual relationships outside of marriage and any perverse or coercive sexual acts within marriage." He quotes a host of *Book of Mormon* passages and cites the *Doctrine and Covenants* instructions "collectively known as the law of chastity" to back this up. He argues that the *Twilight* novels are essentially the

17 Meyer, *Twilight*, page 140: Making decisions was the painful part for me, the part I agonized over. But once the decision was made, I simply followed through – usually with relief that the choice was made. Sometimes the relief was tainted by despair, like my decision to come to Forks. But it was still better than wrestling with the alternatives.

law of chastity in story form: "To show the importance of sexual purity, she makes the romance between Bella and Edward, and their use of agency to avoid sexual temptation, the central story line in the *Twilight* Saga" (pages 37-48).

- **Marriage:** Arnaudin spells out implicitly that for Mormon believers marriage is *the* means to eternal life and the principal, even exclusive spiritual vocation for Latter-day Saints. Calling LDS marriage "an unending union for time and eternity" in contrast with the 'til death do us part' vows of conventional marriage, he quotes Brigham Young as authority for the belief that Mormon marriage is "the thread which runs from the beginning to the end of the holy Gospel of Salvation — of the Gospel of the Son of God; it is from eternity to eternity." And at death, if man and wife have chosen to adhere to LDS faith and practices, "the reward is a never-ceasing spiritual life after death, consisting of living a life equal to God and continuing to have children, known as spirit children, with one's spouse"(Page 49). Arnaudin believes the Cullen couples, especially Carlisle and Esme's efforts to be sure their children all have spouses and the quasi-eternal nature of their lives and bonds, make them "role models" for Mormon beliefs about marriage (Pages 49-51).
- **Family:** Arnaudin very quickly touches on the LDS doctrine of Pre-Existent life in the context of explaining the importance of family to Latter-day Saints as an echo or reflection of that other-worldly existence:

> LDS believe that before coming to Earth, everyone lived with Heavenly Father and Heavenly Mother and was individually loved and taught by them as a member of their eternal family.... Therefore, the concept of a family existed before mankind and continues to endure after death of the body.

This explains why "the basic unit of the Church of LDS is the family." Arnaudin quotes David O. McKay's *Family Home Evening Manual* to make the point that the "home is the basis of a righteous life, and no other instrumentality can take its place nor fulfill its essential functions"(Page 52). Arnaudin argues that the Cullen family closeness, the Quileute pack, even Bella's protective feelings for and loyalty to her human parents are reflections of Mrs. Meyer's LDS beliefs about the eternal family. (Pages 52-60)

- **'Harmful Language: Lying, Profanity, and Gossip'** : Arnaudin quotes Mormon guides that instruct LDS faithful not to swear because "[p]rofane, vulgar, or crude language and inappropriate or off-color jokes are offensive to the Lord" and "capable of harming one's spirit and degrading the speaker." He dismisses the "sparsely used" profanity of the *Twilight* books and makes the valid observation that "the Twilight Saga complies with [LDS] standards" on profanity. (Pages 70-74)
- **'Diet and the Word of Wisdom'**: Arnaudin believes that LDS dietary rules, derived from "Section 89 of the *Doctrine and Covenants,*" "a revelation known as the Word of Wisdom" are what "outwardly distinguish active LDS more than any other practice."

  The decree limits the use of alcohol to sacramental wine and hard liquor for washing the body, deems tobacco good for only treating bruises and sick cattle, and labels hot drinks, later defined by Joseph Smith's brother Hiram as coffee and tea, not for "the body or belly" (Lyon 1584). The use of meat, of "beasts and of fowls in the air," is allowed, but suggested to only be used in winter or during famine, while grains, namely wheat, should be the center of the human diet alongside in-season fruits and vegetables (D&C 89:12-13). (Page 75)

Arnaudin thinks *Twilight* characters, though none of them are Mormons, observe these rules in large part: "Meyer is careful not to betray her faith by including even minute details that violate the Word of Wisdom." Understanding that vegetarianism is a Mormon ideal rather than real-world practice, he says "the choice of diet [Meyer] portrays [in *Twilight*] are true to LDS living and, as a result, honor the Mormon faith. (Pages 75-77)[18]

18 Elizabeth Baird Hardy, Private Correspondence 2 November 2009: On the subject of food, I started to think back over what Bella eats and when (which isn't often; I think she has an eating disorder), and I noticed a trend. For her father, she cooks meat. Steak is her first meal for him; later she prepares him chicken enchiladas and beef stroganoff (of which she is not particularly fond). She also orders (and does not eat) a burger with him when they go out after graduation. At the Quiluete bonfire, Jacob and his friends consume massive numbers of hot dogs. With Edward, the menu is meat-free: apple and pizza (probably just the cheese version that cafeterias usually have), mushroom ravioli at Bella Italia, and omelets on the honeymoon. Though Rosalie cooks a steak for Jacob, Edward, Food TV aficionado, doesn't cook meat. Also, in the film, Meyer has a cute little cameo in a diner scene: the waitress specifically says, "Here's your veggie burger," while Bella eats a salad and criticizes Charlie for eating too much steak.

- **Persecution:** Arnaudin argues that "due to the beliefs that define their faith, Mormons have regularly faced ostracism from society" and that "persecution has been rampant throughout their existence." Incredibly, in perhaps something only someone suffering from Provo Paranoia could write, he asks us to feel sympathy for the vampires of these stories as Mormon analogues, the same monsters whom you recall are super powered creatures that live by eating human beings. Vampires are, according to Arnaudin, "the epitome of a persecuted people."

> Mythic monsters of old, their legends have been distorted for centuries with the overwhelming majority judging them to be evil creatures. Yet when Bella meets Edward, she quickly falls in love with him without a discriminatory care for what he really is. Instead of menacing, shadow dwelling drinkers of blood, she sees him and his family for what they are: kind, loving, tolerant people attempting to escape the negative connotations of their race by coexisting with humans and contributing to society. By taking time to befriend them and understand their way of life, she accepts them as humans, worthy of respect and love from all others, and in bonding with them, she sheds all possible preconceptions to the point that she intends to live with the Cullens as one of them forever. (Page 79)

I think Arnaudin is right that Mrs. Meyer's vampires and especially the Cullens are Mormon stand-ins, but it is a remarkable stretch to think of them as "persecuted" or "misunderstood," with the possible exception of the Cullens. Even Edward understands that he is a monster by definition and notes that the "myths" about vampires are wrong in the details but absolutely spot-on in fostering fear of his kind.

Despite small gaffes like this, Mr. Arnaudin's *Mormon Vampires* is invaluable for its sober introduction to Mormonism and the workmanlike way it combs through the first three books of the series to detail exactly how the text conforms to the LDS doctrine. I am equally delighted by learning the more arcane things he shares about the life and teachings of Mormons – and by *his* having presented them so they that I can quote him rather than make the assertion myself.

For example, would you believe me, *qua* gentile, if I were the one telling you that Mormons believe that baptism transforms the blood of converts, an experience bringing on fits? Here is what Mr. Arnaudin writes on that subject:

- **Conversion**

LDS: Mormons also believe that when a non-Mormon is baptized into the Church, the convert's Gentile blood is cleansed from their body and they are given a new internal makeup. The Prophet Joseph Smith said that the Holy Ghost "purge[s] out the old blood" to turn the Gentile into a "seed of Abraham" and that such a "new creation" is a necessary part of the transformation (*History of the Church*, v.3, 380). The Prophet Brigham Young confirms that "[Smith taught] that the Gentile blood was actually cleansed out of their veins, and the blood of Jacob made to circulate in them; and the revolution and change in the system were so great that it caused the beholder to think they were going into fits" (Young, v.2, 269). (Page 64)

***Twilight*:** An additional striking similarity is that of each respective conversion's relation to blood. Despite Edward's insistence that she not know, Bella eventually catches Alice off guard and convinces her to tell how one becomes a vampire:

> It takes a few days for the transformation to be complete, depending on how much venom is in the bloodstream, how close the venom enters to the heart. As long as the heart keeps beating, the poison spreads, healing, changing the body as it moves through it. Eventually the heart stops, and the conversion is finished. But all that time, every minute of it, a victim would be wishing for death (Meyer, *Twilight* 414).
>
> With the exception of the heart stoppage and inclusion of pain, the perceived blood change of a newly-baptized Mormon is almost identical to that of a human freshly bitten by one of Meyer's vampires. (Page 67)

Fascinating. Vampire transition in the *Twilight* books is almost a description of how Mormon Prophets understand how an LDS baptism affects a convert. Keep this in mind when I explain at chapter's end how Bella's story is an allegorical depiction of her conversion to the LDS faith and consequent divinization.

As grateful as I am to Mr. Arnaudin, though, *Mormon Vampires* just scratches the surface of the LDS subjects to be discussed. Even with this bloody baptism head-shaker, all of the points he chooses to address are "milk before meat" selections from Mormon life that are least likely to cause folks to draw back in surprise or disapproval. He practices his own method of "progressive truth" in exploring the Mormon backdrops to Mrs. Meyer's artistry.

A simple, funny example: most Americans think they know that Mormons don't drink caffeinated drinks (Saints themselves joke that LDS stands for 'Let's Drink Sprite'). The truth is that the Prophet revealed that they shouldn't indulge in "hot drinks," which interpreted meant "coffee and tea," which, interpreted, has come to mean "avoid caffeine," even if your coca-cola is ice cold. But the drinks which *Twilight* characters enjoy reflect just how Mormon Mrs. Meyer's imaginative landscape is.

That is "very, very Mormon." In what other mental and spiritual universe could there be clandestine teen parties without alcohol, an Olympic Peninsula town without coffee shops and bars, and a secret lover's tryst in which a woman drinking two Coca-Colas in a rush is the gateway both to the dropping of inhibitions and to their frank conversation?

More seriously, Arnaudin's *Mormon Vampires* leaves out a host of important "hard teaching" LDS doctrines that give Mrs. Meyer's *Twilight* books their Mormon edge. The "milk" of Arnaudin's discussion misses the greater part of Mormonism *and* how these esoteric doctrines inform *Twilight.* Here are eight "meaty" points he neglects:

- **The Pelagian Doctrine of Free Agency:** Mr. Arnaudin discusses choice as Mormons understand it. He neglects to mention the roots of this doctrine in the interpretations of the Fall of Man peculiar to Mormon Prophets. In brief, Adam's fall in the Garden of Eden is a *good* thing and human beings, rather than being depraved, are capable of liberating choice or "free agency." This is important because *Twilight* is essentially a re-telling of the Eden story from an LDS perspective. More on this below.

- **The Divinity of Mormons in the Celestial Kingdom:** Arnaudin all but says in his discussion of "persecution" and in his *Mormon Vampires* title that the Cullen vampires are story stand-ins for LDS faithful. In this allegory, becoming a Mormon Vampire is the goal of the hero's journey Bella Swan is making. It seems only fair, then, to discuss at some length the Mormon teaching that a life spent in heroic conformity to church teaching will make the adherent a god or goddess with a world to rule with their spouse and in which to create spirit children. The goal of Mormon life is individual divinization or attaining godhood which is essentially the life of a Meyer vampire.

- **The Finite Personhood of God:** These Cullen 'Mormon Vampire-Gods,' however super-powered, were once mortals and still have human qualities and appearance. This story item is a pointer to the LDS truism, taught by the fifth LDS President Lorenzo Snow in June of 1840 as a summary of Smith's King Follett Discourse, "As man is, God once was; as God is, man may become." That God the Father is a finite person, a human being – and that he has a wife – is tough meat, indeed, for readers who do not believe in an anthropomorphic God but a Transcendent one. The story-picture of the finite-but-divine Cullens, however, presents the doctrine of the finite Mormon god graphically.
- **A Woman's Salvation is Only Through Her Husband:** Bella is certainly anything but marriage-mad, but she cannot get through life without Edward. She even puts her life at risk brazenly rather than live without her beloved. Accepting the Cullen Coven as vampire ciphers for Mormons invites a longer discussion of a woman's dependence on her spouse in LDS teaching than Mr. Arnaudin offers. As marriage is the sacred Mormon path to godhood and the husband knows his wife's secret name to pull her through the curtain to the Celestial Kingdom, Bella's sacrificial devotion to Edward makes more sense.
- **The Fullness of the Faith:** The Cullens are anything but proselytizing about their 'vegetarian' and humane way of life among other vampires (their passivity about vampire slaughter of human beings, frankly, is a little unnerving, no?). The conflict between the Cullens and the Volturi, though, clarifies that each has a defining vision they think is the correct and fullness of understanding about the right way to live. Mormons likewise teach a definitively exclusive and anti-ecumenical doctrine about what life is about and how it should be lived.
- **Cousin Lemuel:** The Volturi only appear at the end of the second and fourth books; in contrast, the Quileute Protectors, especially Jacob Black, and their antagonism and eventual

alliance with the Cullen Coven is the backdrop to the last three books. Mormon history, especially in the western migration after the move from Kirtland, Ohio, involves Mormon relations with Native Americans, whom they understand as dark-skinned, fallen Lamanites because of *The Book of Mormon.* (Native Americans were often called 'Cousin Lemuel' after the brother of Laman in BoMor.) LDS racial teaching about Native Americans is a touchy subject, certainly, and one that does not reflect well on Mormonism, but it is meat served on the *Twilight* table in the Cullen-Quileute and Edward-Jacob relationships.

- **Eternal Progression: Immortality and Exaltation** The 'end-game' of Mormon faith is to gain exaltation to the Celestial Kingdom, the third heaven above the Terrestial and Telestial Kingdoms. Human life ends in one of these three Kingdoms, but life involves "eternal progression" in growing likeness to God. Traditional Christianity, in contrast, believes that spiritual development is essentially closed at death (see the Parable of Lazarus and the Rich Man, Luke 16:19-31). The Cullens' immortality and belief in Carlisle's "vision" of asceticism and service point to the doctrine of Eternal Progression, as the human-wolfman-vampire strata suggest the three Kingdoms in the afterlife.
- **Pre-Existent Life as Spirit Children:** The 'imprinting' of the werewolves and their mates and the 'destined love' of the Cullen couples both reflect LDS teaching of our pre-existent life as God's immortal 'spirit-children' or 'intelligences.' Our design for our loved ones is our remembering our relationship with them in pre-existence. That's a stretch for most gentiles, but it is Mormon teaching the *Twilight* plot points bring to the fore.

Spotlight is the beginning of serious literary discussion of Mrs. Meyer's artistry and meaning and I offer these eight points to supplement the "milk before meat" "progressive truth" in *Mormon Vampires.* The continued discussion of Mrs. Meyer as a Mormon artist needs to include those LDS doctrines that are very different and even contrary to traditional and conventional Christian understanding.

I say "continued discussion" because except by gaining what Mr. Arnaudin correctly calls "Mormon literacy" there is little hope of grasping the backdrop of these books, namely, the LDS beliefs of the author. And we are a long way from having that. I know just enough about Mormon history and doctrine to ask what I hope are informed questions and not to be satisfied with pasteurized answers or self-serving "progressive truths." I look forward to reading the next stage of LDS critical scholarship on *Twilight* that will pick up where Mr. Arnaudin left off and talk about the implicit Mormon doctrines he neglects.[19]

I think, though, that Mr. Arnaudin and I are in full agreement about *Twilight* being the fruit of Mormon artistry and that it is written in conformity to LDS teaching. I agree with him when he concludes *Mormon Vampires* by pointing out the inevitability of Mrs. Meyer writing LDS fiction, whatever her conscious intentions:

> Mormonism, the mysterious religion that has eluded general public comprehension since its existence, continues to baffle non-believers, resulting in a population uninformed of one of the world's fastest-growing faiths. Only with a knowledge of religious literacy, and more specifically Mormon literacy, can the series be interpreted for what it really is.
>
> Though Meyer admits to allowing her faith to somewhat influence her writing, her claims of having not yet written a Mormon novel are unfounded. The truth is that by remaining a faithful member of the LDS Church, she cannot help but write Mormon novels. Her values and beliefs are ingrained in every aspect of her life, including her fiction. Betraying any of her Church teachings in her writing is unacceptable, and therefore, though the *Book of Mormon* and other Church doctrine are never mentioned by name, she has created characters and situations that adhere to LDS tenets. (Pages 90-91)

As valuable and interesting as making the common sense connections between Mrs. Meyer's faith and her work is, it's not very satisfying in itself. This type of critical work brings to the surface only the implicit or passive Mormonism in the *Twilight* novels, the colors and shading that must be in the books because they are the way Mrs. Meyer thinks and understands the world.

Mrs. Meyer's faith, however, is more important in understanding the artistry and meaning of *Twilight* than just being the mental landscape from which she draws her ideas. I think the dream she has in June 2003 suggests the *Twilight* Romance was inspired by her desire to defend her

---

19 Maxine Hanks, I know, is working on an LDS exegesis of *Twilight* which exploration will be worth reading.

LDS beliefs against attacks made by gentile critics. Having established that Mrs. Meyer is a Mormon Artist, let's look at *Twilight* as the work of a Mormon Apologist.

The first step in that process, the subject of the next chapter, is in picking up the suggestion made implicitly by Arnaudin in *Mormon Vampires* that the Cullens are allegorical Latter-day Saints. Imagine everyone in Forks is a character out of the Mormon pantheon of heroes and demons and that Bella's story is the journey of a spiritual seeker wanting to join the LDS Coven, I mean "family."

Twilight as the LDS *Pilgrim's Progress*: A Tale of Mormon Vampires

Mrs. Meyer in interviews is pretty touchy about suggestions that her religious beliefs have heavily shaped her work. When a woman asked her asked at TwilightMoms.com if a friend's suggestion that *Twilight's* vampires were modeled on Mormon ideas of the human body in the afterlife reflected Mrs. Meyer's intentions, she shot back: "Unintentional and rubbish 😐No offense to your friend. It is possible to read TOO deep into a book. They're just vampires."[20] A Phoenix reporter, too, wrote that "she does remember one Mormon woman who reviewed *Twilight* and analyzed how it tied into the *Book of Mormon*. She was dead wrong on every tie-in, Meyer says."[21]

As interesting, in that interview Mrs. Meyer said she might one day write an explicitly Mormon novel:

> She may write a Mormon novel someday, but for now, she's happy working with her vampires.
>
> "I have a novel I started that would be a Mormon comedy

---

20 http://www.twilightmoms.net/viewtopic.php?f=99&t=3354&sid=6834d48aa2f72e374926385347f67460

TM: I am not LDS, but I have some friends who are (here and in real life!) and one of them pointed out to me that the Twilight vampires share some qualities with the LDS concept of the human body in the afterlife (bloodless, perfect, immortal) and with the LDS concept of Satan (beautiful, alluring, enticing, difficult to resist). Was this deliberate, or unintentional, or is the comparison just a bunch of rubbish altogether?!

Steph: Unintentional and rubbish 😐No offense to your friend. It is possible to read TOO deep into a book. They're just vampires

21 Megan Irwin, 'Charmed: Stephenie Meyer's vampire romance novels made a Mormon mom an international sensation, *Phoenix New Times*, July 12, 2007; http://www.phoenixnewtimes.com/2007-07-12/news/charmed/

> romance," she says. "I do wonder what it would be like, because I have these girls who will read anything I write, so I know they'll read it, and I can't imagine what their reaction would be. And what parents will think about their kids reading stuff that has quite a lot of Mormon doctrine in it."[22]

Since that time, she seems to have reconsidered and is careful to downplay her Mormonism. Her website's "unofficial biography" used to include this simple profession of faith:

> I am also a member of the Church of Jesus Christ of Latter-day Saints (or Mormon, as we are commonly called – for more info on what that means, see www.mormon.org) and that has a huge influence on who I am and my perspective on the world, and therefore what I write (though I have been asked more than once, "What's a nice Mormon girl like you doing writing about vampires?")[23]

The current "bio" page at StephenieMeyer.com has no reference to her religion. I doubt we'll be seeing that "Mormon comedy romance" anytime soon.

I should say "*another* Mormon comedy romance," though, because I think we already have one in *Twilight*.

Mrs. Meyer was asked once what questions she would ask her favorite authors and she answered:

> I'd love to talk to J.K. Rowling about secrecy and crazy antagonistic fans and her writing process and what her everyday life is like. I'd love to listen to Orson Scott Card talk about anything, but I wouldn't be able to formulate questions, as I have learned from experience. I'd like to ask Jane Austen how much of herself is in her stories.[24]

To the two living authors, she asks puff questions. To the dead author she is never going to meet, she asks a scary one with heavy implications: "how much of herself is in her stories." As a reflective person well aware of her insecurities, I don't doubt that Mrs. Meyer has looked at her books as if they were a mirror of her concerns, hopes, fears, and faith and been startled by what she sees.

22 Op.cit.

23 Quoted in Edwin B. Arnaudin's *Mormon Vampires: The Twilight Saga and Religious Literacy.* A Master's Paper for the M.S. in L.S degree. April, 2008. Page 11; http://www.ils.unc.edu/MSpapers/3348.pdf

24 Page 2: http://www.twilightmoms.net/viewtopic.php?f=99&t=3228

And, if I agree with Mrs. Meyer that *Twilight* is not a second telling of *The Book of Mormon*, I don't think that looking at these vampire Romances as a mirror of her faith gives us anything but a clear reflection of Mormon beliefs and practices. The books can be seen, as Arnaudin implies in *Mormon Vampires*, as something of an LDS *Pilgrim's Progress*, an allegory of the Mormon religious path from beginning to end.

Here's a scorecard for that allegory with the stick-figure transparencies matched up with their Mormon-world referents, tit-for-tat:

Bella Swan, the awkward ugly duckling with a pure heart, is the sincere gentile seeker who is willing and able to see through the myths and misconceptions of the world and what she has been taught. She won't get stuck in the lies people have told her about Mormons or in her own preconceptions. Her name, 'beautiful swan,' points to her destiny of transcending her awkward, fragile humanity for life as a goddess.

The Cullen Family members can be understood as the Holy Trinity: Father/Mother are Carlisle and Esme, Holy Spirit Alice and Jasper, and God Incarnate Rosalie and Emmett. To get this you need to remember from the 'meat' points above that according to Mormon revelations, God isn't transcendent and immaterial or a Trinity that is Triune, that is to say, three-in-one. Their Holy Trinity is physical or at least finite – and the three persons of the Godhead are individual, distinct persons. And, better, there is a Mother God as well as a Father God.

To conventional Christians, the Cullens can be experienced as a story *symbol* or transparency for body, mind, and spirit or of the Holy Trinity; to Mormons, the Cullen family looks an awful lot like the "real thing."

I prefer just to think of the Cullens, though, as the Celestial Mormon Church, its realized spiritual directors living in their third Heaven. Their house is as white as it is and filled with light because it is a story equivalent of any Mormon Temple's upper rooms, the place in the world that Saints go to experience imaginatively their anticipated celestial life.

Edward Anthony Masen Cullen, Jr. in this drama is not only God's Word or *Logos* as we discussed in the iconological chapters but more obviously he is the Mormon Prophet, Joseph Smith, Jr. Bella, the gentile seeker, falls in love with him and wants to be sealed to him forever.

Here it helps to understand that "whiteness" has a special meaning to Mormons. In *The Book of Mormon*, the good guys are the descendants of Nephi or Nephites and the bad guy apostates from the true faith are called Lamanites after Laman, one of Nephi's rebellious brothers. Both tribes were white, Semitic people before crossing the Atlantic, but as the Lamanites apostatized a "skin of blackness [fell] upon them" (2 Nephi 5:21).

> "And he had caused the cursing to come upon them, yea, even a sore cursing, because of their iniquity. For behold, they had hardened their hearts against him, and they had become like unto a flint; wherefore, as they were **white**, and exceedingly fair and delightsome, that they might not be enticing unto my people the Lord God did cause a **skin of blackness** to come upon them."
>
> 3 Nephi 2:12-15 continues to teach that dark-skinned Lamanites who converted unto the Lord had their **curse** "taken from them, and their **skin became white** like unto the Nephites."...
>
> For much of its history, the Salt Lake City-based LDS Church edition of the *Book of Mormon* taught that dark-skinned Lamanites (Indians) would eventually experience a change in the color of their skin should they embrace the *Book of Mormon*. Except for a single edition (1840), 2 Nephi 30:6 has read:
>
> "...their scales of darkness shall begin to fall from their eyes; and many generations shall not pass away among them, save they shall be a white and a delightsome people."[25]

When gentiles and Native Americans accept and convert to the LDS faith, Mormon tradition teaches, they become white or just *more* white and a "delightsome people." Say, like the Cullen vampires?

I think Edward's skin color, though, comes straight from the Prophet, about whom it is said he was supernaturally white:

> Emma was probably quick to notice what many of his followers later believed had a supernatural cause, that when [Smith] was speaking with intense feeling the blood drained from his face, leaving a frightening, almost luminous pallor.[26]

---

25 Bill McKeever and Eric Johnson, Mormonism Research Institute, 'White and Delightsome or Pure and Delightsome? – A Look at 2 Nephi 30:6' (emphasis in original); http://www.mrm.org/white-and-delightsome#at

26 Fawn Brodie, *No Man Knows My History*, Alfred Knopf, New York, 1993; page 32

This is to skip over the Mormon Prophet's hypnotic gaze and psychic powers which also are reflected in Edward's abilities. Edward Cullen, as the gentile seeker's true love and her means to join the Holy Family in the Celestial Heaven, is the story cipher for Joseph Smith, Jr. That his real name is 'Edward Masen, Jr.,' points to Smith both in the "junior" and the esoteric nature of the Masons. More on that in just a bit.

Carlisle Cullen is the first Mormon or 'vegetarian' vampire. Note that LDS believers are supposed to eat meat "sparingly," that is, only in times "of winter, of cold, or of famine."[27] This is a rule that has never been a matter of strict obedience as are the other provisions of the Word of Wisdom, but, as we learned from Arnaudin, vegetarianism remains the Mormon ideal.

Back to Carlisle. If Edward is the story stand-in for Joseph Smith, Jr., the Prophet and founder of the Mormon faith, who can Carlisle represent? How can the Prophet have a forerunner who was born and raised by a Protestant minister in 17th Century London? Shouldn't Carlisle be the Smith figure because he is first?

You'd think that would have to be the case if you accepted that Joseph Smith, Jr., was the true beginning of Mormonism in modern times. Historians, though, have broken down that idea and replaced it with a different theological starting point for the faith Smith forged in the 19th Century. They point this origin in, you guessed it, 17th Century London.

Modern historians, believe it or not, have traced almost every belief and practice of the Latter-day Saints to Radical Reformation sects of 17th century England. The remnants of these sects survived in the 19th Century American religious world that Smith knew. John L. Brooke writes in *The Refiner's Fire: The Making of Mormon Cosmology, 1644-1844* that:

> As we have already seen and as several scholars have noted, the ideas brought together by the radical sects in the English Revolution reappeared in strikingly similar form almost two hundred years later at the hands of Joseph Smith.

27 *Doctrines and Covenants*, 89:12-13: 12. Yea, flesh also of beasts and of the fowls of the air, I, the Lord, have ordained for the use of man with thanksgiving; nevertheless they are to be used sparingly; 13 And it is pleasing unto me that they should not be used, only in times of winter, or of cold, or famine.

None of the seventeenth-century sects anticipated the totality of the Mormon cosmology, but, taken collectively, there are some remarkable similarities.

• Lawrence Clarkson, divining for treasure, looks a lot like the young Joseph Smith.

• Smith also looks a lot like John Reeves and Lodowick Muggleton, the prophets bearing a new text announcing a new dispenstion.

• So too, we can see echoes of George Starkey's announcement of the birth of the prophet Elias in the visions of Elias and Elijah received by Joseph Smith and Oliver Cowdery in the Kirtland temple.

• Smith's church would militantly advance the cause of the Kingdom of God just as had the Fifth Monarchists.

• Something of the antinomian behavior of the Ranters, including their spiritual wifery, and the biblical polygamy of the Munster Anabaptists (and of John Miulton) would be repeated among the Mormons.

• The "two seeds" of the Muggletonians and their descent from Adam and Cain would have an echo in the saga of the Nephites and the Lamanites in the *Book of Mormon*.

• Winstanley's communal economy would be reproduced in Smith's United Order of Enoch.

• The hermetic quest for the natural Adamic language of universal knowledge would be repeated in Smith's fascination with ancient languages and in the Mormon gift of speaking in tongues.

• Mormon prophets and priests would receive visions and revelations and have powers of healing and exorcism like those of the early Quaker leaders.

• The finite God of the Muggletonians would be reproduced in the Mormons' similarly finite God, as would be the hermetic reverence for Adam, the *magus*-man.

• The Mormon equation of spirit and matter, their vision of a living earth, and their doctrine of pre-Creation spiritual existence echoed the hermetic cosmology in its many forms.

• So too, there would be hints of a Mormon conception of an androgynous God, simultaneously male and female, replicating a central hermetic doctrine.

• Mormon baptism for the dead would reproduce the Spiritualist doctrine of the Christianity of the Old Testament prophets.

> • The Mormon cosmos would include three heavens, and the Mormon faithful would rise as gods to the highest heaven, reproducing the doctrines of universal salvation and divinization that ran through many of the movements influenced directly or indirectly by the writings of Boehme, Paracelsus, and Hermes.
>
> • Mormon divinization would be achieved by the "sealing powers of Elijah" restored to the Mormon priesthood, powers that, like the sacred experiments of the alchemical *magus,* put divine grace into human hands.
>
> • And like the Quakers and Muggletonians, the Mormon leadership in Utah would labor long and hard to establish and to maintain a firm boundary between their theology and the story of occult influences deeply embedded in their early history.
>
> Are these relationships spanning centuries simply analogues, revealing but essentially unconnected? The reigning interpretations of Mormonism would force this conclusion. On the one hand, the Mormon believer would argue that Smith's was simply the most perfect of a sequence of revelations of a restored church. Conversely, the functionalist social scientist might argue that similar convictions of revelation emerge from analogous experiences of social upheaval.
>
> But these answers are inadequate, because they fail to engage with history, experience, and memory. If social disorder may explain the form of religious movements, it cannot explain their content. The Mormon theology and cosmology were not simply products of "freedom's ferment" in a new land. Recoverable trails of popular experience and enduring, revitalized texts – the focus of the following chapters - suggest that the hermetic dispensationalism of important elements in the Radical Reformation was not merely analogous with but antecedent to the theology framed by Joseph Smith centuries later on a distant frontier.[28]

Brooke's conclusion, shared by other historians,[29] is that Mormonism is less an authentic revelation given to an American 19th Century Prophet than an inspired amalgam of 16th and 17th century Christian heresies current in Smith's day. I quote *Refiner's Fire* at such length not because it undermines the claims of Mormon apologists (though obviously it does) but because it points both to the facts of

28 John L. Brooke, *The Refiner's Fire,* Cambridge University Press, Cambridge, 1994, pp 28-29

29 See Hansen, *Quest for Empire,* Vogel, *Religious Seekers,* and Quinn, *Early Mormonism and the Magic World View*

and the origin of Mormonism's hermetic and alchemical beliefs. The alchemical content of her artistry and specific plot points suggest Mrs. Meyer is aware of LDS foundations in esoteric 17th century London.

We will have to come back to this when we get to how Mrs. Meyer has such a wealth of hermetic ideas and images on which to build her *Twilight* books; here, though, the point is that Carlisle is the story symbol for Mormonism's Reformation roots.

In addition to being a wonderful God the Father stand-in, the senior Cullen's biography points to Mrs. Meyer having read *Refiner's Fire* or other histories detailing the roots of Mormon cosmology and theology in 16th and 17th century Christian sects. Carlisle Cullen, the *real* beginning of virtuous vampirism, is a Christian Protestant of 17th Century London, a devout Christian who was able to keep himself from murdering human beings in the agonies of 'newborn' vampire life.

As the real original Mormon, Carlisle "creates" Edward Masen, Jr., as his spirit child, begotten Son, and as a Prophet to bring gentile seekers of pure hearts into his Holy Family. The story of Carlisle's first "conversion" of a human being to Mormon vegetarian vampire is a story picture of Smith's revelations springing from 17th Century Christian beliefs.

Hard to see? Edward says the Cullen family live in conformity to Carlisle's "vision," and, as you may know, Mormonism is founded in the "First Vision" or "Grove Experience" of the then 14 year old Joseph Smith, Jr., in 1820. Smith is visited there by God the Father and the Son in their glorified bodies.[30] The opening chapter of *Twilight* in which Bella first sees the Cullen kids and Edward in particular is called 'First Sight.' Edward the *Twilight* Prophet lives according to 17th century Carlisle's understanding.

Note, too, that Carlisle moves from England to Rochester, New York, to western North America with his "family." This is the historical path of Mormon migration, especially for the 19th century English converts and "Handcart Pioneers."

Rosalie Cullen's given name is 'Rosalie Hale,' she lived in Rochester, New York, and was made a vampire by Carlisle. He did this to save her life, certainly, but also to create a partner or bride for Edward.

30 Smith gave several different accounts of this visitation, none of which agree with the others with respect to his age at the time, who the personages were that he saw, and what was said. Despite the contradictions and subsequent confusion, it remains in LDS hagiography of Smith, the beginning of the Restoration of the Gospel.

An aside: let me confess here that Carlisle's decisions to make people vampires "to save their lives" strikes me as something of a head scratcher, even in an allegorical tale. He has no way of knowing if the vampire he is creating will be able to become "vegetarian" and refrain from the slaughter of humans on an almost daily basis. To save one human life by making him or her into a vampire, he puts at risk an indefinite number of human lives. That is a bizarrely illogical and uncharacteristically risky choice for sober and circumspect Carlisle, except perhaps in a story that is largely idealized and allegorical.]

Anyway, the Rosalie-Mormon connection is in Rochester, first, because Mormonism's birthplace is Palmyra, New York, and Rochester is the closest city of any size to that hamlet. More interesting, Rosalie, the intended "bride of Frankenstein" if you will, has the same last name as Joseph Smith, Jr.,'s first wife, whose maiden name was Emma *Hale.* Believe me, this name is something that every Mormon knows very well.

This affirms the Edward-Prophet connection, but it also points to Rosalie's conflicted nature as a vampire. She wishes she could be human, even an ugly, poor human, rather than a drop-dead gorgeous vampire. If she could make the jump back, she would. Emma Hale Smith, Rosalie's real world LDS referent, left the Church of Latter-day Saints after her husband's death and denied he was a polygamist until the day she died. She made the jump out of the life of Mormon vampires, if you will.

We'll come back to Rosalie's origins and its links to the Prophet shortly.

The Quileute Wolf Pack is fairly straightforward to place in the LDS Morality Play or Salvation Drama because Mrs. Meyer has told interviewers they are the virtuous **Lamanites**, the dark-skinned warriors from *The Book of Mormon.*

> Growing up, Meyer's favorite *Book of Mormon* story was the one about the 2,000 stripling warriors, from the book of Alma. In the story, the parents of a small group of boys are under attack but have taken a blood oath never to fight again after their conversion to Christianity. They consider breaking the oath but are persuaded not to by a prophet. Their sons, who never took the oath, go to fight instead, and because of their faith, not a single one is harmed.

Meyer sees her werewolves as her stripling warriors.

> "In the history of the Book of Mormon, they [the warriors] would have been dark-skinned, the ancestors of the Native Americans who are here now. So for me, the Quileute [tribesmen, the wolves in her books] are kind of these sons who have taken on the responsibility of taking care of their families."[31]

The white-skinned **Cullens** in this relationship would play the parts of the "white and delightsome" **Nephites** who are in a state of cautious antagonism with these virtuous dark-skinned Lamanite protectors. I offer for your consideration this possibility: if the Cullens are the idealized Mormons, the Prophets or New Gods living in Celestial Heaven, that the La Push Native Americans are the Mormon church "on the ground," the Salt Lake City lead institution with its "group mind" that is both home and something of a prison to those born there.[32] Again, more on this point in a minute.

The **Volturi** bad-guys? They are the institutional Western Church, which is to say, Roman Catholicism. Mormons and Catholics today often fight side by side in the culture war battles over abortion and gay marriage but historically they each consider their own faiths to be the one true faith and do not consider the other even to be Christian (each requires converts to be re-baptized because the sacraments of the one are not valid to the other).

---

31 Irwin, *Charmed,* op.cit.; about the "stripling warriors," Mrs. Meyer has said that it wasn't a deliberate placement: TM:As an author do you really consider the things like theme, archetypes, foreshadowing, symbolism, etc. or are you just writing a good story?
Steph: As an author, I consider NOTHING, ha ha ha. I just tell a story. All the symbolism and themes and archetypes are things I discover after the fact. All that stuff in the above paragraph--I didn't think of any of those things until after the story was done. Then I would read through it and think, "Hey, the pack kind of reminds me of those Ammonite kids. Wonder if that's where I got it from?" TwilightMoms.com, Page 3: http://www.twilightmoms.net/viewtopic.php?f=99&t=3309

32 That Mrs. Meyer has no desire to achieve "True Believer Mormon" status, see her comments about the super-faithful that she made at TwilightMoms: Page 3: http://www.twilightmoms.net/viewtopic.php?f=99&t=3309
TM: Have [you] gotten any grief in your ward or stake from over protective/over-zealous parents?
Steph: I haven't gotten any grief to my face, though I know it exists. My husband takes perverse delight in reading negative blogs to me. Things with titles like: "With what she writes, can Stephenie Meyer be a good member of the church?" That kind of thing only happens in Utah, where I will never, never live.

Joseph Smith, Jr., Orson Pratt, and the Presidents of the 19th Century LDS Church routinely referred to the Roman Catholic Church as "the Whore of Babylon" and many believe that the prophecies referring to the "great and abominable church" to come, "the mother of abominations" in *The Book of Mormon* (1 Nephi and 2 Nephi) are allusions to the Vatican.[33]

New York State in the 1830s was the cradle of both Mormonism and the 'American Republican Party' or "Know Nothings" who were fiercely anti-Catholic and specifically opposed to Irish and German Catholic immigrants. In this historical context, I don't find Mormon anti-papism unusual or even unexpected, if its survival into our times of ecumenical tolerance is extraordinary.

I also don't find it surprising that the chief Black Hats of the book are the "ancient" vampires who live in Italy, have all the power amongst vampires, that they are the ghouls whom vampires revere as authorities and peacemakers, and, most important, that the chief baddies are vampires who persecute the White Hat Cullen Coven. This is a fair representation of how Mormons have viewed themselves historically *vis a vis* their relationship with conventional Christianity and especially with the Catholics: as persecuted martyrs. Hence Arnaudin's bizarre suggestion that the murderous vampires are "the epitome of a persecuted people." Mormons have a collective persecution complex out of all proportion to their historical injuries – and it centers on their differences with conventional Christian sects, especially the Catholic Church.[34]

If you doubt the Volturi are Catholic mannequins, you're missing one of the better laughs of the story in the 'gathering of witnesses' chapters of *Breaking Dawn*. The two **Romanian vampires** are story stand-ins for the Orthodox Church; they think the Cullen-Mormons are foolish freaks but they have a visceral and boundless hatred for the Volturi-Catholics who stole their power eons ago. Great fun, that one, especially if you have heard Orthodox Christians from Bulgaria, Romania, and Greece talk about Roman Catholics.

---

33 See http://www.exmormon.org/mormon/mormon327.htm for a quick selection of Prophet and BoMor passages that are supposedly anti-Catholic.

34 Elizabeth Baird Hardy suggests that Alec and Jane, the abused, perverse children in the Volturi talent arsenal, could be a slap at the Catholic Church's recent scandals with pedophiliac clergy and sexually abused young people. Private correspondence, 2 November 2009.

And the rest of the witnesses gathered to "speak truth to" the Volturi? I suggest each group that comes to the Cullen Temple is one that Mrs. Meyer believes represents a real world group who is, in her mind, a natural ally of Mormons against the power and privilege focused Western Church. The Orthodox Romanians are the most obvious, but the others play out:

- Virtuous Muslims are fronted in the story by the Egyptian Coven;
- American Patriots, individualists, and freedom lovers have Garrett;
- Feminists, real exotic folk to the marriage-focused Mormons, have the Amazon coven as their stand-ins (feminists as Mormon allies is a real reach given the anti ERA position of the LDS hierarchy years ago); and
- The Denali Coven are Alaskan vegetarian vampires much like the Cullens, who represent the problematic Mormon look-alikes, the Canadian fundamentalist-polygamists.

If that last seems a stretch, you need to know that, just as the Denali vampires brought the whole issue of Cullen-LDS differences with the Volturi-Vatican to a confrontation in *Breaking Dawn*, so the Canadian Mormon fundamentalists with their many wives embarrass mainstream Mormons and cause frequent confrontations with the law and media exposure. The Denali as polygamist allegory is why Mrs. Meyer casts them as one man and the rest women and their being sexually charged *succubae*.

In a Mormon imagination, all these "witnesses" are potential Cullen-LDS allies against Aro the Pope and his Evil Trinity that stands in such harsh contrast with Forks' Holy Family.

I didn't forget the Irish Coven. They're the best transparency except for the Romanian-Orthodox "creep-tacular" vampires. How could the Irish turn against Roman Catholicism? Because their native Gaelic spirituality has much more in common with the hermetic beauty, love, and virtue of the Cullen-Mormons than with the Volturi-Catholics.

Score the Nomads as Protestant sectarians and the human beings as clueless, non-believers. It's all about religion, right? Now that we have all the allegorical figures in this LDS *Pilgrim's Progress* identified, we can trace Bella's conversion/divinization story-inside-the-story, the heart of Twilight's allegorical meaning and artistry.

Chapter 6

Twilight as the Work of a Mormon Apologist

Wish Fulfillment Resolutions of Gentile Criticisms about LDS
Or
The Mountain Meadows Massacre Re-Visited

Have your Allegorical Score-card in hand? Great. Now for reading the story as Bella's becoming-a-Mormon-goddess hero's journey!

The first hurdle for the human serious seeker to clear in becoming a Latter-day Saint is gaining proximity to the Prophet. Edward, Smith's story stand-in, lies to Bella after saving her life, won't be open with her about what or who he really is, and the only thing he shares openly and truthfully is that being close to him will be very dangerous for her. She gets a Lamanite to spill the beans about the "cold one" Nephites and has her Mormon moment in the forest behind her house. She reaches him by her own seeking and "free agency." He does not compel or even encourage her love and faith but teases her with "progressive truth," "milk before meat."

To understand Bella's actual conversion scene in the forest, you have to remember that Smith's "grove experience" where he has the "First Vision" is in the woods behind *his* house in Palmyra, New York. Bella doesn't pray the "show me the true faith" prayers that the Prophet claimed he did before the 'First Vision;' she has an interior dialogue in which she asks herself the classic missionary one-two closer:

- "Do you believe in your heart that these claims (Christ died for your sins, Joseph Smith is the Prophet, Edward is a vampire...) are true?"
- "If you do, what must you do now to act on what you know?"

Her answer to these questions? "Admit you love Edward heart, soul, mind, and strength, even though it will mean the end of your life as you know it!" Because marrying a Mormon vampire *will* certainly end your life. From the moment she has her epiphany and conversion experience in the forest, though, it's all over for Bella (Edward, appropriately, takes her back to this exact spot in *New Moon* to end their relationship where it really began: "Sorry, you can't be a Mormon vampire – conversion over – goodbye.")

The Cullens may be beautiful, happy, and otherworldly rich but nobody likes them or wants to spend time with them. Bella, of course, has the necessary noetic discernment to see through the myths about Mormon-vampires that silly humans believe. She pierces the Salt Lake glass ceiling of mistaken beliefs about these people and begins her serious relationship with Edward, the God-Man, the Mormon vampire Prophet.

He takes her to the grove, of course, not behind her house but the perfectly circular meadow, for the next stage of her walk in the faith. It is not only an Adam and Eve allegory as explained in previous chapters, but a true Mormon experience. Listen in on their key dialogue in the grove. In that circle, Edward and Bella describe their love for each other in the language of the Prophet Isaiah. Or is it?

> "You already know how I feel, of course," I finally said. "I'm here... which, roughly translated, means I would rather die than stay away from you." I frowned. "I'm an idiot."
>
> "You *are* an idiot," he agreed with a laugh. Our eyes met, and I laughed, too. We laughed together at the idiocy and sheer impossibility of such a moment.
>
> "And so the lion fell in love with the lamb..." he murmured. I looked away, hiding my eyes as I thrilled to the word.
>
> "What a stupid lamb," I sighed.
>
> "What a sick, masochistic lion."[1]

Edward is almost quoting Isaiah 11:6, "The wolf also shall dwell with the lamb, and the leopard shall lie down with the kid; and the calf and the young lion and the fatling together; and a little child shall lead them." Almost.

---

1 *Twilight*, Chapter 13, page 274

Edward says to Bella in their *Twilight* meadow conversation that his love for her is like "the lion [who] fell in love with the lamb." For Christians, that is a distant echo of Isaiah but for Mormons "the lamb and the lion" are words taken from a favorite LDS hymn, 'The Spirit of God.' This song was written for the opening of the first Mormon Temple, is sung with the Hosannah Shout, the LDS 'Rebel Yell,' at every Temple opening, and is something of a Mormon anthem. As every Mormon knows, the hymn ends:

How blessed the day when **the lamb and the lion**
Shall lie down together without any ire;
And Ephraim be crown'd with his blessing in Zion,
As Jesus descends with his chariots of fire!

We'll sing we'll shout with His armies of heaven:
Hosanna, hosanna, to **God and the Lamb!**
Let glory to them in the highest be given,
Henceforth and forever: amen and amen.[2]

The lion lying down with the lamb. Talk about "resolution of contraries."

But this is not hermetic lore, it is Paradise and the Garden of Eden. The core allegory of *Twilight* discussed in previous chapters – the love story of God and Man – deriving from the Genesis story, though, is **not** the story as Moses told it or as Christian saints and sages have understood it. The *Twilight* idea of what happened in the Garden is, for obvious reasons, the Mormon version of that story.

And it is a very different story than the Fall of Man story you may have learned in Sunday School.

Western Christians after St. Augustine understand the events in the Garden of Eden as historical or mythic cause of everything that is wrong in the world. To simplify boldly, Adam and Eve's disobedience to God's instruction about eating the fruit from the Tree of Knowledge, their "original sin," caused human beings to be sinful by nature and required

2 I first heard *The Spirit of God* 'Lion and the Lamb' connection at a lecture by Maxine Hanks at 'Summer School in Forks' ("Mormonism and Twilight," Maxine Hanks, SSIF, June 2009). Emma Smith's Hymnal, Collection of Sacred Hymns (Kirtland, Ohio: W. W. Phelps & co., 1835; reprint, Independence, Missouri: Herald Heritage 1973), hymn 90 http://www.kirtlandtemple.org/hymns/thespiritofgod.html

the incarnation and sacrifice of a divine, sinless Savior to restore and redeem them. Orthodox Christians and many Protestants reject this "ransom" theology and "original sin" as juridical but they, too, accept the Fall of Man in the Garden as the beginning of man's distance from God, if not the causal origin requiring Christ's Crucifixion for atonement.[3]

Mormons reject both these views in keeping with the hermetic heresies of the Radical Reformation that were accepted and advanced by Joseph Smith, Jr. In theological language, Latter-day Saints are called "Pelagians" after the fourth century Christian named Pelagius who asserted that there were no "original sin" consequences to the Fall and that human conscience and free will were sufficient for salvation. Mormonism, after the Christian hermetic *magi* of Carlisle's London, takes this a step further and asserts that the Fall was not only *not* a bad thing but that it was *good*, even necessary for human salvation.[4]

In various streams of Mormon tradition, Adam, in fact, is the finite God of earth or the Archangel Michael and Eve his celestial wife from another planet. The fall and expulsion from Paradise, according to this view, is good and necessary in order for Adam and Eve to marry and reproduce. Celestial marriage is a core ordinance for Mormon exaltation (salvation) so, because there were no sexual relations in Paradise, without the Fall which is not a Fall, man could not take this important step in the eternal progression from pre-mortal existence, mortality, to post-mortal life as a god in the Celestial Kingdom.[5]

This is a remarkable departure from orthodox, creedal Christianity with respect to sexuality and in understanding how human beings relate to God. Traditional Christianity and the other revealed orthodox faiths consider celibacy to be the normative sexual condition that human beings of spiritual achievement or ambition assume. Mormonism, in contrast, considers sex within marriage as a spiritual exercise and the human means both to procreation and to experiences that are spiritually edifying, even salvific. 'Single Mormon' is something of a 'square circle' and monastic vocation is to them something like a sacrilege.[6]

---

3 From this view, it is Christian participation in Christ's Resurrection rather than the sacrificial events on Calvary themselves that are man's means of salvation and divinization.

4 Sterling McMurrin, *The Theological Foundations of the Mormon Religion,* University of Utah Press (Salt Lake City) 1965, pp 57-67 'On Original Sin'

5 http://www.lightplanet.com/mormons/basic/afterlife/progression_eom.htm

6 'Mormon Vampires,' op.cit, page 49
"[I]f Mormon beliefs are followed throughout life, the reward is a never-ceasing

The doctrines of Eternal Progression and the sufficiency of human will and conscience in Joseph Smith, Jr.'s restoration of Christian faith, too, break with Christian tradition. Instead of man working in synergy with God to receive and be transformed by His Graces, Mormonism advocates a can-do spirit of works, which, if done in conformity with God's teachings in the LDS church, will result in our drawing ever nearer to God in this life and in the next.

Which is what we see in the *Twilight* version of the Garden story.

In a nutshell, Bella is Eve and Edward is the Adam-God of Brigham Young's theology. Their "fall" in Bella/Eve/Man's choosing the apple in the Forks High School cafeteria from Edward/Adam/God's tray, although rife with dangers and difficulties, is the only way that she can begin her spiritual transformation through an alchemical wedding with the God-Man. The story is a romance and allegory depicting the roles and responsibilities of the divine and human lovers but it has the specifically Mormon hermetic twist that sex within marriage is the end game and the only means to personal salvation and immortal life.

Note that I said "sex within marriage." Sex is a great, necessary, and spiritual thing to Latter-day Saints but only between man and woman and only in a marriage sealed in the Temple. Sex outside of marriage is the quick road to hell. Mormons have been taught by their Prophets that a young woman is better off dead than to have lost her virginity outside of marriage.

I'm betting that at least the last bit sounds crazy to you. The Law of Chastity, though, really is that big a deal in Mormon families:

> LDS leaders have repeatedly spoken out in defense of the law of chastity. Prophet Heber J. Grant says that "[t]here is no true Latter-day Saint who would not rather bury a son or a daughter than to have him or her lose his or her chastity — realizing that chastity is of more value than anything else in all the world" (Grant 55). Prophet Spencer W. Kimball speaks of the far-reaching...effect of loss of chastity. Once given or taken or stolen it can never be regained. Even in a forced contact such as rape or incest, the injured one is greatly outraged. If she has not cooperated and

---

spiritual life after death, consisting of living a life equal to God and continuing to have children, known as spirit children, with one's spouse (Ricks 465). The great bounties of life that Mormons wish to attain are only truly realized through marriage, an expectation of all Church members since **celibacy is "foreign to LDS life" (Inouye 260)**, and because the key aspects of family and eternity rest on marriage, it is a decision to be made wisely." Emphasis added.

> contributed to the foul deed, she is of course in a more favorable position. There is no condemnation when there is no voluntary participation. It is better to die in defending one's virtue than to live having lost it without a struggle (Kimball 196).[7]

Hence Edward, standing in for the Prophet, insists he cannot make love to Bella. He relents at last, once they are engaged to be married at the end of *Eclipse*, but Bella the true seeker realizes then that they must wait for the wedding lest she endanger Edward's soul. The LDS Law of Chastity is the invisible, sure, guiding hand in Bella and Edward's physical relationship from 'First Sight' to their Alchemical Wedding.

Twilight was meant to be a stand-alone novel so I'm guessing the original ending had something of a marriage scene in the Phoenix ballet studio. Mormon marriages take place in the upper rooms of Mormon Temples after bride and groom have completed their initiation into the mysteries of the Garden of Eden and what really happened there according to Mormon Prophets. A big feature of these rooms are the mirrors which face each other so bride and groom, being sealed to one another for all eternity, can see in the mirrors' endless imaging of their marriage a picture of that "forever." I suspect the "forever"s that Edward and Bella exchange at the end of both *Twilight* and *Breaking Dawn* were originally meant to be shared in front of the ballet studio wall mirrors.

Instead, the Man-God couple are joined together at the Cullen home/Temple in a Mormon ceremony with a nominal pastor officiating (LDS ceremonies have officiants rather than professional clergy). Bella and Edward exchange vows without the "til death do us part." This omission is not surprising, of course, because of Bella's incipient vampire status but "til death do us part" is also absent from Mormon weddings because death is only a new beginning for married couples who are sealed unto eternity.

Marriage is the means to a woman's salvation which comes through her husband. He knows her secret name that will allow her to pass through into the Celestial Kingdom, a drama performed with curtains in the Temple. But if marriage is the *sine qua non* of LDS spiritual life, then childbirth is a woman's crown of glory. Bella, appropriately, then in this allegory about Mormon conversion, becomes a vampire-Mormon goddess, rising from the dead after three days in heroic apotheosis, after carrying a child sacrificially and dying in the act of giving birth.

7 Arnaudin, *Mormon Vampires*, op.cit., page 29

The intertwined events of Renesmee's birth and Bella's transformation are the real point of the whole series because they depict the glorious conclusion of LDS life. The battle of the Volturi-Catholics with the Nephite-Lamanite Cullen-Quileute alliance and a host of LDS friendly witnesses at *Breaking Dawn's* conclusion is almost an after-life after-thought and anti-climax. The story ends as it must with the hermetic mental union and physical congress of Bella the divinized convert with her personal Prophet soul-mate as explained in the conclusion to Part 1.

The *Twilight* Saga is the story-picture or allegory of the life in the this world and the next of a Latter-day Saint convert-become-goddess.

Twilight as a Mormon Midsummer Night's Dream

The natural question after reading this allegorical LDS divinization drama within the surface story of Bella and Edward's Romance is "Was it intentional on the author's part?" That's the nice way, at least, of asking whether I'm not just making it all up, which is to say, seeing Mormon meaning where there are, as Mrs. Meyer says, "just vampires."

That's certainly a possibility, of course, but as imaginative as I am I doubt I could have made up the detailed correspondences between the biggest part of Mrs. Meyer's mental landscape and the story she tells. Rather than blaming the exegete if one wants to deny conscious intent on the author's part, a more likely explanation of the LDS allegorical content is Mrs. Meyer's claim that she discovers the greater meaning of her work after the fact of writing, i.e., this is subconscious artistry.

Frankly, I find that more of a stretch than deliberate allegory because of the details involved. What are the odds that these story details weren't recognized by a dyed-in-the-wool Latter-day Saint as having explicit and implicit Mormon meaning?

- Carlisle Cullen's origins being in the exact place and time that historians assign to LDS' Radical Reformation beginnings;
- Edward Cullen having Joseph Smith, Jr.'s hypnotic eyes, white skin, auburn hair, and psychic abilities;
- Edward's beautiful intended bride, Rosalie *Hale*, having the same last name as Joseph Smith, Jr.'s first wife and her coming from Rochester, NY, the birthplace of Mormonism; and
- The Capulet-Montague divide in the series, the tension between the Cullens and the Quileutes, Edward and Jacob, would be a

> tit-for-tat parallel with the white-dark division of Nephites and Lamanites in *The Book of Mormon,* the book Mrs. Meyer teaches adolescents in Sunday School and says is the biggest influence in her life.

Forgive me, but what I think stretches the limits of credible possibilities is that Mrs. Meyer wasn't writing this allegory into her 'vampire with human girlfriend' story with some degree of conscious intention. A better question than "Is this really in there?" then is "*Why* would Stephenie Meyer write a Mormon 'Ugly Duckling' Divinization Allegory?" For that, we have to go back to June 2003, the time of Mrs. Meyer's original dream inspiration and take a look, first, at her life, and, next, at what Mormons were talking and thinking about at that time.

Frankly, her condition in June 2003 was not good. Her life was a liberal caricaturist's nightmare picture of the stay-at-home Christian mom:

> The Meyers were coming off a depressing year. While she was pregnant with her youngest son, Eli, she'd fallen over —"I was realllly pregnant," she says — and broken her arm badly. Five weeks later, her husband, Pancho, was diagnosed with Crohn's disease.
>
> "It wasn't a great time in my life. I'd put on so much weight with the two babies. My 30th birthday was coming up and I was so not ready to face being 30," she says. "I didn't feel I had much going for me. I had my kids, but there wasn't much I was doing."
>
> Meyer needed a creative outlet. She'd painted in college, but with the kids, it was too hard, and the scrapbooking parties she went to with friends from church were fun but not exactly fulfilling.
>
> "When I switched to writing, it was a much fuller outlet for me," she says. "There was a whole lot of pleasure in that first writing experience. It felt like a dam bursting, there was so much that I couldn't get out, and then I could." ...
>
> She didn't tell anyone what she was doing. She dropped out of her scrapbook club and didn't even go to the movies because the thought of three hours away from the computer was unbearable.
>
> "I lost a lot of friends that summer," she says, laughing.
>
> She didn't even tell her husband, though he'd started to wonder what she was up to.

> "I was really protective and shy about it because it's a vampire romance. It's still embarrassing to say those words — it sounds so cheesy," she says. "It's not like I was going to tell him that I was writing this story about vampires, because he was just going to be even more perturbed." [8]

In other interviews she has said "my brain was nothing more than mushy oatmeal by the time my third was a toddler,"[9] that she and her husband argue about everything,[10] and that one of the great blessings of being a successful writer is that he no longer tells her to get off the computer and do something productive with her time.[11]

Ouch.

Overweight and under-challenged. Post-partum mother recovering from a broken bone. "Perturbed" argumentative husband with chronic illness. An oatmeal-mush brained woman feeling the need for a "creative outlet" beyond scrap booking with the neighborhood moms.

As Mrs. Meyer has said frequently, she didn't write *Twilight* for publication or for a specific audience. "I did not intend for Twilight to be YA – I intended it to be for ME."[12] She didn't think about publishing it until after she had finished the book and her only reader, her sister Emily, suggested it.[13] The first book was written for an exclusively Mormon audience, two LDS stay-at-home mothers, one of whom was really just a sympathetic and supportive reflection of the author.

---

8 http://www.phoenixnewtimes.com/content/printVersion/481142

9 TwilightMoms.com Q&A, Page 3: http://www.twilightmoms.net/viewtopic.php?f=99&t=3309

10 "We're not either of us very docile people," she says. "We argue all the time because that's our personalities. We didn't get in mean arguments, but I'm sure we argued over it because we argue about everything — we argue about milk." http://www.phoenixnewtimes.com/content/printVersion/481142

11 "The good part [of waking up as a 'famous' writer] is getting to write whenever I want and no one can tell me to get off the computer and go do something productive." http://www.twilightmoms.net/viewtopic.php?f=99&t=3310&sid=4121c76701101a5ff2db13f0d1a7666d

12 TwilightMoms.com Q&A, Page 1: http://www.twilightmoms.net/viewtopic.php?f=99&t=3222

13 "My older sister, Emily, was the only one who really knew what I was up to. In June, I'd started sending her chapters as I finished them, and she soon became my cheerleading section. She was always checking in to see if I had something new for her. It was Emily who first suggested, after I'd finished, that I should try to get *Twilight* published. I was so stunned by the fact that I'd actually *finished* a whole, entire book, that I decided to look into it." http://www.stepheniemeyer.com/twilight.html

So, if the book is Mormon and a divinization allegory because it was conceived by a Mormon housewife trying to save her mind from further decomposition (into cream of wheat?), why write it as a "cheesy vampire romance"? And how do we get a sparkling vampire with girlfriend in a meadow? For answers to those questions we need to remember June 2003 and what Mormons were talking about then.

Let's start with her Mormon Midsummer Night's Dream:

> I woke up (on that June 2nd [2003]) from a very vivid dream. In my dream, two people were having an intense conversation in a meadow in the woods. One of these people was just your average girl. The other person was fantastically beautiful, sparkly, and a vampire. They were discussing the difficulties inherent in the facts that A) they were falling in love with each other while B) the vampire was particularly attracted to the scent of her blood, and was having a difficult time restraining himself from killing her immediately. For what is essentially a transcript of my dream, please see Chapter 13 ("Confessions") of [*Twilight*].
>
> Though I had a million things to do (i.e. making breakfast for hungry children, dressing and changing the diapers of said children, finding the swimsuits that no one ever puts away in the right place, etc.), I stayed in bed, thinking about the dream. I was so intrigued by the nameless couple's story that I hated the idea of forgetting it; it was the kind of dream that makes you want to call your friend and bore her with a detailed description. (Also, the vampire was just so darned good-looking, that I didn't want to lose the mental image.)
>
> Unwillingly, I eventually got up and did the immediate necessities, and then put everything that I possibly could on the back burner and sat down at the computer to write—something I hadn't done in so long that I wondered why I was bothering. But I didn't want to lose the dream, so I typed out as much as I could remember, calling the characters "he" and "she."[14]

Mrs. Meyer's inspiration, then, for *Twilight* was a dream she had on June 2, 2003, about a vampire, an "average girl," and their "intense conversation" in a meadow about falling in love. The key word in Mrs. Meyer's dream is not "vampire" or "girl," though, but "meadow."

In chapter 4 of Part 1 above, we talked about all the Mountain Meadows in these books because of the perfectly circular meadow of

---

14 http://www.stepheniemeyer.com/twilight.html

Mrs. Meyer's dream. Remember all the things that happen in Mountain Meadows?

If you were living in Bella's world and you *really* wanted to find a vampire, I'm thinking your best bet, based on the *Twilight* novels, is to spend time in mountain meadows, especially those well off the beaten track. Think about it.

- It's where they play baseball and football;
- They seem to run into each other in meadows as often as not (think of James, Victoria, and Laurent just happening by the Cullen Coven's game in the Rainier meadow);
- Meadows seem to be the venue of choice for vampire battles, as the *Eclipse* showdown with Victoria's newborns has its main arena in one and the Volturi come *en masse* to the same spot in *Breaking Dawn* to deliver their ultimatum about Renesmee;
- Carlisle has a painting in his office that catches Edward's interest on Bella's first visit when he tells her about Carlisle's new attempts as a newborn vampire to destroy himself. The painting is of "an empty, shadowed meadow in a forest, with a craggy peak in the distance;"[15]
- Bella happens upon Laurent in *New Moon* in a mountain meadow and she is saved from becoming his lunch only by the appearance of the Quileute Protectors. She sees Jacob Black in his wolf form here for the first time.

Mountain meadows play a huge part in *Twilight*, obviously, because they are Mrs. Meyer's preferred locale for key story confrontations and revelations. For her gentile readers I doubt this means anything more than her need for an open and isolated space.

"Mountain Meadows," however, means something much less pastoral and positive and much more visceral and painful to American Latter-day Saints. The summer of Mrs. Meyer's dream was a high-water mark for gentile attacks on Mormonism through published explorations of the 1857 *Mountain Meadows* Massacre. 2003 saw three books published with national exposure and distribution that focused on the Mountain Meadows Massacre, in which tragedy Mormon faithful in

15 *Twilight*, page 336; Meyer says about the painting, "That painting was significant only to Carlisle. It reminded him of the way the world looked to him during the first part of his life as a vampire--very lonely." TwilightMoms.com Q&A, page 5, http://www.twilightmoms.net/viewtopic.php?f=99&t=3353

Southern Utah executed more than 120 men, women, and children on their way to California.[16] All three books paint LDS beliefs and history unsympathetically, to say the least, as a cult of blood-thirsty violence; seeming like a joint assault, their publication caused a strong reaction from and a new awareness of Mountain Meadows in the Mormon community.

The murder of more than 120 blameless Arkansas men, women, and children travelling through southern Utah in 1857 by Latter-day Saints pretending to be Native Americans is an atrocity with few equivalents in American history.[17] All three books published on the subject in 2003 argue that the attack was ordered by Brigham Young; LDS Church historians have always denied this, if they are unable to deny that President Young covered-up the crime and protected the murderers for decades until he was obliged to serve up a scapegoat as a sop to gentile opinion and the Federal government. 'Mountain Meadows' has become a short-hand synonym in arguments made by those criticizing LDS beliefs and practices for their founders' violence, megalomania, and disregard for the lives, beliefs, and property of non-believers.

The phrase "Mountain Meadows" to Mormons is painfully meaningful, then, and never was this disgraceful, horrific event from their history as much in the public mind among gentiles and LDS faithful as it was when Mrs. Meyer had the dream that inspired the *Twilight* series. I think it more than likely that Mrs. Meyer's dream was her subconscious attempt to come to terms with the monstrous slaughter of innocents in that Utah mountain meadow. The *Twilight* books inspired by this dream carry the embedded argument that the Mormons were not the bad guys the 2003 gentile books about the massacre say they were but the victims of American aggression and persecution of the LDS faithful.

As crazy as that must sound, the events in her Mountain Meadows bear it out.

As noted above, Mrs. Meyer's Mountain Meadows in *Twilight's* four books are places in which the paranormal and supernatural quality

16 *Blood of the Prophets: Brigham Young and the Mountain Meadows Massacre* (Bagley), *American Massacre: The Tragedy at Mountain Meadows, September 1857* (Denton), and *Under the Banner of Heaven: A Story of Violent Faith* (Krakauer)

17 At least as white-on-white atrocities go; it needs to be noted that LDS militias and the US Army in this period killed as many and often more Native Americans in single raids on their camps but little is made of these massacres, at least in comparison with Mountain Meadows.

of the Nephite and Lamanite Mormons, as represented by Edward as sparkly vampire and Jacob as werewolf, are revealed. More telling, the Meadows are the places where it is the innocent Cullen Mormon-vampires who are attacked, ambushed really, twice by invaders in great numbers whom they are only able to repel by heroic effort and something like miraculous intervention.

The only Mormon defenses for the Mountain Meadows massacre, beyond the valid question of then-Prophet Young's foreknowledge, have been the unfounded insistence that the Arkansas families somehow provoked the attack and that all Utah (then 'Deseret') was in a panic that they were about to be killed by the U.S. Army and California militias gathering at their borders. Mrs. Meyer gives story form to this quality of claiming persecution for religious beliefs as justification for murderous "self-defense" in each of the Meadows confrontations in her books.[18]

The *Twilight* Saga is in several important ways, beyond its generically human allegorical and anagogical meaning, a very specific exercise in Mormon self-defense and self-justification against gentile criticism. Mormons are good and, like their vampire stand-ins, "the epitome of persecuted people;" gentiles, in contrast, are power-hungry crazies who intentionally misunderstand them and want to destroy them. LDS violence, in this view, is only self-defense and above reproach. *Twilight's* Mountain Meadow events make this allegorical argument without exception.

Before detailing the other defenses of Mormon history, faith, and practice that Mrs. Meyer makes against gentile criticisms within her stories, though, we need to clarify how this works. It's a function of, echoing Mrs. Meyer's question for Jane Austen, how much an author puts herself into her stories.

The Mormon 'Mary Sue:' Bella Swan as Mrs. Meyer's Story Double

In the world of fan-fiction, stories in which authors inject themselves into their stories as a wish fulfillment exercise are called "Mary Sue"

18 Bella Swann's birthday, 13 September, was the date in 1870 on which the trial of the only Mormon prosecuted for Mountain Meadows, John D. Lee, began. I have been able to find no other historical correspondent for this date in Mormon history; I concede, of course, that this connection with Bella's birthday is unlikely. The date could have been assigned arbitrarily, for plot reasons, astrological meaning, or a date otherwise significant to the author.

stories or, if written by a man, "Gary Stu"s. It is a deprecatory term for unconscious and unintentionally auctorial self-insertion, by which projection the author puffs him or herself up by giving the character acting as surrogate or psychological proxy remarkable powers, attractiveness, and heroic victory.

I don't think it's much of a reach to see that *Twilight* is Mrs. Meyer's "Mary Sue" book in which Bella Swan is her story stand-in. It's evident in the story and Mrs. Meyer has said as much herself. "Physically, I'm most like Bella (being human and all). Also, I've got the pasty-white brunette thing down. And I'm not very graceful."[19] And all those boys loving Bella, the new girl at Forks High School?

> Some parts of Bella's experiences are modeled after real life (my life, to be exact) in order to ground the fantasy aspects of the story in solid reality. Ironically, many of the details that are one hundred percent reality are the ones that are called into question the most (as illustrated by some of my angry Amazon reviews). In this particular case, I modeled Bella's move to Forks after my real life move from high school to college. (Personal story alert!) I mentioned in my bio that I went to a high school in Scottsdale, AZ, which is Arizona's version of Beverly Hills (picture the high school in the movie *Clueless*). In high school, I was a mousy, A-track wall-flower. I had a lot of incredible girlfriends, but I wasn't much sought after by the Y chromosomes, if you know what I mean.
>
> Then I went to college in Provo, Utah. Let me tell you, my stock went *through the roof*. See, beauty is a lot more subjective than you might think. In Scottsdale, surrounded by barbies, I was about a five. In Provo, surrounded by normal people, I was more like an eight. I had dates every weekend with lots of really pretty and intelligent boys (some of whose names end up in my books). It was quite confusing at first, because I knew there was nothing different about me. (Side note: don't ever let anyone tell you that high school is supposed to be fun. High school is to be endured. College is fun.)[20]

Without straining credulity, I think even the sympathetic reader who knows the details of Mrs. Meyer's life in 2003 that she has shared in interviews will find it hard not to see the wish fulfillment quality of

---

19 TwilightMoms.com, page 4: http://www.twilightmoms.net/viewtopic.php?f=99&t=3310

20 http://www.stepheniemeyer.com/twilight_faq.html#pretty

Bella's life *vis a vis* the author's situation.

- Mrs. Meyer tells us she was not very attractive in high school ("a mousy, A-track wall-flower"); Bella is a boy magnet, though supposedly of only average beauty, and, *mirabile dictu*, effortlessly wins the heart of the previously asocial boy Adonis on campus;
- Her real world husband has Crohn's Disease, a chronic inflammation of the bowels that is incurable and painful, and, as we've seen, she describes him as "perturbed" and their relationship as one largely about "arguing." Bella, in contrast, is married to a "perfect" and "angelic" superman who cares for her every need, who never needs medical attention, to be fed, or to be cared for himself, and who, while over anxious about her well-being at times, is relatively imperturbable.
- Mrs. Meyer married at age 20 and suggests it was only because of the peculiar demands of her faith;[21] Bella marries young, too, but has to choose between two supernaturally handsome, slavishly devoted, sacrificially loving men.
- She had no creative outlets beyond failed efforts to learn "scrap-booking;" Bella, in addition to her adventures in Italy, Phoenix, Seattle, and the meadows of the Olympic Peninsula, reads the books she loves, and writes papers on Shakespeare's misogynistic treatment of his female characters.
- The author has three boys and wants a girl – but no more babies after breaking an arm and having weight trouble with her last pregnancy; Bella gets the girl Mrs. Meyer didn't, a super-powered girl no less, and has around the clock child care from both her sister-in-law and her former heart-throb (straining the believability limits even of fantasy fiction…).

This is not to mention the universal childhood fantasy we get in *Twilight*; teenage Bella is essentially the mother-and-father caretaker and decision-maker for both of her clueless, childish parents. The father, Charlie, with only small misgivings, accepts the marriage and supernatural transformation of their daughter (not to mention the

21 "On our second official date was when he proposed. He proposed a lot. Over 40 times. He would propose every night and I would tell him no every night. It was kind of our end-of-date thing. Mormons get married a lot faster. The no-sex thing does speed up relationships." http://www.phoenixnewtimes.com/content/printVersion/481142

Baby Bean-stalk, Nessie). The mother, Renee, is all but Bella's legal dependent.

I suspect, too, though I have no evidence from interviews, that Mrs. Meyer had the usual unfortunate and unpleasant experiences while delivering her children in hospitals. Bella delivers at home surrounded by protective, loving family, almost all of whom are much more concerned with her health and comfort than with the baby she is carrying. Her fictional pregnancy includes broken bones just as Mrs. Meyer's did, and I suspect there were complications during at least one of her deliveries with an epidural and anesthesia; Edward's punching a venom needle into her heart to save her and her inward near-death experiences while she transforms from human to vampire have many of the characteristics of patients who are resistant to sedation.

Unlike the humiliating and mechanical, not to mention painful, experience in real life maternity wards, Bella's experience in *Breaking Dawn* is painful, yes, but, more important, a heroic act of sacrificial love that not only leads to her apotheosis, i.e., becoming a deathless vampire raised above human needs for sleep, food, even oxygen, but also to the transformation of the world. Nessie's birth as hermetic hermaphrodite, half-human and half-vampire, and Jacob's imprinting with her join the vampire and werewolf communities as well as the human-vampire worlds.

The temptation here after recognizing that the author is writing a wish fulfillment fantasy is to dismiss the consequent work as necessarily worthless because it had therapeutic value and inspiration. That would be an unfortunate and very silly mistake.

Most obviously, it is a mistaken impulse because, if we threw out as soiled bandages every "Mary Sue" novel in which the author acts out satisfying, compensatory dreams, we'd lose a lot of great books. Start out with Shelley's *Frankenstein* and Bronte's *Jane Eyre* and work your way through English fiction up to Montgomery's *Anne of Green Gables* and including Joanne Rowling's *Harry Potter.*

All of these books have their reflection in *Twilight* but none as much commented on as Harry's influence on Bella. In addition to magical or paranormal settings and characters, the two series are both 'Mary Sues.'

We can see Harry as a stand-in for Ms. Rowling, for example, in noting that they share green eyes, a birthday, and a beloved dead mother. Ms. Rowling's painful estranged relationship with her own father is revealed and acted out in the books via the violent deaths suffered by almost every father figure in the narrative line; she admits that she only had Mr. Weasley survive the snake bites he received in *Order of the Phoenix* because she had killed all the other daddies in Harry's adventures.

A character, especially the main character, serving as an author surrogate is no measure of a work's value. It means only that the writer is human. All books, perhaps even all artistic endeavors, have a significant psychological component of the inside being expressed on the outside in therapeutic narrative. Especially, it seems, in first novels.

Every novel as a creative work represents in varying degrees a psychological exercise of its author to work through unresolved interior conflicts. The subconscious content of Mrs. Meyer's *Twilight* Saga, though, asks for our reflection more than most books both because it is her first book and because its core inspiration is dream material.

Robert Anderson, a psychiatrist whose *Inside the Mind of Joseph Smith* (Signature Books, 1999) explores Smith's *Book of Mormon* as an exercise in psychobiography, explains the importance of an author's first composition:

> It is a general truism that the first artistic creation of an artist or writer is usually most revealing of his personality, for it is hoped that the artist's work will also be psychotherapeutic work and contribute to resolving original conflicts and problems.... If the creative work of the artist or author is psychotherapeutic (as one hopes it will be and does sometimes seem to occur), then subsequent work will become more and more removed from the original struggles and conflicts....
>
> The creative artist may reveal aspects of his life throughout his works, but it is hoped that the artistic work will be therapeutic and maturational for the artist. When this is so, the first work of the artist is usually most revealing of his personality, and the problems or conflicts most transparent.[22]

22 Robert D. Anderson, MD., *Inside the Mind of Joseph Smith*, Signature Books: Salt Lake City, 1999, pages xxx, 30

In June 2003 Mrs. Meyer has three sons and feels heavy, old, fragile or broken, and weighed down with responsibilities that keep her from her self-expression. She is inspired and feverishly writes a story in which her character has one daughter (there will be no more…), her love for the baby is acknowledged and praised by everyone as sacrificial and heroic, and the fruit of her labors are peace on earth or, at least, a stop in the fighting around Forks.

Anderson calls this sort of reversal in a psychobiography a "fantasy conquest" in which the author is "compensating for a horrible real-life experience by displacing it with a conquering fantasy." Mrs. Meyer works out her personal issues through her story proxy Bella and writes, as Anderson believes the Mormon Prophet did in *The Book of Mormon*, a "fantasy compensation for [her] real life incompleteness and loss."[23]

Mrs. Meyer writes *Twilight* after being inspired by a dream, she writes it without thought of publication, and, perhaps most important in seeing the work as auto-therapy, she writes it and *Forever Dawn,* the first sequel or "epilogue," for herself and her sister, the closest likeness to a mirror's reflection she could find in another person. Her work reflects the several psychological tensions and conflicts she was working though at the time of her inspiration for the series.

While from her interview statements we can only guess at the individual issues with parents, husband, and community Mrs. Meyer was working through in 2003, we can see gentile-Mormon points of conflict like Mountain Meadows much more clearly. Subconsciously or deliberately, the *Twilight* novels have been written in such a way that they answer non-Mormon criticism or debunking of LDS claims with "fantasy conquests" and story inversions. Just as the Mormon vampires in Mrs. Meyer's mountain meadows are not murderers of innocents but the heroic victims of Catholic and American persecution acting only in self-defense, so her stories turn upside-down the common-place perceptions of LDS beliefs that many Americans have.

Meyer as Mormon Apologist: Romance *is* Literary Wish Fulfillment

Northrop Frye writes that Romance fiction "is nearest of all literary forms to the wish fulfillment dream."[24] Mrs. Meyer, as have seen, is a writer whose world-view and thinking has been shaped by an LDS family,

23 Robert Anderson, op cit., page 47

24 Frye, *Anatomy of Criticism.*, page 186

church, and education and whose fiction, consequently, is suffused with Mormon beliefs. The *Twilight* novels, because they are her first books and were inspired by a dream, not surprisingly, are Romances that include wish fulfillment responses to hard questions gentiles have about Mormonism.

Here are what I think are the most important controversies Mrs. Meyer writes about within her 'Mormon vampires' allegory. Please note that I am not offering gentile assertions or Mormon defenses as valid and invalid arguments. I lay out each controversy because Mrs. Meyer has made a story response to it.

Genetic Evidence: In a 2002 anthology of essays on the *Book of Mormon,*[25] in a Winter 2003 *Dialogue: A Journal of Mormon Thought* article,[26] and again in a February 2003 *Anthropology News* piece,[27] LDS anthropologist Thomas W. Murphy argued that genetic studies of Native Americans in North and South America:

> [lend] no support to traditional Mormon beliefs about the origins of Native Americans. Genetic data repeatedly point to migrations from Asia between 7,000 and 50,000 years ago as the primary source of Native American origins. DNA research has substantiated the archaeological, cultural, linguistic, and biological evidence that also points overwhelmingly to an Asian origin for Native Americans. While DNA evidence shows that ultimately all human populations are rather closely related, to date no intimate genetic link has been found between ancient Israelites and the indigenous peoples of the Americas—much less within the time frame suggested by the BoMor [Book of Mormon]. After considering recent research in molecular anthropology, summarized here, I have concluded that Latter-day Saints should not expect to find validation for the BoMor in genetics.[28]

---

25 Murphy, Thomas W. "Lamanite Genesis, Genealogy, and Genetics." In Vogel, Dan and Brent Metcalfe, eds. *American Apocrypha: Essays on the Book of Mormon.* Salt Lake City: Signature, 2002: 47-77. http://mormonscripturestudies.com/bomor/twm/lamgen.asp

26 Murphy, Thomas W. "Simply Implausible: DNA and a Mesoamerican Setting for the Book of Mormon." *Dialogue: A Journal of Mormon Thought* 36(4) [Winter, 2003]: 109-131.

27 Murphy, Thomas W. "Genetic Research a 'Galileo Event' for Mormons." *Anthropology News* 44(2) [February, 2003]: 20.

28 http://mormonscripturestudies.com/bomor/twm/lamgen.asp

Dr. Murphy called this a "Galileo moment" for Mormon believers in 2003 because, like the astronomer's revolution that turned geocentric Western Christian cosmology on its head, these genetic findings appeared to invalidate Latter-day Saint beliefs that Native Americans are the descendants of Abraham through the children of Lehi. The Mormon world was rocked, as you might imagine.

Mrs. Meyer's answer to this scientific assault on the LDS Prophet, his revelation, and core Mormon beliefs is in the climax of *Breaking Dawn.* The Volturi have come to the Cullen's Mountain Meadow for a showdown with the vegetarians and their allies – and it looks very bad for the white hats, to say the least. What saves the good guys from the Vampire-papists is an inversion of the genetics argument contra *Book of Mormon* revelation. In a wish fulfilling reversal of reality's conflict so typical of dreams, the Cullens are saved by the *ex machina* appearance of a South American aborigine whose DNA proves the Mormon vampires are telling the truth.

Genetics isn't the enemy; it's the savior. Cullen Carlisle, vampire God the Father, turns out to be a geneticist, who figures out everyone's chromosome count.[29] Mormons aren't stooges whose faith claims are proven false by genetic research; they are genetic experts who defeat unbelievers by their superior knowledge.

Joseph Smith, Jr. as Prophet, Con Artist, or "Pious Fraud:" The fulcrum or crux of the historic disagreement between Mormons and gentiles hasn't been genetics but the character of the LDS Prophet, Joseph Smith, Jr. Mormons believe that in his restoration of Christian faith and translation of *The Book of Mormon* that Smith is second only to Christ as a person and as object of veneration. Critics argue that he was history's greatest con man and fraud, from his youth as a treasure-digger to his mendacious "prophecies" and "translations" with and without "seeing-stones." Until recently there was very little middle ground between the two ends of this spectrum.

The mean being argued now by a diversity of scholars – literary critic Harold Bloom, psychotherapist Robert Anderson, and historians Dan Vogel and Michael Quinn among others – is that, rather than the "either-or" exclusive positions of "Prophet" and "Con Artist," Smith was something not quite so grand or so jet-black wicked. Bloom, for example, thinks that the Prophet was "Gnostic" and sees Smith as a "religious genius:"

29 See the genetics discussion in chapter 12 of *Breaking Dawn*

> Joseph Smith did not excel as a writer or as a theologian, let alone as psychologist or philosopher. But he was an authentic religious genius, and surpassed all Americans, before or since, in the possession and expression of what could be called the religion-making imagination.[30]

Bloom cites Paglia's definition of charisma as "the Numinous aura around a narcissistic personality" with approval, and argues that "the Mormon prophet possessed that quality to a degree unsurpassed in American history."[31] He believes that Mormonism is a gnostic or kabbalistic Christianity and that only Smith's "genius or daemon" made its survival of the several crises of its early years possible.

Dan Vogel's historical argument in *Joseph Smith: The Making of a Prophet* and Robert D. Anderson's parallel and more clinical look in his *Inside the Mind of the Prophet* argue that Smith's childhood traumas and family situation made him a narcissist who could not see beyond his own psychological malformation. They come to the same conclusion from the contrary perspectives of the historian and psychoanalyst: Smith was a narcissist and "pious fraud." Smith was clearly an extraordinary man of great achievements and profound personal failings who was capable of both selfless piety and destructive deception and selfishness.

Vogel and Anderson keep the ends in tension without denying or endorsing the exclusive validity or total error in either the "Prophet" or "Con Man" positions about Smith. Both believe, though, that Smith's perception of reality, physical or spiritual, seems to have been not true discernment but largely subject to his psychological issues.

This understanding of Smith does not seem to contradict or exclude, though, the conclusion that he was a "pious fraud," which is Vogel's conclusion, a fraud who was aware of his deceptions but convinced they were justified in the benefits they gave believers, as internal evidence in Smith's life and *The Book of Mormon* strongly suggest was the case.[32]

---

30 Harold Bloom, *The American Religion*, Simon & Schuster, New York, 1992; pages 96-97

31 Op.cit., page 98

32 Dan Vogel, *Joseph Smith: The Making of a Prophet*, Signature Books, Salt Lake City, 2004 (pages vii-xxii), Robert D. Anderson, *Inside the Mind of the Prophet: Psychobiography and the Book of Mormon*, Signature Books, Salt Lake City, 1999 (pages 218-242), D. Michael Quinn, *Early Mormonism and the Magic World View*, Signature Books, Salt Lake City, 1998 (pages xx-xxxix, 321-326), Richard Lyman Bushman, *Joseph Smith: Rough Stone Rolling*, Vintage, New York, 2007

Mrs. Meyer's story response to the growing consensus among non-Mormon academics that Joseph Smith, Jr., was a "pious fraud," not necessarily a con man but certainly not a second Mohammed or Christ, is Edward Cullen, *Twilight's* version of Smith. Noble Edward, the great-souled man albeit perhaps without a soul, is anything but a narcissist, and, if he does lie (and somewhat brazenly as Smith was wont to do, too), he only does so for the good of his family, for Bella's welfare as he understands it, and to deceive the evil.

Which is to say, Mrs. Meyer's story presents Edward/Smith as both Prophet *and* pious fraud. Mrs. Meyer embraces the Smith of Mormon belief and offers a story apology or explanation for his deceptions.

Vogel and Anderson, along with the geneticists, find *The Book of Mormon* to be a fantasy born of Smith's painful childhood experiences and his need to compensate in story as well as an amalgam of early 19th century religious beliefs and controversies. In this last, they echo critics of Smith's time. Contemporaries like Alexander Campbell, founder of the Disciples of Christ, were convinced that *The Book of Mormon*, rather than being a record of a South American 'Lost Tribe of Israel' from the time of Christ as it claims to be, was really only Smith's distillation of religious thinking and controversies of his time. Campbell wrote in 1831, soon after *The Book of Mormon* was published:

> This prophet Smith, through his stone spectacles, wrote on the plates of Nephi, in his book of Mormon, every error and almost every truth discussed in N. York for the last ten years. He decides all the great controversies - infant baptism, ordination, the trinity, regeneration, repentance, justification, the fall of man, the atonement, transubstantiation, fasting, penance, church government, religious experience, the call to the ministry, the general resurrection, eternal punishment, who may baptize, and even the question of freemasonry, republican government, and the rights of man. All these topics are repeatedly alluded to. [33]

Mrs. Meyer's retort about the veracity of *The Book of Mormon* to these skeptics is simple and bold. The revelation that forces the Volturi to abandon the field of battle in *Breaking Dawn* is a magical South American aborigine whose existence and magical hybrid genetics the Aro-Pope and his minions thought impossible. The faith of Mormons rests in large part on the historical existence of Semitic tribesmen in

---

33 Alexander Campbell, *Millennial Harbinger*, Vol II, N. 2, Bethany, Virginia, February 7th, 1831: http://www.lds-mormon.com/campbell.shtml

South America – and that one such latter-day South American is played as a trump card in the series finale is a transparent thumb in the eye to gentile disbelievers.

The Freemasonry Foundation of Mormon Temple Endowments: Mormonism in its beginnings lacked the ritual foundation it has today with its secret ceremonies, anointings, and initiations that are performed in Temples only for members with a 'Temple Recommend' from their Bishop attesting to their fidelity and purity. (Mormons only attend Temple ceremonies on rare occasions to receive Endowments; their regular meetings for worship and study are held in Ward Meetinghouses.) Though there were several ceremonies that Smith revealed in the Kirtland (Ohio) Temple, the most important Temple Endowments were first performed in Nauvoo, Illinois, and showed remarkable similarities with Masonic rituals of that time.

Critics of Mormonism say, flat-out, that Smith's use of Masonic symbols, handshakes, secret words, and the like on Temple buildings and in Mormon sacraments ('Endowments') amounts to nothing more than religious plagiarism, even fraud. They point out the leaders of the early church community were all Freemason lodge members and that Smith had become one himself only several weeks before rolling out his look-alike Temple ceremonies.

They also believe that Smith modeled the whole buried "golden plates" revelation from which plates he claimed to have translated *The Book of Mormon* on the model of the Masonic "Legend of the Secret Doctrine" (or "The Treasure of the Widow's Son"). The Prophet Enoch is a central player in the legend and Smith styled himself a second Enoch and Prophet. Critics of Mormonism believe he created this faux faith from whole cloth using Enoch's mythic life as the Masons told it as his template.[34]

LDS apologists respond that the Prophet restored the true Temple services from before Solomon's time of which the Masons had only degenerate, shadowy forms. In the Mormon Temple rites, believers are joined to God rather than to a collegial fellowship. As Heber Kimball, one of Smith's Apostles wrote, "We have the true Masonry. The Masonry

34 See Dr. Reed C. Durham, Jr. 'Is there no help for the Widow's Son? ('Presidential Address, Delivered At The Mormon History Association Convention, April 20, 1974) for the legend and the parallels with Smith's discovery of the plates and their translation. http://www.cephas-library.com/mormon_is_there_no_help.html

of today is received from the apostasy which took place in the days of Solomon and David. They have now and then a thing that is correct, but we have the real thing."[35]

Richard Lyman Bushman, emeritus professor of history at Columbia and believing Mormon, writes in his biography of Smith, *Rough Stone Rolling*, that the influence of Freemasonry is not as cut and dried as either disbelievers or apologists would have it.

> Intrigued by the Masonic rites, Joseph turned the materials to his own use. The Masonic elements that appeared in the temple endowment were embedded in a distinctive context – the Creation instead of the Temple of Solomon, exaltation rather than fraternity, God and Christ, not the Worshipful Master. Temple covenants bind people to God rather than to each other. At the end, the participants entered symbolically into the presence of God.
>
> Endowment, Joseph's name for the temple ceremony, connected it to promises made long before his encounter with Freemasonry. In early revelations, the word "endowment" referred to seeing God, a bequest of Pentecostal spiritual light. The use of the word "endowment" in Nauvoo implied ritual rather than a transcendent vision. This transition gave Mormonism's search for direct access to God an enduring form.
>
> David Hume, the eighteenth-century empiricist and critic of "enthusiastic" religion, had observed that outbursts of visions and revelations soon sputtered out. They lacked form to keep them alive. They could not endure because they had "no rites, no ceremonies, no holy observances, which may enter into the common train of life, and preserve the sacred principles from oblivion." To remain in force "enthusiasm" had to be embodied in holy practice. Ann Taves, a modern scholar of religion, has added that "direct inspiration survives only when it is supported by a sacred mythos embedded in sacred practices." The Mormon temple's sacred story stabilized and perpetuated the original enthusiastic endowment.
>
> The resemblances of the temple rites to Masonic ritual have led some to imagine the endowment as an offshoot of the fraternal lodge movement. Between 1840 and 1900, membership in lodges leapt from around 2,500 to over 6,000,000. The lodges' success attested to the need for bonding among American males. In

35 Quoted in Durham, op.cit. see also Tim Canfield and Bob Moore, 'Was Joseph Influenced by Masonry?,' http://www.zarahemlabranch.org/masonry.htm

> the hard world of emergent capitalism, the lodges set up an alternative universe of virtue and friendship encased in imagery and ancient rites. On the surface, the temple resembles the cloistered brotherly world of the lodges. But the spiritual core of the Nauvoo endowment was not male bonding. By 1843 women were sitting in the ordinance rooms and passing through the rituals. Adam and Eve, a male-female pair, were the representative figures rather than the Masonic hero Hiram Abiff. The aim of the endowment was not male fraternity but the exaltation of husbands and wives.
>
> The Nauvoo endowment is more akin to aspects of Kabbalah, the alternative Jewish tradition that flourished for centuries alongside rational Judaism. As one commentator explains, Kabbalah's central impulse was a desire to encounter God: "The position of classical Judaism was that the essence of God is unknowable: 'Thou canst not see My Face.' The Kabbalists sought not only to define and characterize the Godhead – through a kind of spiritualized cosmogonic physics – but to experience it." Joseph's governing passion was to have his people experience God. To be sure, Joseph was not seeking a mystic God known through some transcendent fusion. Joseph's God existed in time and space in a bodily form. Nonetheless, the fundamental trajectory of the endowment coincided with the passions and expectations of mystics for centuries past and especially with the Kabbalistic dream of conjunction with the divine.[36]

Prof. Bushman cedes to the critics that Smith "turned [Masonic rites] to his own use" and that the effect of these borrowed rituals was to ground or "stabilize" his evolving religion in sacramental practice. He counters accusations of plagiarism and fraud, though, with the assertion that Smith "embedded" Masonic rites in a different context, to a different, gnostic end, and for both men and women. Bushman believes that Smith's identification with the Prophet Enoch came from his own inspired translation of Genesis, which expanded Enoch's 5 *Genesis* verses to 110 verses in Smith's *Book of Moses*, rather than from the Masonic story about "The Treasure of the Widow's Son."[37]

Mrs. Meyer's LDS allegory addresses this Masonic problem creatively and deftly. Carlisle Cullen is the theological heart of Mormonism, you'll recall, born in the English Radical Reformation. He

---

36 Richard Lyman Bushman, *Joseph Smith: Rough Stone Rolling*, Vintage, New York, 2007, pages 450-451

37 Bushman, op.cit, pages 137-142

lives alone, though, until a widow begs for mercy for her son. Carlisle transforms his first begotten son, Edward, who is the story's Prophet figure, the means by which Bella is able to join the Holy Family.

The Freemasonry connection here is that the widow and her son Edward *are* Masons; their last name is "Masen." Meyer's resolution of the controversy about Smith's using Masonic elements in Temple Endowments is to have the Father restore and revive the dying Masen/Mason and bring him to perfection in the Prophet. The story acknowledges that without Freemasonry there is no Mormonism as we have it today, but asserts it is only in their transformation and divinization as the Father worked this miracle in his beloved Prophet that what was a 'Masen' became a means to apotheosis.

I think, too, that Mrs. Meyer knows her LDS history and the importance of Masonry in it, not only because she named her Mormon protagonist lead 'Masen, but because she makes him "the widow's son" and has him talk about the "Lion and the lamb."

Joseph Smith, Jr.'s, last words as he fell from the window of the Carthage Jail were "O Lord, my God!" This was not a simple piety or prayer to God but a cry for help to any Masons that may have been in the mob assembled to kill him.

> The Masonic Legend of Enoch concludes with the murder of Hiram Abif, the hero of modern Masonry. Hiram Abif, a Mason, was murdered for not revealing "the hiding place and the contents of the hidden treasure." While he was being slain Hiram lifted up his hands and cried "Oh Lord, My God, is there no help for the widow's son?" His cry became the universal Masonic call of distress, to be used in times of dire emergency.[38]

A Mason who hears this cry was obliged by oaths made in their brotherhood rites to come to the aid of his distressed brethren, if his own life were not also put at risk by the attempt. No one in Carthage stepped forward. (John Taylor, who was in the room in which Smith was shot, testified that Smith made this cry and that it was the Masonic distress cry rather than act of piety.) That Mrs. Meyer makes Edward the "widow's son," and, more important, that it is the widow begging Carlisle to have mercy on her son which makes Carlisle do what he had not done for almost 300 years points to the LDS-Mason link.

---

38 Paul Trask, *Part Way to Utah: The Forgotten Mormons*, Refiner's Fire Ministries, 1997, page 76; http://www.help4rlds.com/pwtu/PWTUChap6.pdf

Not convinced? In a letter Smith wrote to Joseph Hull, a Mason and Congregational Minister in Lempster, New Hampshire, he describes in occult language how the completion of the Temple in Nauvoo will complete the square of Masters in the world, an event that will usher in the Millennium. His conclusion: "when the above Described Lodge is duly formed & Begins to work we may ex have peace on Earth & Good will to men & no dought the Lion will lye down with the lamb & the Sucking Child will play with the Asp & not be Stung."[39]

"The Lion will lye down with the lamb," Edward's description in the perfect meadow circle of his love and life with Bella, is Masonic language for the perfection of the world. Edward Masen Cullen is Mrs. Meyer's story depiction of Masonry perfected in the Prophet and her apologetic response to gentiles who believe that Mormonism is just warmed-over Masonry.

Man-Child Marriage and Polygamy: Much of Jon Krakauer's *Under the Banner of Heaven* is specifically about the Mountain Meadows Massacre but he is after bigger game than historical tragedies. He talks about Mountain Meadows only to argue that the Mormons have always been bloodthirsty and dangerous. His focus is on the *present* day murders and misogyny of polygamous LDS fundamentalists who live for the most part above and outside the law in the Mormon belt. Krakauer's most damning anecdotes are about the suffering of child-brides wed to much older Fundamentalist LDS men practicing Smith-inspired "Celestial Marriage" (plural marriage or polygamy) when the girls are only in their early teens.

When Bella meets Edward in January, 2005, he is well over 100 years old, though he seems to be 17.[40] Their relationship is hurried along because of Bella's fear that, if she isn't transformed into a vampire soon, she will become an old woman while he does his Dorian Gray schtick. Edward, the older man, of course, says his love has nothing to do with age; he is blind to Bella's youth and the possibility his love will cool as she ages. (Polygamy is given something of a joking bye in *Twilight* through the harmless idea of 'plural marriage' shown in Rosalie and Emmett marrying repeatedly as human conventions require when they move to new places.)

39 Durham, op.cit., Appendix A

40 All dates and ages are derived from the invaluable TwilightLexicon.com timeline: http://www.twilightlexicon.com/?page_id=9

Man-child marriage, as seen in the Edward-Bella relationship, is something to which Bella only agrees because Edward insists on it as a condition for his making her a vampire. As her whole life *and* her apotheosis depends on her fixed relationship with Edward, the nightmare reality and crime of man-child marriage that Krakauer lays at the feet of Mormonism is re-packaged as a child-*saving* spiritual practice the good-guy insists on to protect the child at risk.

Going a step further, Quil, one of the Quileute shape changers, "imprints" on a small child, binding them for life. Jacob Black, too, imprints on Bella's newborn baby, about which Bella is at first enraged but ultimately accepts as right. Both events only further confirm the *Twilight* subtext that man-child relationships are supernatural goods rather than psychological perversion. Jacob's discussion with Bella about how little girls on whom wolfmen have imprinted "choose" their much older mates when they grow up, wolves who have been "sealed" to them (using LDS marriage language here) regardless of the girls' supposed future free-choice, is especially unnerving in this light.

Misogyny or 'Why Being a Mormon Woman is a Downer:' On the one hand, LDS women have it all over women in more traditional and conventional Christian churches. There is a God the Mother, Eve may still be the cause of man's fall but that is a great thing, not a failing, and their families, sealed to them in the Temple, will live together eternally in Celestial Heaven.

But there is a down side for Mormon women. And it's steep.

In the Temple drama before the marriage sealing ordinance, the bride and groom witness a play depicting the events of the Garden of Eden story. Eve makes a covenant to obey Adam, "the law of the Lord," and "to hearken to your counsel." In the endowment room, the couple walk through a veil ceremony during which the bride acts out her dependence on her husband for her salvation. She tells her husband-to-be behind the curtain her sacred Temple name and he draws her into the room representing the Celestial Kingdom.

This is a one-way street. The husband pulls her through the veil at the resurrection by calling her name. She is not calling his name. And if he doesn't call (because he fell away from the faith), then she does have other means to resurrection through another priesthood holder, but it's dicey. LDS men have all the priesthood and familial authority and their wives live in full obedience to them, if they are only bound, according to the rules at least, so long as the husbands "hearken into the Father."[41]

A woman's salvation, in essence, is had only through her husband. If they enter the Celestial Heaven, they have promises of eternal life together and of producing an indefinite number of spirit children just as our God the Father and Mother produced us as spirit children in our pre-existent life. The husband may have additional wives married to him in the third heaven; women do not have corresponding polyandrous opportunities (responsibilities?) once beyond the veil.

Critics of Mormonism claim this creates a misogynist culture unique to the 21st century West, albeit similar in several ways to Islamic culture, which shares a polygamist tradition with the Latter-day Saints. Mormon apologists argue that this is nonsense and, though marriage and child-bearing are central to the spiritual life of LDS women and they are not eligible for the Priesthood or church leadership positions, that they enjoy equal or greater freedoms and opportunities than gentile feminists have.

Mrs. Meyer's story stand-in, Bella Swan, is a dutiful Mormon woman, who is obedient to her parents[42] but devoted to, even worshipful of her beloved. She's not unaware of sexism in the world or even in her relationships; think of the paper she wrote on misogyny in Shakespeare's *MacBeth* or her breaking her hand slugging Jacob Black to communicate to the macho dude that he had crossed the line by kissing her.

The moral of Bella's story is that of the faithful Mormon wife. By adhering to the law of chastity until marriage, by fidelity to her man, and by giving birth to children, not just sacrificially but in her case *suicidally*, the ugly duckling and awkward, mousy woman becomes a super-powered near-immortal who is even stronger than the strongest sexist boor (yes, I mean Emmett). Bella Swan, the 'beautiful swan' goddess, in this transformation saves her family from the threat of the Volturi.

There is a back side to Mrs. Meyer's views on this subject we'll get to in a moment, but the front is an LDS Morality Play. Good girls like Bella who play by the rules until the end get everything they could ever want, "forever."

---

41 http://www.mormoncurtain.com/topic_womeninmormonism_section1.html#pub_1454734794

42 Bella takes care of her parents for the most part if she is obliged to deceive them about her closet life as a Mormon wanna-be.

"No on Proposition 8" The New Mormon Cross to Carry: If the man-on-the-street today knows three things about Mormons, my guess is that it would be that they live in Utah, they used to be polygamists, and they are against gay marriage. I think a lot of people may know about Glenn Beck and Gladys Knight being LDS, too, and that Mormons don't drink alcohol or coffee, but the gay marriage opposition is what they talk about and see on the television news.

I can only scratch my head on this one, because all traditional, orthodox faiths (none of which consider Mormonism a valid faith) also are against gay marriage. I think the Mormons get singled out on this because marriage itself is so important to their spiritual lives that their campaigns against legal homosexual unions is more open, dynamic, and much more well funded than other churches' efforts.

They worry that if gay marriage is legalized that they will be required to perform weddings for same sex couples in their Temples if they want to remain open. Homosexuality, however, is a ban to receiving the 'temple recommend' anyone who wants to enter the Temple must have. Therefore, the thinking goes, the state might close Mormon Temples if they refuse to perform same sex weddings.

'Homosexual Mormon,' even outside the marriage issue, though, is something of a 'square circle.' The church officially takes the position that believers are to "condemn the sin and love the sinner," but, given the centrality of marriage and reproduction in LDS spiritual and community life, being gay is something like being a non-person.

There are no homosexuals in the *Twilight* series. I think, though, that Mrs. Meyer offers the LDS teaching on homosexuality in Carlisle's hope that his abstinence from preying on human beings, "doing the best he could with the hand he was dealt," will "count for something" with God.

Jacob Black, too, is slightly bitter that he was made a Quileute Protector without a choice in the matter and he just does his best. Take a second and turn the page at an angle so you can think of these two characters as good Mormons who have homosexual desires. Cullen and Jacob are doing exactly what the church says LDS believers with same sex attraction must; abstain and do your best with those unnatural desires.

'The Race Card' – White is Right: When I introduced Edward as the allegorical stick figure for Joseph Smith, Jr., in *Twilight* above, I was obliged to discuss why the pallor of the Cullens' skin was a marker that they were Mormons. The Nephites in *The Book of Mormon* are pale Semites and the Lamanite apostates in Mormon scripture are dark skinned as a consequence of their fall from grace.

What I didn't get into there was that the belief that the righteous are white and non-whites are that way for a reason morphed into institutional racism under Brigham Young. For more than a century, black men could become Mormons but they could not enter into the Priesthood (as almost all 12 year old boys do in an important rite of passage), serve a mission, or receive other Temple endowments. In effect, they could not enter into the highest of three heavenly kingdoms or become gods because they were ineligible for Celestial Marriage.

This changed in 1978 when the Quorum of 12 had a revelation that black men could become LDS priesthood members. Cynics said this revelation was timed to coincide with the opening of a Temple in Brazil or that God was forced to speak up because BYU's football program was suffering in the recruiting wars for big league talent. However it was timed or inspired, the revelation has significantly broadened the missionary field and the reach of the Church of Latter-day Saints, though few black Mormons have reached decision making positions in the Salt Lake hierarchy in the 30 years since the change.

The only non-white people in Mrs. Meyer's Olympic Peninula are the Quileutes, a tribe of Native Americans. I lived on the Olympic Peninsula for five years and visited the West End a few times during that stay. I was there again last summer for a *Twilight* conference. The absence of black people isn't a function of anything but true-to-life realism.

Mrs. Meyer, though, carries the postmodern banner for tolerance and against prejudice with enthusiasm. As discussed in the morality chapter in Part 1 above, one of her themes is that the Nephite-Cullens and Lamanite-Quileutes have to get over their traditional hatred (and olfactory aversion – "you stink!") to one another. This victory comes about in the end through Renesmee's birth, Jacob's imprinting, and Edward's acceptance of him as his "son." I believe this racial resolution of contraries in her stories is Mrs. Meyer's depiction of the end of the institutional racism founded in the prophetic vision of Brigham Young and *The Book of Mormon* and ended by revelation in 1978.

Wait a minute! What about Polygamy?

Multiple marriage has to be in any Mormon drama somewhere. It's the great scar on the LDS body politic and the first thing that gentiles want to talk about. Though it has been a century since the Salt Lake City hierarchy – the First Presidency – announced it had had a revelation and polygamy was no longer the "Principle" of Celestial Marriage (in this life) very much the way the church renounced racism in the 70's, non-Mormons are still fascinated by it. Mrs. Meyer says one of her editors in New York asked her if she had sister-wives, blissfully unaware that mainstream Mormons are monogamous.

Fundamentalist LDS, of course, have never abandoned polygamy and it is their communities that, though largely tolerated and kept off-stage by the embarrassed larger church, keep the practice in the gentile mind as a Mormon marker. Again, Jon Krakauer's book was largely about the crimes committed by individual polygamists and by the nightmare existences in their communities, in which women, especially young women, are all but slaves.

Mrs. Meyer inserts the peculiar practice with which most people associate historic and current Mormons, however inappropriately, in her immortal children subplot. "Immortals" were babies and very small children that had been made into vampires and survived the transition. It is implied that vampires made these children to satisfy their longings for family which they could not satisfy by normal reproduction; vampires can and do copulate – endlessly and ecstatically we're told – but it is fruitless exercise.

Unfortunately, immortal children are unable to restrain their thirst at any given moment and have no capacity for learning to speak of. They represent, consequently, a constant threat of exposure to the human-gentile population. The Volturi decided, as Carlisle explains to Bella, that, because "they were incapable of protecting our secret," "they had to be destroyed." And destroy them the Volturi did, though covens with these beautiful, deadly children fought to the last bloodsucking family member to protect their loved ones.

The Denali Coven had an immortal child that Tanya's mother loved and the Volturi killed her and the child. Her orphaned children are especially sensitive, consequently, to the idea of immortals. When Irina sees Renesmee from a distance, then, her first thought is "It's an immortal!" and she reports to the Volturi, which precipitates the confrontation in the Mountain Meadow in *Breaking Dawn's* big finish.

The polygamy connection in *Twilight* with immortal children is that the historical cause of the U. S. Army and California militias coming to the northeast and southwest borders of Deseret (Utah) in 1857 was American outrage about polygamy. The Principle of Celestial Marriage at that time was very much in practice among Mormons, even the rule of the devout, though missionaries in the United States and United Kingdom either did not mention it or just denied it ("milk before meat"). Not a few of the people slaughtered in the Arkansas company caught at Mountain Meadows were female Mormon converts who were escaping the life as a "sister bride" by joining the wagon train. The LDS murderers worried that these women "apostates," the victims of polygamy, would cause greater scandal in California, a state already forming its militia to move against the Mormon inland empire.

Of course, when the Volturi come to the Mountain Meadow, the supposed immortal child Renesmee is only a pretext for their aggression. It is the defining, humanistic vision of Carlisle that they really want to stamp out. This is revealed when the invasion does not turn back as soon as Aro learns from both Edward and from Renesmee that she is not an immortal.

The parallel the discerning reader is meant to draw in the Mormon vampire allegory is that persecution of Celestial marriage was never about religious or civil objections to polygamy but the surface excuse for an attack on the Lord's righteous people. The truth of Mormonism is a threat to the religious status quo and power holders, so they are ever eager to find a good reason to attack the righteous and to smear them with charges of horrific impropriety and law breaking.

Again, this is dream-like inversion and "victory conquest" by which the Mountain Meadows Mormon murderers are not insane religious zealots who slaughtered as many as 157 people that had surrendered to them as the three books and history says they were. These LDS faithful are instead the victims of misrepresentation and of attack by much larger and more powerful forces.

In the final *Twilight* wish fulfillment re-telling of the 1857 massacre, the Native Americans are again alongside the Mormons as they were in Utah but here there is no battle or death because the gentile invaders meet an army of witnesses able to battle them on almost equal terms; Bella Swan's postmodern superpower that protects the White Hats from the metanarrative mind control of the Volturi evens everything up. We are shown the allegorical revelation that *The Book of Mormon* was correct – there *are* South American Indians with the supposedly impossible genetic make-up! – and the Volturi retreat to lick their wounds and perhaps fight another day.

Mountain Meadows isn't the only Mormon public relations nightmare that Mrs. Meyer recasts as a 'plus' by turning it on its head. Man-Child marriages, Genetic arguments against *The Book of Mormon*, charges of racism, misogyny, homophobia, even religious fraud and plagiarism a la Masonry are all LDS points of conflict with gentile critics that Mrs. Meyer 'resolves' by re-writing them in her dream-inspired Romance with almost somnambulant disregard for facts.

But *Twilight* isn't just Mormonism in the mirror or "LDS Apologetics 101." There is also a layer of critique Mrs. Meyer offers the hierarchy in Salt Lake City as well as those who sanctify Joseph Smith, Jr. Turn the page for that and, finally, for what conclusions we can make from the Mormonism in these novels about why we love Bella and Edward's love story.

Chapter 7

Twilight as the Work of a Mormon 'Apostate'

How Mrs. Meyer's Criticisms of LDS Shape Her Twilight Novels

So Stephenie Meyer is just an unthinking, True-Believer-Mormon?

Hardly.

It is understandable, though, after this extended exposition of how much LDS apologetic material there is in the Mormon vampire allegory embedded within the *Twilight Saga* that the serious reader might scratch his or her head and ask that. I don't think, however, it is fair to conclude more about her than what we knew already after reading Arnaudin's *Mormon Vampires* and thinking about the Mormon elements of Mrs. Meyer's fiction.

The author's mental and emotional landscape was all formed and continues to receive daily booster shots from her Mormon family, church, community, and *alma mater.* What else could she write in her first book except a total Mormon fantasy that addresses the subconscious and surface concerns of the LDS faithful and advances their view contra the gentiles?

That doesn't mean, of course, that the woman is a humorless, religious fanatic handing out tracts at the mall or petitioning the City Council to make bikinis and speedos illegal at the local pool. If her interviews are any guide, Stephenie Meyer is an independent thinker, refreshingly open and honest, with a self-deprecating sense of humor and candor about her failings and insecurities. Pigeonholing her or her books as the Saturday Night Live caricature of 'The Church Lady' is a big mistake.

Her independence from the LDS party line, if you think I'm contradicting myself, along with a remarkable comic touch is as evident in the *Twilight* books as are her apologetic notes and dream defenses. She can laugh at LDS history and problems as creatively as she defends her church from critics. Check out Rosalie Hale again, something of a story stand-in for Emma Hale Smith, the Prophet's wife. There are few cows more sacred in the LDS round-up than Joseph Smith, Jr., but almost certainly Mrs. Meyer takes a roundhouse shot at the Prophet in Rosalie's origin story.

Rosalie Hale, you recall, is the beautiful woman whom Carlisle turned into a vampire on her deathbed in 1933, half-hoping she would be a match for his "son," Edward. This is fun because "Hale" is the maiden name of Joseph Smith, Jr.'s first and only legal wife, Emma. The joke here works on two levels. Emma Hale Smith didn't ever accept the Prophet's Principle of plural marriage, so Rosalie's match with Edward not having worked out can be a pointer to this historic conflict. But the criticism of Smith is much sharper in the story of her near-death and her actions after Carlisle transforms her.

Rosalie was the very beautiful daughter of an ambitious family in Rochester, New York, and she becomes engaged to the most eligible bachelor in the city, the rich and flamboyant Royce King, II. The city and name both translate to the Mormon Prophet because Mormonism is born just outside Rochester, the "2nd" is a transparency for "Jr.," and "Royce King," because *roi* is the French word for "king" and the last name is also "King" points to a man from upstate New York who was twice coronated. Joseph Smith, Jr., was twice ordained king, first in 1843 and then as "King of the World" in 1844.[1] I kid you not.

Rosalie never marries Royce King, II, because she is gang raped and left for dead in the street by drunken Royce and his friends (as a vampire, she has her revenge on them all). Mrs. Meyer's opinion about the Prophet's "Principle," his treatment of his first wife, and that he deserved the death he received, in history and her fiction, are all well laid out in Rosalie's story – "Emma Hale Smith was wronged and very much in the right to leave her polygamous, unfaithful husband!" – an opinion that is well outside LDS orthodoxy, I probably don't need to add.

---

1 http://www.mormonapologetics.org/topic/37524-the-1843-and-1844-ordinations-of-joseph-smith-as-kingthe-1843-and-1844-ordinations-of-joseph-smith-as-king/; cf., also Richard Lyman Bushman, *Rough Stone Rolling*, Vintage (New York), 2005, p. 536 for a democratic apology for his ordination from the LDS historian.

And there are other notes of criticism of Mormonism in the books, which, if not as telling as the Rosalie story and its beneath-the-radar attack on Mormonism's sacred cow, are as meaningful. This writer is clearly no TBM Temple worker whose life is dedicated to baptizing dead Holocaust victims *in absentia*.

The biggest thing is the most obvious. Edward and the Cullen Holy Family, however admirable, even heroic, their abstinence from eating humans may be, are still bloodthirsty vampires. *By nature* they are lethally dangerous to conventional humans whom, for the most part, they disregard or hold in disdain. Jon Krakauer's book *Under the Banner of Heaven* labors to paint just this picture not only of Mormons but all religious believers. He focuses, though, on the LDS 'blood atonement' theology and oaths in the original endowment ceremonies as the cause of the Mountain Meadows massacre and continued Fundamentalist violence. Mormons are dangerous folk.

Mrs. Meyer's dream picture of Mormons in the Cullen coven doesn't deny Krakauer's postmodern atheism and portraiture of God-believers as bloodthirsty crazies who might kill their neighbors at the drop of a hat. Incredibly, really, given her upbringing, she adopts this view as her own with the only slight adaptation that the Mormon vampires, in stark contrast with the Volturi-Catholics and Nomad-Protestants, fight the impulse compelling religious believers to be inhuman monsters. The Cullen-Mormons can never escape their nature, though, as Edward's revulsion at the idea of Bella wanting to become like him reveals that he understands.

This postmodern view of religion – that it is a dangerous vehicle of the mind-and-freedom-destroying cultural narrative – is an amazing perspective to find in a novel written by a Mormon or any believer. Especially as it is perhaps *the* vital conflict of the book. Bella Swan is on a hero's journey to become a goddess but she has to come to terms with the reality that this apotheosis comes at the cost of her humanity. She will leave the community of normal people for a seeming paradise but at the price of becoming something of a monster.

Not exactly missionary material for Mormonism.

Rosalie is a relatively unsympathetic character (perhaps a bit of a dig at Emma Hale Smith, alas) who is self-important and superficial compared to the other Cullens, even Emmett. But Mrs. Meyer, though she clearly has Bella as her psychological surrogate in the series, presents another woman as her proxy who presents a story picture of the dark side of Mormon life. Leah Clearwater, like Rosalie, is unhappy with the paranormal hand she has been dealt that deprives her of a normal woman's life and joys.

The Quileute tribe is, like the Cullen Coven, a group of allegorical Mormons in the story, the good Lamanites. They are introduced in *New Moon* which story is all but a re-telling of *Twilight* with werewolves standing in for vampires.

- Sam Uley, the first wolfman to change over, is the Quileute Carlisle.
- His pack, like the Cullens, have no secrets from one another because they share the same mind (the Cullens have this openness because of Edward's ability to hear thoughts).
- The werewolves understand themselves as "monsters" and "other."
- They are mythic creatures who are misrepresented and misunderstood.
- They act as Bella's sleepless protectors through the night.

Like the Cullen vampires besides Bella, none of the wolfmen protectors chose their pack life; it is forced upon them by their genetic code, their community, and their proximity to vampires. Jacob Black, something like Rosalie Cullen, resents his loss of freedom and humanity and that he had no choice in the matter.

Jacob's misgivings, though, are nothing compared with Leah's, the only woman in the La Push wolfpack. The pack shares a mind, so all her feelings – love, bitterness, and resentment – about her former lover, now the pack's alpha male and imprinted on another woman, are out in the open every time she becomes lupine. The men resent her and have little idea of what to do with her. And having become a wolfman protector, she has lost her menses, a poetic picture of losing her feminine identity.

I think Leah is Mrs. Meyer's picture of the intelligent woman born into the LDS faith. As Orson Scott Card noted, there is no more escaping Mormon belief than there is 'getting out of' being Jewish. It's an immersive culture and full-time identity. Leah, though, like talented LDS women whose abilities put them into competitive and close contact with misogynist Mormon macho-men, has little choice but to leave if she wants to be fully human, a woman, and to use her talents freely. Her life is the tragedy of the books because all of her choices involve self-destruction at some level. If Jacob Black's sisters had not fled the reservation, the same trap might have caught them.

Leah could be Mrs. Meyer's second story proxy.[2] She is no TBM, but she is caught on the 'can't live with the madness' and 'cannot leave all that I know and am behind' divide. Bella embraces everything about Mormonism and achieves apotheosis and the perfect life in Cullen paradise; Leah moves to the periphery of pack life in Jacob's almost private sect in which she has some hope of freedom from the group-think of Mormonism and institutional discrimination against women. She, alone among all the characters in the books, is not at home with either the LaPush wolfpack or the Cullen Coven.

Again, Mrs. Meyer is not a Salt Lake robot. She has sworn she would "never, never live" in Utah because of the fervor of the faithful there[3] and we see her awareness of the front and back of her faith in her Mormon vampires. They are blood-thirsty monsters indifferent in large part to human-gentile life but whose beauty and nobility are nonetheless sympathetically drawn.

The Cullens are not the *Stregoni benefici* Bella reads about online who are "said to be on the side of goodness and a mortal enemy of evil vampires."[4] The Forks vampires have a "live and let live" vampire policy, which is to say, they allow the vampires they know to kill humans without objection, only asking that they not do what they do in the Cullen backyard. This is a "let die" policy towards human beings, of

2 It should be noted that, like Leah Clearwater, Mrs. Meyer has a brother named Seth. If the real world referent Seth struggles with conventional LDS church life, the pack, but longs for the Celestial Church represented in the story by Edward and the Cullens, as Seth Clearwater does, the Stephenie-Leah link would be that much stronger.

3 TwilightMoms.com Q&A, Page 3: http://www.twilightmoms.net/viewtopic.php?f=99&t=3309
TM: Have [you] gotten any grief in your ward or stake from over protective/over-zealous parents?
Steph: I haven't gotten any grief to my face, though I know it exists. My husband takes perverse delight in reading negative blogs to me. Things with titles like: "With what she writes, can Stephenie Meyer be a good member of the church?" That kind of thing only happens in Utah, where I will never, never live.

4 *Twilight*, page 135; Mrs. Meyer says this "myth" is one that Carlisle made up "all by himself" about himself; http://twilightlexicon.com/2006/03/11/personal-correspondance-5/

course. No one moves to help the busload of human tourists being herded into the Volturi "cafeteria" in *New Moon.* Carlisle and Edward are nice guys but they are not at war with vampires who choose to kill humans for breakfast, lunch, and dinner.

Ouch.

That Mrs. Meyer has mixed feelings even about the Mormon vampires she obviously loves came out in a discussion of her several influences at *Entertainment Weekly.* She explains there that she always loved the film *Stranger than Fiction* and says:

> "There's a scene where [the fictional character] Emma Thompson's character created ... tracks her down and walks into her living room and he goes, 'Hey, I'm Harold Crick.' And she collapses to the floor and says, 'I know.' That moment makes me cry. Imagine what that would be like! I actually did have a dream after *Twilight* was finished of Edward coming to visit me – only I had gotten it wrong and he did drink blood like every other vampire and you couldn't live on animals the way I'd written it. We had this conversation and he was terrifying."[5]

The *Twilight* books, in other words, are stuffed with Mormon content because they are the artful expression of thoroughly Mormon Millie, Mrs. Meyer. She, however, is not a shill for anyone, qua skeptical postmodern, and, though she defends her church against gentile criticism with dream-like echoes of church positions, she also has her reservations about LDS history, faith, and practices. The book is largely a response to the three Mountain Meadows history books that were published in late 2002 and 2003, yes, but, in making her story Mormons, the Cullens, into blood thirsty vampires who are no different except in choice from their monstrous brethren, she largely accepts the consensus gentile view of Meadows historians about LDS beliefs and inherent violence.

I don't mean to say that this makes Mrs. Meyer a heretic or a non-believer. Far from it. If I have called her an "apostate" in my chapter title, that is only in alliterative excess to make the point she is Mormon Artist, Apologist, *and* Apostate, i.e., her work reflects, defends, *and* criticizes

5 Maxine Hanks discussed the possible meaning of this comment in her talk at 'Summer School in Forks' ("Mormonism and Twilight," Maxine Hanks, SSIF, June 2009). Stephenie Meyer, 'Stephenie Meyer: 12 of My 'Twilight' Inspirations, Entertainment Weekly.com;' http://www.ew.com/ew/gallery/0,,20234559_20234565_20237747,00.html

the church which is her life. If we're looking for a historical analogy or literary parallel, it is Dante and his relationship with Catholicism in his 'Gary Stu' book, the *Divine Comedy*. His church is his means to the beatific vision but it doesn't keep him from laying into churchmen, even pontiffs located in Hell.

So with Mrs. Meyer. She sees the front and back of her faith: its promise of divinization as well as the realities of misogyny, cult-like entrapment, and an inhuman quality that borders on indifference if not violence towards non-believers. Understanding how Mormonism suffuses her work means seeing all three LDS hats Stephenie Meyer wears simultaneously as a Mormon Artist, Apologist, *and* 'Apostate.'

Mrs. Meyer's Mormonism Reveals Why Her Books are So Popular

So, we've come to the end of the road on this first trip through the Twilight Saga wearing LDS tinted glasses. I don't think any part of what we've seen is especially controversial or over-wrought. Starting with the foundation facts that Mrs. Meyer is Mormon by birth, choice, faith, and prolonged study and that LDS thinking and community life color all her experience, it shouldn't be a surprise or stretch to find that:

- her imaginative 'other world' – Bella's adventures in Forks - has all the elements of LDS beliefs and practice embedded in it;
- Bella Swan's hero's journey is an allegory of her body and soul conversion to Mormonism and her apotheosis into a Mormon goddess;
- the stages include wish fulfillment resolutions of gentile criticisms of her faith, always with the Mormon-counter argument presented as an inversion and fantasy conquest; and
- the four *Twilight* novels also include her misgivings and critiques of her church's past and present failings.

The Romance was inspired by a Mountain Meadows dream the summer the Mountain Meadows Massacre reached its high-water mark in American thinking because of three books being published on the subject. Mrs. Meyers's 'Mary Sue' novel, written for herself and one other Mormon stay-at-home mom, is laden with LDS meaning from start to finish.

So what?

Well, it's not a big deal in the sense that she is trying to smuggle the Mormon gospel to unsuspecting readers in a subliminal subterfuge. Let me repeat what I said way back in the beginning of Part 2: Mrs. Meyer is not writing as a missionary or with intent to propagate the faith or proselytize her readers. *Twilight* is not a Mormon tract inviting us to the local Ward Meeting house; it would be a shame if the books were pigeonholed as 'LDS lit' and neglected by critics consequently even more than they have been.

I can say "they're not Mormon books" with a straight face after going on for three chapters about the importance of their latent and explicit LDS content because it should be obvious Mrs. Meyer's novels aren't read and enjoyed by millions because these Twihards are Mormons looking for a faith-fix. Far from it.

As I explained in Part I, Mrs. Meyer's novels sell the way they do because they satisfy a reader's needs. I disagree with the 21st century consensus that all people are born with an entertainment-diversion chromosome that must be satisfied for us to know inner peace and fulfillment.

Human history and present reality confirm that the species *homo sapiens*, as Eliade believes, should more properly be called *homo religiosus* because we seem to have been designed for the pursuit of myth and self-transcendent experience more than we are for either rational thinking or watching television. We make time for the teevee 'soaps,' for fantasy fiction, and for blockbuster movies, again per Eliade, because in a secular culture, these avenues serve a mythic or religious function.

Mrs. Meyer's stories resonate with readers' hearts because they satisfy this need (1) by confirming and re-affirming our core beliefs that are peculiar to this historical period, and, (2) by giving us an imaginative experience of timeless, transcendent truths in allegorical and anagogical symbols and stories.

The author's Mormon beliefs and how they shape and inform her stories aren't important because deep in our hearts we secretly want to drink the Salt Lake City Kool-Aid. Most Americans know little about Mormon history and beliefs and I'm pretty sure many of them wish they knew even less.

The LDS content of the *Twilight* Saga, though, does help explain why people love these books because their more profound meaning reflects the hermetic foundation and borderline occult beliefs of Mormonism.

The four *Twilight* novels also conform to and confirm mainstream American beliefs about what constitutes an authentic spiritual life.

I hope you remember in the chapter on the anagogical layer of meaning in Part I of this book all that we discussed about the translucent meanings of the circle, alchemy, and mind as light and the unity of existent things. Given that most readers, especially critics, think of Mrs. Meyer, *qua* "Mormon Mom," as two steps down on the intellectual ladder from former Governor Sarah Palin, this profound stuff was no doubt hard for some to believe. "Where would she learn all *that*?" the skeptic asks.

The answer is straight forward and, frankly, almost undeniable. She gets it from her LDS faith. Mormonism is forged in the hermetic crucible of the Radical Reformation, its "endowments" were in large part lifted from Freemasonry rituals and adapted to sacramental needs, and it continues to be about a world-view that is psychic or "magical" rather than rational or empirical.[6]

If there is a single key to opening the lock that keeps us from understanding the popularity of Mrs. Meyer's books, I think it is the "shared mind" theme of the *Twilight* novels. This anagogical meaning that we discussed in the Conclusion to Part 1 derives from the Christian understanding of the uncreated *Logos* as the substance or "inner principle" of every created thing as well as "the light of men," i.e., their thinking and "inner heart." I explained how the Prologue to the Gospel of St. John was the basis of this relatively esoteric understanding of the interconnectedness of God, Man, and the world in mind.

It is possible that Mrs. Meyer gets this through English literature, as I'll explain in a second. The more obvious explanation, though, is that she learned it in Mormon Sunday School or at BYU. *Logos* epistemology and cosmology are something of a stretch for conventional Christians but not for Latter-day Saints. For Mormons, the idea that the universe is mental, as C. S. Lewis put it, and that "intelligence" is uncreated and eternal are essential teachings of their Prophet.

There is a lot more to Mormonism than *The Book of Mormon*. Most of the ideas discussed in these three chapters, for example, come from interpretation not of *The Book of Mormon* or Joseph Smith, Jr's

6 See *D. Michael Quinn, Early Mormonism and the Magic World View*, Signature Books, Salt Lake City, 1998, and John L. Brooke, *The Refiner's Fire: The Making of Mormon Cosmology, 1644-1844*, Cambridge University Press, New York, 1993.

other supposed translations from plates and texts but from his inspired prophecies, most of which are collected in the LDS *Doctrine and Covenants* (hereafter 'D&C'). In D&C Section 93, a "Revelation given through Joseph Smith the Prophet, at Kirtland, Ohio, May 6, 1833," Smith speaks in the name of both Jesus Christ and John the Evangelist largely reviewing the content of the Prologue of the Gospel of St. John. As John he says:

> 7 I saw his glory, that [the Lord] was in the beginning, before the world was;
>
> 8 Therefore, in the beginning the Word was, for he was the Word, even the messenger of salvation—
>
> 9 The light and the Redeemer of the world; the Spirit of truth, who came into the world, because the world was made by him, and in him was the life of men and the light of men.

Speaking as Christ, he explains that He was "the Firstborn" of God the Father, that man was "in the beginning" with Him in God, and that intelligence, "the light of truth," is also uncreated and a cause of "existence."

> 21 And now, verily I say unto you, I was in the beginning with the Father, and am the Firstborn;
>
> 22 And all those who are begotten through me are partakers of the glory of the same, and are the church of the Firstborn.
>
> 23 Ye were also in the beginning with the Father; that which is Spirit, even the Spirit of truth;
>
> 24 And truth is knowledge of things as they are, and as they were, and as they are to come....
>
> 29 Man was also in the beginning with God. **Intelligence, or the light of truth, was not created or made, neither indeed can be.**
>
> 30 All truth is independent in that sphere in which God has placed it, to act for itself, **as all intelligence also; otherwise there is no existence.**
>
> 31 Behold, here is the agency of man, and here is the condemnation of man; because that which was from the beginning is plainly manifest unto them, and they receive not the light.
>
> 32 And every man whose spirit receiveth not the light is under condemnation.
>
> 33 For man is spirit. The elements are eternal, and spirit and element, inseparably connected, receive a fulness of joy;

34 And when separated, man cannot receive a fulness of joy.

35 The elements are the tabernacle of God; yea, man is the tabernacle of God, even temples; and whatsoever temple is defiled, God shall destroy that temple.

36 **The glory of God is intelligence, or, in other words, light and truth.**[7]

This is a loaded passage that speaks plainly of Christ as a created being rather than a "begotten" Son of the Father, of a "pre-Creation spiritual existence" echoing "the hermetic cosmology,"[8] and of the centrality of human "agency" in the divine plan of salvation. What I want you note here, though, is just that Smith's esoteric ideas about intelligence echo with a Radical Reformation occult accent the Johannine and orthodox Christian teaching about the Word as continuous with if not identical to the fabric of existence and human conscience.

As Hyrum Smith, a member of the LDS Quorum of 12 Apostles, noted in his commentary on D&C Section 93, "Christ is the real genuine light that illuminates everyone born into the world. Whatever intelligence man possesses emanates from the Divine Source."[9] The Word, the "Firstborn" of God, is the common substance and cause of Mind and Existence.

Mrs. Meyer, LDS Sunday School teacher and BYU graduate, grew up hearing these ideas about human life being tied to uncreated, pre-existent "intelligence" as the foundation tenets that gave "free agency" and "knowledge" the importance they have in Mormon life. That her fictional characters – the Cullens and the Quileute wolfpack – who stand-in for the Celestial Church and for Salt Lake City's hierarchy both have a "shared mind" and that Bella "sees" every mind as a light and Edward's light as "the brightest of all" is little surprise; Mrs. Meyer's idealized romance plot points are drawn from the paranormal ideas of her faith.

I suspect, too, that the ideas she learned at the Ward Meetinghouse were "recognized," correctly or incorrectly, and confirmed in her reading English literature at the most Mormon of schools, Brigham Young University.

7 *Doctrines and Covenants*, Section 93, 7-9, 21-24, 29-36 (emphasis added)

8 John L. Brooke, *The Refiner's Fire*, Cambridge University Press, Cambridge, 1994, pp 28-29

9 Hyrum M. Smith and Janne M. Sjohdahl, *The Doctrine and Covenants with an Introduction and Historical and Exegetical Notes*, Deseret Book Company, Salt Lake City, 1971 (originally published 1915); page 588-589

Alchemical Drama

How could she see Smith's ideas about pre-existence intelligence as the cause of existence in English poems, plays, and novels? Mormonism is born in 16th and 17th century hermetic Christianity, but so is English literature, believe it or not. If the Western Canon is based in Shakespeare, as no less an authority than Harold Bloom (Shakespeare authority *and* fan of Joseph Smith, Jr.!) says he is, and Shakespeare is the alchemical dramatist and spring feeding the great stream of literary alchemy running from Elizabethan England to Hogwarts School of Witchcraft and Wizardry, it seems that much of the mythic function of literature is hermetic or Masonic.

And I think Mrs. Meyer understands this common source of her faith and the symbolism and power of better books, as hard as that may be to believe for those who think her necessarily dimwitted because she is a Mormon housewife. She was, after all, an English major at Brigham Young University, the Oxford *and* Mecca of LDS higher learning. In an environment that is "all Mormon, all the time" and the faculty must not only be Mormon but have current 'temple recommends,' I doubt very much that her Shakespeare courses – or any of her reading – was done without attention both to postmodern issues like 'misogyny' and to hermetic content that is echoed in Mormon core beliefs.

I'm hoping that doesn't seem a big leap to you. If it does, think about the Forks High School teacher's names. Mrs. Meyer seems to enjoy making the names do double duty; they serve as character markers so we know who we're talking about and as hints about their classroom or the sort of person they are. The gym teacher is named 'Clapp,' for instance, which is a vernacular term for venereal disease (if you haven't guessed, Mormons don't admire folks with VD and Mrs. Meyer and Bella hated gym class). The biology teacher is named 'Mr. Banner,' which is the name of the Marvel Comic book scientist who must control his passions carefully or he will morph into the mindless, rampaging 'Incredible Hulk.' That's a match with the struggle for control Edward has to exercise in that classroom as he sits next to Bella in *Twilight.*

My favorite teacher's name, though, is the English teacher: Mr. Mason. I think that name is a Meyer hat-tip to her experiences in BYU classrooms learning the hermetic and esoteric meanings of traditional English literature in Shakespeare, the Metaphysical poets, William Blake, Charles Dickens, Percy Shelley, S. T. Coleridge, George

MacDonald, W. B. Yeats, and the Inklings, among others. Her Mormon teachers as LDS believers no doubt emphasized the parallels between alchemical literature and the Masonic backdrops of Mormonism.

Mrs. Meyer's faith, then, answers the question, "Whence the profound stuff in these books?" but that is a different question than "Are Mrs. Meyer's Mormon beliefs why her books are so popular?" They are not directly responsible, of course, because the Church of Latter-day Saints has roughly the same appeal to millions of Americans as Scientology and the Unification Church (which is to say, "no appeal, whatsoever").

The esoteric content of Mrs. Meyer's books resonate with readers, what I presented as their allegorical and anagogical layers of meaning, not because they are Mormon per se, but because these ideas are either true or they echo the beliefs of our times.

I think a significant number of the esoteric translucencies and story transparencies that Mrs. Meyer borrows from her faith and the traditions of English literature work as well they do for the same reason they have worked for centuries. They reflect transcendent and transpersonal realities with which divine referents the "inner heart" of the reader identifies and longs for. The unity of existence in *logos* and our conscience, our communion with what is most real – love, life, peace – in the resolution of contraries, and the possibility of eternal life available to each person through sacrificial love aren't "LDS truth" or "Christian truth" or "New Age truth" but just "truth."

I suspect the high-ground *homo religiosius* argument-from-design is not as credible as the pitch that this kind of thinking is like our own and that's why we like it, so let's go that route as we did with postmodern morality (see Part 1, chapter 2). In brief, readers respond to hermetic fiction and literary alchemy because Americans are conditioned from birth to think of the world the way Englishmen of Shakespeare's day did.

Huh?

Remember Aristotle's dictum from *The Politics,* as true today as it ever was, that the polity fixes the architecture of the soul. Citizens of a monarchy think about and perceive the world, themselves, and their place in the world differently than those raised in a socialist country, democracy, or bicameral Republic. What is bizarre about American Constitutional government is that it reflects (a) the nostalgia for

Tudor and Elizabethan governance the Puritans felt, those democratic traditionalists who fled England in the early 17th Century, and (b) the non-conformist religious beliefs of the Radical Reformation, whose German, English, Dutch, and French adherents were persecuted in Europe of that time.

The Puritans, like Shakespearean Tudors, held that law was above government, an immutable 'Ancient Constitution' of checks and balances that restrained the centralization and abuse of power by any one faction. The Stuarts who expelled them were royal absolutists and they were supplanted eventually by Parliamentarians who made the King a gelding and took all the power – government over law and precedent – to themselves. The religious nonconformists, like the Puritans, saw the world as shadows of immutable truths, the inner light theology of the Quakers and the alchemical spirituality of the various Behmenist sects.

The government these European outcasts create in Philadelphia[10] in 1787, is a government that features fixed houses of contraries (the House of Representatives and Senate) whose legislative powers are fixed, checked, or overturned by a Judicial and an Executive wing. Nothing happens unless the contraries of the Legislative branch are resolved, the President doesn't veto it, and the Supreme Court says it is constitutional. All of this reflects the divine reality as understood by the Elizabethan hermeticists in which the Unmoved Mover presides over a world of non-dualist, complementary tendencies in obedience to Natural Law.

Constitutional scholars believe that the greatest obstacle to "effective" government in the United States is our devotion to the Elizabethan nostalgia of the Puritans and the nonconformist spirituality of the human refugee flotsam that settled in the American colonies in the 17th Century.[11] Our government is this way, and, so, as Aristotle says, we are that way. The only American traditions and conventions are anti-traditionalism and nonconformity, per our ancestors and the institutions they established.

10 Philadelphia, where Jasper meets up with Alice, incidentally, was named for one of those Radical Reformation English universalist and Christian mystic cults, this one led by John Pordage. The United States could not choose a more apt place to found its experiment in alchemical governance – and what a place for Jasper and Alice to meet their "resolution of contraries."

11 Daniel Lazare, *The Frozen Republic: How the Constitution is Paralyzing Democracy,* Harvest Books: New York, 1997, pages 11-35, See also Tillyard, *Elizabethan World Picture,* Vintage

Which, of course, is why writers like Joanne Rowling, Dan Brown, and Stephenie Meyer are all the best selling writers of the 21st century. The Potter and Swan novels have a Masonic universalism and literary alchemy as their scaffolding, and Brown uses them as the gist and guts of his potboiler anti-Papist plots. Americans are hard-wired by government, history, and our nonconformist conventions, secular and religious, to eat this stuff up.

Really, given our cultural predisposition for hermetic fantasy, I wonder why there aren't more standout writers like Orson Scott Card and Stephenie Meyer who are thoroughly LDS in their thinking.

What makes Mrs. Meyer's *Twilight* books rank with *The Da Vinci Code* and *Harry Potter* is probably the love-story angle of their spiritual allegory and alchemical symbolism. Frankly, the carnality of the Edward-Bella relationship, however restrained, is a great match with American spirituality.

Most Americans, sad to say probably all of us at various times, have anthropomorphic conceptions of God as a finite person, usually an old man with white robes, a long beard, and a nice place to sit in the clouds. It's a lot easier to picture and worship Father Time than the invisible center or Transcendent Absolute, right? Certainly, that most Americans are Christians and restrict their Christology to devotional adoration of the historical Jesus of Nazareth rather than the Word, Incarnate and as Creative Principle, predisposes us to a kind of spiritual materialism.

Just being materialists, of course, also pushes us in that direction. Most immigrants to America in the 19th and 20th centuries were not political or religious refugees but those folks with more mundane, economic hopes. Our conceptions of God, not too surprisingly, then, tend to the finite, personal God rather than the metaphysical.

Twilight's God and Man love-story, rewritten with Vampire and Girlfriend stand-ins, is a natural match with our theological conceptions, especially because the love between Edward and Bella is not conceptual, however chaste it is for the most part, but erotic and, eventually, sexual. Sex is America's religion, to which all other faiths are only shadows.

Malcolm Muggeridge said it best. "Sex is the mysticism of materialism and the only possible religion in a materialistic society."[12] That may sound positively Puritanical but it is logical. If the human

12 Also, along these lines: "Sex is the ersatz or substitute religion of the 20th Century" and "The orgasm has replaced the cross as the focus of longing and fulfillment."

person is only a physical body, whose mind is only a biochemical reaction in the brain with no independent existence and whose soul, like everything immaterial, is delusion, then the only way to transcend the self and experience freedom from ego and some hint of eternity or a greater reality is physically and in physical congress especially. Making "the beast with two backs" to the materialist is the height of selfless love because it is the physical equivalent of selflessness or transcendence.

All traditional religions, of course, see this very differently. They understand the human person as a psychosomatic unity, in which the immaterial aspect of the person, the soul, is prior to and greater than the physical body, the person's material and visible aspect. The soul has this priority in the soul-body unity called "flesh" in Christian scripture because it opens up to the much greater reality, the Spirit, in the person's 'inner heart.' The spiritually mature person, contra the materialist, then, is the person *least* focused on sex; the celibate monastic in every orthodox tradition is the model of sanctity.

In most American conventional church life and especially in Mormonism, however, marriage is the only authentic religious vocation (Catholic priests and nuns would be the exception, if, sadly, priests are misrepresented, as often as not, as being sexually repressed or perverted for their abstinence). To those legions among us who are "spiritual but not religious," sexual license, that is, freedom from all restraint not bondage, is something of a sacrament.

Traditional faith disciplines the soul-body flesh to give it the necessary orientation to commune with the Spirit; materialist faith is flesh-friendly because it believes the physical person is more real as a measurable quantity of mass and energy than the non-material realms. The psychic and the spiritual, the magical and the truly transcendent, are categories without distinction to the materialist because these realms are both essentially immaterial and, consequently, relatively unreal. Sex rules, consequently, and supplants authentic spirituality.

American Christianity in this flesh-friendly tide has morphed into something that has been aptly labeled as 'Moralistic Therapeutic Deism,' in which feel-good faux-faith believers hold that:

1. "A god exists who created and ordered the world and watches over human life on earth."
2. "God wants people to be good, nice, and fair to each other, as taught in the Bible and by most world religions."

3. "The central goal of life is to be happy and to feel good about oneself."
4. "God does not need to be particularly involved in one's life except when God is needed to resolve a problem."
5. "Good people go to heaven when they die."[13]

Number three on that list trumps all the others. "Happiness" as in self-satisfaction rather than blessedness or sanctity, is the new human *telos* or *summum bonum.*

Twilight's God-Man relationship allegory played out as a love story with a "perfect" male lead and a devoted girlfriend resonates with the tenets of sexual spirituality a la Muggeridge and with Moralistic Therapeutic Deism (MTD), the *de facto* American faith. Mormonism, while anything but MTD, with its finite gods and focus on marriage and reproduction, is why Mrs. Meyer is able to write this *Harlequin* Song of Songs so compellingly and why it is the match it is with American readers.

From looking at Mormonism to see what we could learn about the popularity of the four *Twilight* novels, we've learned a bunch. Putting Mrs. Meyer's faith up on the viewer and then thinking about *Twilight* has revealed:

- The backdrop of ideas giving her story its end-game context and meaning: they're about pursuing and gaining immortality through selfless devotion to God;
- The explanation of how the story is a response on several levels to the Mountain Meadows Massacre book glut in 2003 and the attendant controversy;
- How much the novels are "Mary Sue" efforts and therapeutic exercise of author to defend and critique LDS in Romance wish fulfillment; and
- Hermetic sexuality which is a match with American conceptions about reality, spirituality, and sex, and, consequently, a cause of the books' anagogical power.

What I've learned that really strikes me is that the *Twilight Saga* is really two books written for different audiences. Mrs. Meyer wrote the

13 R. Albert Mohler, Jr., 'Moralistic Therapeutic Deism – the New American Religion,' *Christian Post*, Mon, Apr. 18 2005; http://www.christianpost.com/article/20050418/moralistic-therapeutic-deism-the-new-american-religion/index.html

first book and sketched the fourth when she and her sister were the only readers, so we know the series is primarily for Mormon women. The second books are these same novels as they are experienced by gentile readers, male and female, old and young, all of whom are for the most part clueless about the LDS content.

I find this fascinating because I never would have thought that a first effort novel, usually insufferably therapeutic via a story character acting as proxy for the author's wish fulfillment fantasies, and a rookie book by a Mormon at that, could resonate so profoundly with readers of very different beliefs. I think, after doing even this short review of the Mormon story inside *Twilight,* that the success of books can be found in the much greater overlap between American de facto, individualist, 'sexual spirituality' and Mormon faith in a God "who was as Man now is" and remains human, if Master of this uncreated universe.

As the United States, more than any other country, is a nation of nonconformist individuals grown from same spiritual foundation as Mormonism, i.e., the 16th and 17th century Christian sects of the Radical Reformation, I cannot marvel that there is great overlap in conventional American ideas about God (e.g., MTD, atheism, etc.) and Mormonism. They have hermetic and sexual ideas at their core.

There is a division between traditional or orthodox revealed faiths and both MTD and Mormonism in their understanding of the Person of Christ, what Frithjof Schuon calls the "Relative Absolute" or "Personal God." Orthodox Christians know Christ as a transcendent Hypostasis, the *Logos* incarnation, as well as the historical Nazarene. Mormons, and even many believers from other denominations, think of Christ devotionally as merely Jesus the 'divine guy.' The difference is profound because in Mormonism we have the elision of the properly distinct psychic and spiritual realms, the magical with the completely other. This confusion fosters a flesh friendly faith, a sexual spirituality, rather than a true divinization or theosis.

I think it is the Mormon content of the *Twilight* novels, from the Masonic symbols and alchemy to the natural theology of mind, that explains why we love these books. They reflect both metaphysical truths and the world as our Founding Fathers designed that we would see and know it. The Bella-Edward love story works as an allegorical and Pelagian retelling of the Garden of Eden morality play because it is a spiritual tale told in the language of physical love, the "mysticism of materialists." We've come a long way from the allegory of Spencer and Bunyan in this Mormon *Pilgrim's Progress* and love story, that's for sure, if the content is just as religious.

Spotlight, as I wrote in the introduction, is two books corresponding to the experiences readers have. The first part, the chapters on iconological meaning's four layers, is about the experience *everyone* has in Forks. The second part is about what Mrs. Meyer wrote for herself when she had no thought of publishing it for anyone that was not her sister, another Mormon stay-at-home mom. The whole book, both parts, has been about getting at the artistry and meaning of Bella's adventures to figure out why they are as popular as they are.

Having done that heavy lifting, let's take a quick look in The Chapter of Tens at books to read and ideas to ponder that will help us understand better the artistry and meaning of the *Twilight* Saga.

Chapter 8

Twilight Chapter of Tens

Everything That Wouldn't Fit in the Other Parts of This Book

If you're not living on the moon, odds are good that you have one or more volumes in the "For Dummies" series of books published by Wiley. I've got a couple of the rival "For Idiots" how-to guides, but I own a whole shelf of the yellow and black "For Dummies" helpers and it's a rare day I don't reach for one, for some help with chess or MicroSoft PowerPoint or personal finance. I even bought the *Mormonism For Dummies* title when I started researching this book. [1]

My favorite part of these *Dummies* books – and the reason I think I own so many of them – is the closing section in each: "The Part of Tens." Here, no matter what the subject, the Guru who has written the book lays out several lists of ten items that are usually very funny and, at the same time, some of the most helpful and interesting stuff in these information-filled tomes. My bet is this section is where the Subject Matter Expert throws everything he or she wanted to say that didn't fit into the neat outline the editors sent him or her.

Now that I'm at the end of *Spotlight* and have started the conversation about the artistry and meaning that drives *Twilight*-mania, I'm in a bit of a bind. There's a lot more that I want to say but I'm out of room.

For example, I haven't said anything about the meaning of Jacob's first name with respect to the Biblical Patriarch and *The Book of Mormon* hero with the same moniker. I haven't discussed what it means that the series' Joseph Smith, Jr., stand-in has doubts not only about his salvation

1 It was written by Latter-day Saints, so the book's discussions were even-handed as I had hoped, but they were also pasteurized, "milk before meat," as I had feared.

but even that he has a soul. And what about how the LDS doctrine of "Eternal Progression" and how it is reflected in the story line confirm postmodern secular millenialist beliefs? Where does that stuff go?

Well, as I really only had room for the iconological "first look" at the books and for the interpretation of Mrs. Meyer's Mormon Midsummer Night's Dream in *Spotlight,* it has to go somewhere else. The best place for you to find it will be at my *Twilight* weblogs, TwilightSpotlight.com and Forks High School Professor (FHSProfessor.com), where I post my latest thinking on this subject. I hope you will join the conversation amongst serious readers there about what the books mean as well as "current events" in *Twilight* fandom (interviews with the author, *Midnight Sun,* etc.).

I'm also beginning two other *Twilight* book projects: *Bella Swan's Bookshelf,* a survey of the most important books to read to understand the literary underpinnings of the series, and a set of books called *Edward and Bella's Library,* actual editions of classic novels and plays Mrs. Meyer says influenced her artistry with *Twilight*-focused introductions and annotations in each book.

Right now, though, I have a bunch of notes I want to share in order to introduce some of the topics we'll be discussing in those books and on my weblogs. I'm going to do this in the format of the "For Dummies" manuals' closing 'Part of Tens.' Here are five quick sets of ten items each to jump start conversations and whet your appetite for more *Twilight* talk:

Ten Stories That Will Help You Understand *Twilight*'s Artistry and Meaning

I think in journalism school the students are given a notebook during Freshman orientation or at graduation in which binders are "cheat sheets" for interviews with different types of people at certain moments. If true, as I suspect it must be, this is why the winning quarterback of the Super Bowl, Rose Bowl, or local high school team is always asked "how it feels to win the championship" and why the politician who has lost is asked what his or her plans are now that the "voters have spoken."

And every bestselling author is asked what book inspired their blockbuster novel and "Who is your favorite writer?" These are natural questions, certainly, but there has to be some kind of background plot or

J-School handout for the same questions to be asked at every interview, even years after the answers are on the author's Wikipedia page.

Mrs. Meyer has been especially generous in answering questions about the influences and "Greats" that inspired her *Twilight* Saga. Let's look at ten books and plays that she has mentioned or which are embedded into the series or which I think are helpful in "getting" what Mrs. Meyer is telling her readers.

1. **Pride and Prejudice:** "I read Pride and Prejudice, Jane Eyre, Rebecca, and the Anne of Green Gables series all over and over again throughout my formative years."[2] In the Little, Brown publicity interview released with *Breaking Dawn* in 2008, Mrs. Meyer said *Twilight* was "loosely based" on the Austen novel.[3] Jane Austen is in her pantheon of "favorite authors" with Shakespeare and Orson Scott Card. Loosely based is right; the obvious connection is that both feature a handsome lead that seems out of reach to the female protagonist. While *Twilight* and *Pride and Prejudice* are not related the way *New Moon* and *Romeo and Juliet* are or as *Eclipse* is to *Wuthering Heights*, the author's affection for the book is reason enough to revisit the Austen classic.

2. **Jane Eyre:** "I read it when I was nine," says Meyer, "and I've reread it literally hundreds of times. I do think that there are elements of Edward in Edward Rochester and elements of Bella in Jane. Jane was someone I was close to as a child – we were good friends! I think in some ways she was more real to me than any other fictional heroine."[4] The classic 'Mary Sue' dream coming-of-age story for women, *Jane Eyre* is essential reading for *Twilight* lovers.

3. **Romeo and Juliet:** In the *Breaking Dawn* Little, Brown interview, Mrs. Meyer says that *New Moon* is largely built on the story scaffolding of *Romeo and Juliet*.[5] Bella says as much in that book, in which she and Edward watch the film version

2 'A December 2005 interview with Stephenie Meyer, author of *Twilight*.' http://www.yabookscentral.com/cfusion/index.cfm?fuseAction=authors.interview&interview_id=81

3 http://www.youtube.com/watch?v=UVEvEtF08S8&feature=player_embedded

4 Karen Valby, 'Stephenie Meyer: 12 of My 'Twilight' Inspirations,' Entertainment Weekly, September 28, 2009 http://www.ew.com/ew/gallery/0,,20308569_20308554,00.html

5 http://www.youtube.com/watch?v=UVEvEtF08S8&feature=player_embedded

and the play is mentioned repeatedly and discussed at length. Sure enough, the Cullens and Quileutes are set up as Capulet and Montague contraries and Edward and Jacob become the alchemical "quarreling couple" (think Mercutio and Tybalt) in addition to the evident Romeo and Paris parallels. *Romeo and Juliet* is must reading for understanding the finish in *Breaking Dawn* as well as *New Moon.*

4. **Wuthering Heights:** The Bronte Gothic classic is used in *Eclipse* in much the same way as *Romeo and Juliet* is in *New Moon,* which is to say, as story scaffolding. In this retelling, though, Edward recognizes the Edgar Linton and Heathcliff parts he is given and decides not to make the mistakes that they do. The third book in the Saga takes on an entirely different depth and meaning when Edward's struggle with Jacob and with his own pride is read as a recast *Heights.*

5. **Midsummer Night's Dream:** The resolution of the Jacob-Edward-Bella love triangle in Jacob's imprinting on Renesmee parallels the magical end of the Demetrius -Lysander-Hermia trio in Demetrius' enchantment with Helena. The intersection of magic and the paranormal as a given in a romance also makes this Shakespeare classic a "must re-visit" item for serious *Twilight* readers.

6. **Merchant of Venice:** Mrs. Meyer held out that there was a "second book" that influenced *Breaking Dawn* beyond *Dream,* which was revealed both in text (Alice hides her note to Bella in her copy of *Merchant of Venice*) and at her web site post-publication. "I put a clue into the manuscript as well. Alice tore a page from *The Merchant of Venice* because the end of *Breaking Dawn* was going to be somewhat similar: bloodshed appears inevitable, doom approaches, and then the power is reversed and the game is won by some clever verbal strategies; no blood is shed, and the romantic pairings all have a happily ever after."[6] The alchemical content of *Merchant's* finish is also a very big part of this play's importance in understanding Mrs. Meyer's series finale.

7. **Anne of Green Gables:** "The series influenced how my series turned out. Because I was never a fan of the stories where

6 http://www.stepheniemeyer.com/bd_faq.html

everything ends and they kiss at the wedding. *Anne of Green Gables* started out with her as a child, she had a very fully described adolescence, she had a book-long engagement, we got to see her wedding, we got to see her have her first child and lose her first child, we got to see her children grow up. We got the whole life, and I loved that."[7] Bella can be understood as a Catherine Linton/Jane Eyre/ Anne Shirley genetic cross. For wish fulfillment, 'Mary Sue' reading, try *Anne's House of Dreams.*

8. **Speaker for the Dead:** Mrs. Meyer says the book "with the most significant impact on her life as a writer" [8] is Orson Scott Card's *Speaker for the Dead.* It is the second novel in Mr. Scott Card's *Ender's Game* series but it was the inspiration and heart of the award winning *Ender's* books. Serious *Twilight* readers will recognize that the Speaker is a Joseph Smith, Jr., stand-in, that he struggles with the Catholic church and its hold on the mind of the local population, and the Piggies receive a restored gospel in the Speaker's speech that explains their pre-mortal, mortal, and after-life – all wrapped up in a "wow" science fiction adventure and setting. Did I mention the philotics-ansible connection (the shared-mind communication-device of the *Enders* books) with LDS beliefs about "intelligence"? Really, *Speaker* is a template for brilliant postmodern Mormon fiction – and Mrs. Meyer ran with it.

9. **Rebecca:** Mrs. Meyer says du Maurier's classic thriller comes "in as a close second" to *Speaker for the Dead* as the book most influencing her as a writer. The incredible match of Maximilian de Winter and the unnamed narrator, the wealthy lord of Manderley with a young woman who is an American woman's private servant may be the most obvious parallel with the unbelievable Edward-Bella match of all the books she has mentioned. Though Bella is much friendlier a narrator than is

7 Karen Valby, op.cit; http://www.ew.com/ew/gallery/0,,20308569_20308554_2,00.html

8 10 Second Interview: A Few Words with Stephenie Meyer http://www.librarything.com/work/8384326/descriptions/ **Q:** What book has had the most significant impact on your life? **A:** The book with the most significant impact on my life is *The Book of Mormon.* The book with the most significant impact on my life as a writer is probably *Speaker for the Dead,* by Orson Scott Card, with *Rebecca* by Daphne du Maurier coming in as a close second.

the anonymous Mrs. De Winter in *Rebecca*, du Maurier revealed the potential power of a first person speaker in an unlikely Romance, which lesson Mrs. Meyer learned very well.

10. **A Woman of Destiny:** As my list ender, I'll go off the board of Mrs. Meyer's choices for another title from her favorite living writer, Orson Scott Card. *A Woman of Destiny*, also known as *Saints*, is a Romance featuring, incredibly, the polygamous marriage between a brilliant English poetess (an English stand-in for the historical Eliza Snow) and Joseph Smith, Jr. As a work serving as an apology-in-fiction for the infamous past of his church, *A Woman of Destiny*, because of Scott Card's great story telling and remarkable handling of facts contrary to his thesis, is a wonder and certainly a model for *Twilight*'s LDS allegory.

Also-ran books just missing this List of Ten: Bram Stoker's *Dracula*, Joanne Rowling's *Harry Potter*, and any Harlequin serial boy-meets-girl formula love story.

Ten Non-fiction Topics and Writers You'll want to Know More About

The books on the fiction list above, the substantive gut of my 'Bella Swan's Bookshelf' work-in-progress, are my answer to the frequently asked question, "What can I read that I will like the way I like *Twilight*?" I'm not sure these recommendations are an especially honest answer to that question – *Wuthering Heights* is a far cry in mood, difficulty, and meaning, for example, from any of the *Twilight* books and I wonder if there are many Bella Boosters who will like Catherine – but I know reading any or all of them will give that reader a greater appreciation of Mrs. Meyer's artistry and meaning.

Two questions I am asked at lectures that amount to the same thing are "What can I read to help me learn how to read at a greater depth of understanding?" and "How did you learn to read this way?" I don't think this is a request for book titles like *How to Read Literature Like a Professor* as much as it is for the non-fiction books, or, better, the *categories* of reference books that I used in writing *Spotlight*. (See the bibliography for information about the titles on all these Lists of Ten.)

Here are the Top Ten subjects and writers I recommend to anyone wanting to get into *Twilight's* heart:

1. **Literary Criticism:** The Big Three authors I recommend to those wanting to read books at a level beyond "I know what I like" without subjecting themselves to the demeaning work of deconstruction are Northrop Frye, Wayne Booth, and John Ruskin. I've cited Frye's *Anatomy of Criticism* throughout this book, Booth's *Rhetoric of Fiction* is as valuable, and John Ruskin, the last great iconological critic who did the "deep, slow mining" for meaning in books, just as did when interpreting paintings. And there are my books on Harry Potter, too, of course.
2. **Mircea Eliade:** The big question I have tried to answer in this book is "Why are the *Twilight* novels so popular?" and the answer I have given is an expansion of Eliade's thesis that fiction serves a religious function in a secular culture (therefore it is a book's mythic content and its resonance with readers that is the cause or at least gauge for its popularity). Eliade's *The Sacred and the Profane* and *Myth of the Eternal Return* are invaluable works for reflection on what it means to be human and what place story plays in our becoming more human.
3. **Titus Burckhardt:** Understanding alchemy as something more than "stupid chemistry" or "New Age sophistry" is key, I think, in understanding the magic of literature and how reading transforms the human person through anagogical artistry. Burckhardt's *Mirror of Intellect* and *Alchemy* are the best guides for that.
4. **The Traditionalist School:** Burckhardt was a student of Rene Guenon and Frithjof Schuon, both Sufi Sheiks and giants of the Perennialist or Traditionalist school of thought. To grasp the idea of a Creative Principle and what constitutes an authentic revelation and spiritual tradition, books by these men are without equal. I recommend especially:
    - Schuon's *Transcendent Unity of Religions* explains cogently the idea of the Creative Principle:
    - Charles Upton's *The System of the Anti-Christ: Truth and Falsehood in Postmodernism and the New Age* as well as his *Shadow of the Rose: The Esoterism of the Romantic Tradition* detail our age's confusion of psychic and spiritual realities and the role of Romantic literature in the spiritual life;

- Marco Pallis' *The Way and the Mountain* spells out the five measures of what constitutes an authentic revelation and spiritual tradition; and
- James Cutsinger's *Advice for the Serious Seeker* is a road map to escape the materialist and relativist mind-traps of this historical period; *The Form of the Transformed Vision: Coleridge and the Knowledge of God* is the best introduction to Coleridge I have found and the natural theology that informs the English literary tradition.

5. **Mormonism Essentials from the Church of Latter-day Saints:** I urge readers to learn about what constitutes authentic faith because without that understanding it is difficult to understand Mormonism (or any faith) with anything like objectivity. In learning about Mormonism – again, as with study of any revealed faith – it is best to go to the believers first rather than their critics or to look for academic treatment. Mrs. Meyer says *The Book of Mormon* had "the most significant impact on my life" [9] and that is evident everywhere in her books. (If you want to know, for example, where she came up with Denali Kate's electroshock therapy coming out of her hand, check out 1 Nephi 17:53.)[10] I urge you, too, to read a sympathetic book about the Mormon Prophet, Joseph Smith, Jr., before those biographies that take it as a given that he was deluded, a con man, or a "pious fraud." Richard Lyman Bushman's *Rough Stone Rolling* is far and away the best book I found of this type.

6. **Introduction to Mormonism:** Then you'll need something of an overview of the "Mormon Studies" subject just to get a grip on the specific language and categories of doctrines with which you need to familiarize yourself. I found *Mormonism for Dummies* useful here because it was written by Mormons, one an adult convert, both of whom have studied religions other than their own. It had an unfortunate quality of "progressive truth" and neglecting hard teachings and painful facts. Andrew Jackson's *Mormonism Explained* leans in the opposite direction,

---

9 10 Second Interview: A Few Words with Stephenie Meyer http://www.librarything.com/work/8384326/descriptions/

10 "And it came to pass that the Lord said unto me: Stretch forth thine hand again unto thy brethren, and they shall not wither before thee, but I will shock them saith the Lord, and this will I do, that they may know that I am the Lord their God."

if he does go to some pains to be as charitable as possible in describing beliefs he does not share.

7. **Critical Histories:** Carlisle Cullen's birth and chrysalis in the seventeenth century mean to me at least that Mrs. Meyer is familiar with the growing consensus that the birth of Mormon theology is not exclusively in the translations and prophecies of Joseph Smith, Jr. John Brooke's *Refiner's Fire*, D. Michael Quinn's *Early Mormonism and the Magic World View*, Godwin's *Theosophical Enlightenment*, and Dan Vogel's *Religious Seekers and the Advent of Mormonism*, in setting the hermetic and nonconformist religious beliefs of Smith's time in the context of Radical Reformation ideas of Carlisle Cullen's London, open up Mrs. Meyer's hermetic artistry and meaning via her LDS beliefs. I also recommend Richard Anderson's *The Mind of Joseph Smith* and Dan Vogel's *The Making of a Prophet* for alternative views of Joseph Smith, Jr.

8. **The Mountain Meadows Massacre:** Mrs. Meyer had her inspiring dream in June of 2003 when the reading public was caught in an avalanche of titles about the 1857 Mountain Meadows Massacre. Those books were Sally Denton's. *American Massacre: The Tragedy at Mountain Meadows, September 1857*, John Krakauer's *Under the Banner of Heaven: A Story of Violent Faith*, and Will Bagley's. *Blood of the Prophets: Brigham Young and the Massacre at Mountain Meadows*. Of these, Krakauer's is probably the most important because it was excerpted in the *New York Times Sunday Magazine* before publication and had the most pronounced marketing effort. Juanita Brooks' *The Mountain Meadows Massacre*, originally published in 1950, remains an essential reference work and *Massacre at Mountain Meadows* by LDS historians Ronald W. Walker, Richard E. Turley, and Glen M. Leonard is the only book whose authors were given access to Church archived records on the subject. Sadly, this exclusive ability to see documents diminishes rather than augments the authority with which LDS historians write.

9. **Mormon Women:** *Twilight* was originally conceived by a Mormon woman for an audience of Mormon women: Mrs. Meyer for herself and her sister. It's best to know what life is like, then, for LDS women and what they believe and do. Dorothy Allred Solomon's *The Sisterhood: Inside the Lives of Mormon*

Women was very helpful in this regard; Deborah Laake's *Secret Ceremonies: A Mormon Woman's Intimate Diary of Marriage and Beyond* provided the perspective of a woman, having left the church, who views it through a less forgiving lens.

10. **Orthodox Christianity:** Mormon scholars believe that LDS faith is the "restoration" of ancient Christianity and assert that shadows and reflections of the truths revealed by Joseph Smith, Jr., are evident in the ancient Christian faith of the early Church fathers. I recommend that readers wanting to understand why Eastern Orthodox Christians find this view so bizarre read an introduction to Orthodox faith such as Kallistos Ware's *The Orthodox Church* or John Romanides' *Patristic Theology.* A compare and contrast reading of *The Book of Mormon* or any other LDS prophetic statement with the Orthodox Church's *Philokalia,* especially the writings of Maximos the Confessor, or *The Evergetinos* suggests that Smith's "restoration" was instead a remarkable, tragic departure from the Church born at Pentecost.

Ten Things the Critics Got Wrong About *Twilight*

I first became interested in *Twilight,* when after reading and enjoying the first book in the series despite myself, I learned that the author was being dismissed by critics with the venom academics and media elites reserve for the likes of former Governor Sarah Palin. I just didn't get that – and still don't. The woman's books have sold 70 million copies at last count; shouldn't we be asking, as Lev Grossman suggested in *The Wall Street Journal,* what she is doing *right*?

Here is a quick survey of what the critics got wrong:[11]

1. **"Stephenie Meyer is a Hack Writer"** She is one of those hacks who engages the imaginations of millions and hooks them so profoundly into the lives of their characters that they create web sites to discuss plot points, travel across time zones for fan conferences, and go to book stores at midnight when books are published. She also has put together a seamless genre mélange that works on the four levels of meaning, especially the anagogical. But the lack of anything like magisterial prose and the choice of Romance fiction as her core genre means Mrs.

11 A much longer discussion can be read at Forks High School Professor: http://fhsprofessor.com/?p=7

Meyer is a hack. Gotcha.

2. **"*Twilight* readers are all tweenie girls"** For the first time in publishing history, the category of pubescent women is setting sales records in online and bricks-and-mortar stores, records for both number of books and duration on best seller lists. Who knew that 10-13 year old girls bought so many books from Amazon or had such a fever for books 500, 600, and more than 700 pages long? Forgive me this sarcasm. While I mean no disrespect to young women, the dismissal of *Twilight* as a teen girl fad is meant as disrespect by critics to the author, her books, and her readers. This audience obviously includes old and young, men and women, to have generated 70 million sales. Ask a librarian who is reading *Twilight* and he or she will tell you "Everyone." This tween meme doesn't pass the smell test or any logical inspection.
3. **"*Twilight* is a vampire novel"** No one who has read the first book and who is even remotely familiar with vampire canon can say this with a straight face. It's anti-vampire canon in almost every respect, which canon it intentionally sets up as a myth and whose heroes are the most anti-vampire vampires in the novels. The author has said repeatedly that her books are "vampire novels for people who don't like vampire novels." Because they're not vampire novels? I think so.
4. **"The apple on the first book's cover is meaningless"** And so, then, is the epigraph from *Genesis* on the Tree of Knowledge of Good and Evil, Bella's referring to herself as "Eve" when first meeting Edward in the biology classroom, and her choosing an apple from his tray of food in the cafeteria. The book is an Everyman allegory of the Man-God love story, a story of a seeker's love relationship with God and her transformation and apotheosis consequent to this love. The apple on the cover is anything but meaningless.
5. **"The author's faith plays little role in her work"** Making her the first author in history, male or female, whose beliefs (or lack of beliefs) were not the source of her story's substance. The book is about human transformation, but her LDS beliefs about what makes transformation of this sort possible and what it looks like play little role in how she presents this? The assertion

is *prima facie* risible and I can only hope at this point that the discussions in *Spotlight's* chapters 5, 6, and 7 have demonstrated how important her faith is in understanding *Twilight's* artistry and meaning.

6. **"The *Twilight* books are too popular, too current, and too juvenile to be taken seriously"** These are the three 'Deathly Hallows' of academic, literary canon according to Potterphile James Thomas of Pepperdine. As these books, along with Joanne Rowling's *Harry Potter* novels, are the "shared texts" of our generation, the works shaping the imagination and hearts of most readers to one degree or another, these arbitrary standards for what books are to be taken seriously are hard to take seriously. If anything, the appeal of the books to younger readers, their currency, and their unprecedented sales make them more deserving of study, not less.

7. **"The books are best understood as cultural artifacts"** Reading Mrs. Meyer's books as transparencies not of historical or supernatural referents but of sociological or economic meaning (via Marxist, feminist, and deconstructive exegesis) is to skip over why the books appeal to readers. Worse, it explains why they are popular because of readers' politically incorrect or immature understanding, even their sexist, racist and class driven beliefs. This neglects Eliade's thesis in favor of a bizarre, alternate understanding of why people read, say, that the herd reads in order to confirm their moral, political, and social misconceptions. Is that why you read? Me neither.

8. **"The series was ill-conceived and executed"** Mrs. Meyer did not plan these books beginning to end before putting pen to paper (or fingers to keyboard) and the fact that it was conceived as a single novel rather than a series shows in spots, especially the first book. But her artistry in setting up the alchemical finish in *Breaking Dawn* through the second and third books' retelling of *Romeo and Juliet* and *Wuthering Heights* was very well done. Forgive me for thinking those that sneer at Mrs. Meyer's books have missed the genius and evident power in the writing because of the simplicity of the text's language. Her devoted fans see it, though, and are delighted by the experience they have in Mrs. Meyer's books.

9. **"There is nothing in these books that is original; they're derivative."** I'm trying to think of a truly original writer, whose work cannot be understood as an extension or echo of the literature of the age. All I've come up with is "Homer." What have you got? This derivative dismissal is a throwaway criticism, by which I mean it is thrown out to say "I don't like it" and without a thought of arguing the point – and deserves to be thrown away, i.e., into the garbage, for being vacuous. C. S. Lewis wrote about Milton's "good unoriginality" and certainly the greater part of writing well is not "breaking new ground" but rich adaptation and re-invention.[12]

10. **"*Twilight*-mania is a media and marketing driven fad"** Right. So, if manias for over-sized books can be generated by particularly savvy advertising and publicity, why do we have to wait so long for these hysterias for fiction to come along? I would think that the book industry, on its last legs by some reports, would generate midnight release crazes at least once a month if that possibility were a matter of investing in Madison Avenue magic. They haven't: therefore we can feel certain that we'll find the cause of the magic between the covers of the books.

Ten Correspondences Between *Twilight* and *Harry Potter*

If I'm known for anything I've done by any number of people greater than the children in my family, it's for writing books about Joanne Rowling's *Harry Potter* novels. (Go to the Wikipedia page for details, right?) When I talk, consequently, either at *Twilight* fan events or at Potter conventions, I am asked about the other series and if I think they have anything in common beyond stratospheric popularity and sales.

They do. Here are a quick 'Ten Points of Correspondence:'

1. **Mary Sue novel:** Both Ms. Rowling and Mrs. Meyer were first time authors when they launched their respective series and it shows. Their heroes are story proxies to greater or lesser degrees in which they act out their various dreams and psychological issues in "fantasy conquests" and "fact inversion." To their credit,

---

12 See *Preface to Paradise Lost* (Atlantic Publishing, 2006), page 55, as well as his "Even in literature and art, no man who bothers about originality will ever be original: whereas if you simply try to tell the truth (without caring twopence how often it has been told before) you will, nine times out of ten, become original without ever having noticed it."

they do this in such a way that millions of people join them in this cathartic adventure and the reading public experiences some measure of imaginative chrysalis and transformation.

2. **Genre melange with specific core or axis:** Harry Potter's adventures and Bella Swan's transformation are literary boundary busters in being a constellation or an amalgam of disparate categories of writing shaped around a core story type. Ms. Rowling builds her story structure around the School Boy novel tradition which she alters with a heavily Gothic setting and alchemical narrative structure. Mrs. Meyer chooses Young Adult Romance and mixes in International Blockbuster plot points and her own version of alchemy – which brings us to the next point…

3. **Alchemical scaffolding:** The Hogwarts Saga ends with three novels that are a black, white, and red book in sequence, and whose finale features an Alchemical Wedding of the Red King and White Queen, the birth of the Philosophical Orphan, and the resolution of critical contraries. The *Twilight* Saga's last three books, too, are a *nigredo New Moon* featuring Jacob Black, an *albedo* in *Eclipse* featuring albino Edward's return and Bella's preparation for her transformation, and the *rubedo* finale in *Dawn* with Wedding, Androgen baby, and Resolution. These authors swim in the same hermetic literary stream.

4. **Romance – Hero's Journey:** Harry's books follow a fairly strict ten point story formula dictated to some degree by the school year but featuring elements like "journey underground," "figurative death," and "resurrection in the presence of a symbol of Christ." Bella's adventures are nowhere near as formulaic but they do include a story circle in which she makes an out-and-back trip and returns transformed in keeping with monomyth parameters. Harry and Bella also mix in sacrificial love and death for loved ones to give their hero's journeys a distinctly Christian taste, echoing Calvary.

5. **Romance – Love-story inspired fandom:** Harry Potter fandom for the greater part of its pre-*Deathly Hallows* decade was consumed by the so called 'Shipping Wars. Who did Hermione love – Ron or Harry? This question overshadowed all other discussion online and at fan meetings; one was obliged to declare sides or neutrality. Pretty weird for a Schoolboy novel.

Twihards had a similar division, which made a lot more sense in a love story, about whether Jacob or Edward was better for Bella.

6. **Fandom template:** *Twilight* mania began picking up steam in earnest when Potter-mania was reaching its peak because of the almost simultaneous release of the fifth movie and the last Hogwarts novel. Readers falling in love with Edward, Jacob, and Bella created a fandom using the off-the-shelf model of Harry-Ron-and Hermione's fervent followers. Overnight, it seemed, there was a *Twilight*-Lexicon, a host of 'shipping debate sites, fan fiction with a Slash sub-category, and professionally produced fan meet-ups. It took the better part of a decade for 'Wizard Rock or 'Wrock' to catch on; Bella Bands were big almost immediately.

7. **Critical response despising core genre:** Ms. Rowling and Mrs. Meyer were savaged by serious critics largely because academics retch on the axis story around which these authors build their constellation of genre types. UK critics like Anthony Holden and America's Harold Bloom believe the Schoolboy novel is irreconcilable with literature of value and merit – so Harry's adventures, inevitably, were dissed as "slop." Mrs. Meyer's choice of Young Adult Romance, of course, made Harry seem like Nabokov.

8. **Great Books backdrop:** Mrs. Meyer embeds great books in her stories in addition to using thematic and symbolic scaffolding from traditions like alchemy and monomyth (see the first List of Ten in this chapter). Ms. Rowling is a bit more subtle than to have her characters reading the books of her favorite authors which texts she is rewriting with those characters playing parts – but you can read all about the ten types of stories and the specific 'Greats' she uses as models in *Harry Potter's Bookshelf* (Penguin/Berkley, 2009).

9. **Postmodern morality:** They're both writers living in the 21st century, so it is all but inevitable that Ms. Rowling and Mrs. Meyer share very similar world views (if the liberal Anglican and conservative Mormon are obviously and spectacularly different in the particulars of their beliefs). They both advance the ideas common to postmoderns that prejudice is the core evil of our age and that it is unexamined belief in cultural myths or

metanarratives that blind us to things as they really are. Neither author is a relativist, certainly, but there is little mercy shown to power-holders in either series, the wizards and vampires whom the prevalent myth designates as "good." The marginalized, institutional "other" are the heroes and they are heroic in their self-actualizing, individual, sacrificial choices in resistance to prejudice and the myth, "speaking truth to power."

10. **Religious content, allegory, symbolism:** I recommended Eliade's *The Sacred and the Profane* in the nonfiction book list above because I think his idea about the religious function of fiction in a secular culture is so valuable in understanding the phenomena of *Harry Potter* and *Twilight*. This thesis applies to both these series because they are filled to the gills with themes, symbols, and allegories from the authors' religious and literary traditions that meet the spiritual need readers are trying to satisfy through suspending disbelief and entering transpersonal, nonlocal space. Rowling and Meyer deliver the goods so readers return for repeat initiation and deeper experience. Hence, Potter-mania and the TwiHards.

Ten Ideas to Take Away from *Spotlight*

The best way to close this series of lists is with a "doggy bag" or "bento box" sampler of the "Ten Ideas I Hope You'll Take Home" from this book, both as an impromptu review and to encourage you to think about the artistry and meaning of Stephenie Meyer's *Twilight*.

1. **Eliade Thesis and Granger Corollary:** The thesis, once again, is that people read novels because fiction serves a religious function in a secular culture – and, in a community where the spiritual is roughly coterminous with the delusional, reading may be the only place to satisfy spiritual longings. My corollary is simply that the books that meet or satisfy this longing best (and which are, consequently, the most popular) are the ones with religious or spiritual content and meaning that resonate with the reader's heart and spiritual understanding. Mrs. Meyer succeeds spectacularly in this regard.

2. **Layers of Interpretation ~ Ways of Knowing ~ Nature of Things:** I believe that to understand the popularity of Mrs. Meyer's books we need to use an interpretative tool or critical

lens that opens up how and what readers are experiencing in these novels. The common sense approach is not an ideological filter that draws specific strands of meaning from books, say, as a feminist reading reveals gender issues. We want instead to look at these stories in the four ways human beings know anything – as data from sense perception, opinion from our beliefs, as truth transparencies from science, and as sublime, translucent beauty, truth, and goodness we have in wisdom. In books, the corresponding layers of meaning are surface story or plot points, morality or "good guy/bad guy," allegory or story-within-the story, and the anagogical or symbolic meaning. The best books work at all four layers because better reads correspond to the nature of reality and how we experience the world. Let's roll through the layers of meaning in the *Twilight* Saga:

3. **Surface Meaning:** All the story meanings have to come through what the reader understands at the surface, (a) in the plot or lack of same, (b) via the reader's identification or just interest in the narrator's voice or fate of the lead players, and (c) in the story type or genre in play. Mrs. Meyer uses all the elements of a love-story, combines it with a blockbuster international thriller, and wraps it up in paranormal, borderline Gothic elements. With her sympathetic and comic narrator, the reader is hooked deeply into the story and meaning begins to flow from text to reader through this strong line. If the reader does not engage with the surface story for whatever reason, he or she will be unable to experience the other layers of meaning (hence, genre-revulsion causing widespread critical disdain for *Twilight*).

4. **Moral Meaning:** The implicit morality of the story is a combination of postmodern war waged by the virtuous good guys among the disenfranchised "other" against both conventional prejudice and institutional power. See #9 in the list just above this one for a longer explanation of "postmodern morality."

5. **Allegorical Meaning:** Mrs. Meyer serves up allegorical meaning both as satire (Bella as a zombie reading *Animal Farm*) and in the sense that she is writing a relatively idealized almost mythic story in which her readers can identify with the humanoid characters with the supernatural qualities. The core allegory of the book is that Bella and Edward's Romance is a Man-God allegory and retelling of the Garden of Eden story. Bella the

spiritual seeker is transformed in and by her sacrificial love for God and becomes a goddess of sorts herself after a three-day apotheosis.

6. **Anagogical Meaning:** The artistry that hits us entirely beneath the conscious cranial intelligence is the symbolism and story imagery that we take in through the "eye of the heart. Mrs. Meyer delivers this through her remarkable use of circle images, of literary alchemy within each book and in the series as a whole, and of the conjunction of mind with the fabric of reality and the Creative Word and Principle of God – and how we share this *logos* mind and experience it as conscience, literally "shared knowing."
7. **Mormon Artist:** Mrs. Meyer's LDS faith permeates her *Twilight* novels. All the characters (except the "carnivorous" vampires) for the most part eat, dress, act, and speak as if they live in a Mormon compound in conformity with both the Word of Wisdom and Law of Chastity. The author's church, school, family, and community life are LDS focused. As writers draw from their beliefs and understanding of the world, that everything in *Twilight* reflects Mrs. Meyer's LDS background is just common sense.
8. **Mormon Apologist:** Mrs. Meyer's dream that inspired the first novel and the eventual series of books was about a girl and a conflicted vampire in a "mountain meadow." The novels turn out to be an allegorical drama and apology for the 1857 Mountain Meadows Massacre and other gentile-Mormon conflicts, ranging from the character of Joseph Smith, Jr., and the genetics challenge to *The Book of Mormon* to man-child marriages and polygamy.
9. **Mormon Apostate:** She also gets her shots in against the Prophet and goes so far as to suggest, in making her Cullen Family what Edwin Arnaudin calls *Mormon Vampires,* that there is something problematic, even "blood thirsty" and "soulless" about Mormonism. Mrs. Meyer is not a lockstep, proselytizing, True-Believer Mormon, if her rebellion is buried in story beneath the Thoroughly Mormon Millie's Morality Play that is saturated with Mormon content.

10. **Story as Mormon Allegory:** Interpreting the *Twilight* Saga as a Mormon Midsummer Night's Dream, Bella is a gentile seeker who converts to Mormonism through her love of Joseph Smith, Jr., as portrayed by Edward, and joins the Holy Family and Trinity. This family and its natural gentile allies combine to reveal the evil designs and turn back the invasion of the Volturi Catholics while reconciling the Nephite albinos and Lamanite dark-skinned apostates from *The Book of Mormon.*

I will close as I did in the Introduction. *Spotlight* is not offered as the last word on this subject but as a prolonged argument for taking Mrs. Meyer's *Twilight* novels and her readers seriously. This is the beginning of what promises to be a great discussion. I look forward to reading your comments, questions, and corrections in conversations at Forks High School Professor (FHSProfessor.com) and at TwilightSpotlight.com.

And please write to me at the email address below! I have met many of my better friends through just this kind of communication and I look forward to hearing your ideas about what I got right and wrong in *Spotlight* and what you think about Mrs. Meyer's artistry and meaning.

Thank you for reading *Spotlight* and, in advance, for your email note telling me what you think.

Fraternally in the love of a good book,

John Granger

john@FHSProfessor.com

Bibliography: *Spotlight* Dead-Tree Source Material

I have grouped this bibliography into three sections for ease of use. In the first section are those works cited throughout the text. The second section includes those books used as references for the three Mormonism chapters. The third is the small collection of LDS fiction I gathered to give myself some experience of novels by Mormon writers not named Stephenie Meyer.

Abraham, Lyndy. *A Dictionary of Alchemical Imagery.* Cambridge: Cambridge University Press, 1998.

Auden, W. H. *The Dyer's Hand and Other Essays.* New York: Vintage, 1968 (1948).

Austen, Jane. *Pride and Prejudice.* Vol. I: *The Oxford Illustrated Jane Austen.* New York: Oxford University Press, 1988.

Bayard, Louis. *The Pale Blue Eye.* New York: HarperCollins, 2006.

Bloom, Allan (trans.). *Plato's Republic.* New York: Basic Books, 1968.

Bloom, Harold. *The American Religion: The Emergence of the Post-Christian Nation.* New York: Simon and Schuster, 1992.

________. *How to Read and Why.* New York: Scribner, 2000.

________. *The Western Canon: The Books and Schools of the Ages.* Orlando, Florida: Harcourt Brace, 1994.

Booth, Wayne C. *The Rhetoric of Fiction (Second Edition).* Chicago: University of Chicago Press, 1983.

Borella, Jean. *The Secret of the Christian Way: A Contemplative Ascent Through the Writings of Jean Borella.* Translated and edited by G. John Champoux. Albany: State University of New York Press, 2001.

Bronte, Charlotte. *Jane Eyre.* New York: Puffin, 1994.

Bronte, Emily. *Wuthering Heighhts.* New York: Puffin, 1990.

Bunyan, John. *The Pilgrim's Progress.* Chicago: Donohue, Henneberry, 1907.

Burckhardt, Titus. *Alchemy: Science of the Cosmos, Science of the Soul.* Translated by William Stoddart. Baltimore: Penguin, 1972.

________. *Mirror of the Intellect: Essays on Traditional Science and Sacred Art.* Translated and edited by William Stoddart. Cambridge: Quinta Essentia, 1982.

Cahoone, Lawrence (ed.). *From Modernism to Postmodernism: An Anthology.* Malden, Massachusetts: Blackwell, 2001.

Card, Orson Scott. *Characters and Viewpoint: How to Invent, Construct, and Animate Vivid Characters, and Choose the Best Eyes Through Which to View the Events of Your Short Story or Novel.* Cincinnati: Writer's Digest Books, 1988.

________. *How to Write Science Fiction and Fantasy.* Cincinnati: Writer's Digest Books, 1990.

Cirlot, J. E. *A Dictionary of Symbols (Second Edition).* Translated by Jack Sage. New York: Dorset, 1971.

Coleridge, Samuel Taylor. *Aids to Reflection.* New York: Chelsea House, 1983.

________. *Biographia Literaria.* Vol. III: *The Complete Works of Samuel Taylor Coleridge.* New York: Harper & Brothers, 1868.

Cutsinger, James. *Advice to the Serious Seeker: Meditations on the Teaching of Frithjof Schuon.* Albany: State University of New York Press, 1997.

________. *That Man Might Become God: Lectures on Christian Theology.* Unpublished: available at www.cutsinger.net.

________. *The Form of the Transformed Vision: Coleridge and the Knowledge of God.* Macon, Georgia: Mercer:, 1987.

Dante Alighieri. *The Divine Comedy.* Translated by Henry Cary and edited by Ralph Pite. Rutland, Vermont: Everyman, 1994.

________. *The Divine Comedy 1: Hell.* Translated by Dorothy Sayers. Baltimore: Penguin, 1975.

________. *The Divine Comedy 2: Purgatory.* Translated by Dorothy Sayers. Baltimore: Penguin, 1975.

________. *The Divine Comedy 3: Paradise.* Translated by Dorothy Sayers. Baltimore: Penguin, 1975.

________. *The Divine Comedy 2: Purgatorio.* Translated with commentary by John D. Sinclair. New York: Oxford University Press, 1967.

Dostoevsky, Fyodor. *The Brothers Karamazov.* Translated by Constance Garnett. New York: Barnes & Noble, 2004.

Du Maurier, Daphne. *Rebecca.* New York: Pocket Books, 1969.

Eliade. Mircea. *The Forge and the Crucible: The Origins and Structures of Alchemy (Second Edition).* Translated by Stephen Corrin. Chicago, University of Chicago Press, 1978.

________. *Images and Symbols: Studies in Religious Symbolism.* Translated by Philip Mairet. New York: Sheed and Ward, 1969.

________. *The Myth of the Eternal Return: Cosmos and History.* Translated by Willard Trask. Princeton: Princeton University Press, 1971.

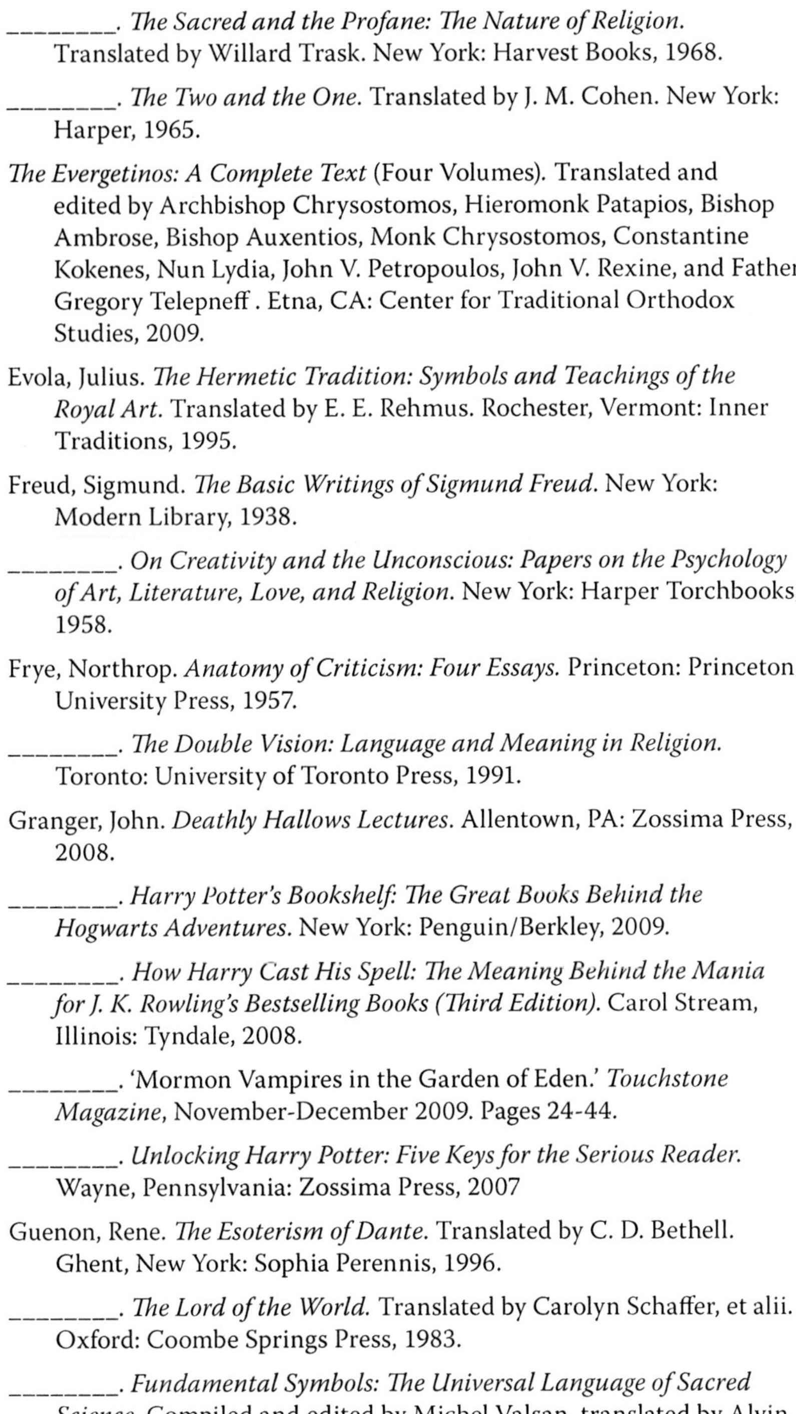

________. *The Sacred and the Profane: The Nature of Religion.* Translated by Willard Trask. New York: Harvest Books, 1968.

________. *The Two and the One.* Translated by J. M. Cohen. New York: Harper, 1965.

The Evergetinos: A Complete Text (Four Volumes). Translated and edited by Archbishop Chrysostomos, Hieromonk Patapios, Bishop Ambrose, Bishop Auxentios, Monk Chrysostomos, Constantine Kokenes, Nun Lydia, John V. Petropoulos, John V. Rexine, and Father Gregory Telepneff . Etna, CA: Center for Traditional Orthodox Studies, 2009.

Evola, Julius. *The Hermetic Tradition: Symbols and Teachings of the Royal Art.* Translated by E. E. Rehmus. Rochester, Vermont: Inner Traditions, 1995.

Freud, Sigmund. *The Basic Writings of Sigmund Freud.* New York: Modern Library, 1938.

________. *On Creativity and the Unconscious: Papers on the Psychology of Art, Literature, Love, and Religion.* New York: Harper Torchbooks, 1958.

Frye, Northrop. *Anatomy of Criticism: Four Essays.* Princeton: Princeton University Press, 1957.

________. *The Double Vision: Language and Meaning in Religion.* Toronto: University of Toronto Press, 1991.

Granger, John. *Deathly Hallows Lectures.* Allentown, PA: Zossima Press, 2008.

________. *Harry Potter's Bookshelf: The Great Books Behind the Hogwarts Adventures.* New York: Penguin/Berkley, 2009.

________. *How Harry Cast His Spell: The Meaning Behind the Mania for J. K. Rowling's Bestselling Books (Third Edition).* Carol Stream, Illinois: Tyndale, 2008.

________. 'Mormon Vampires in the Garden of Eden.' *Touchstone Magazine*, November-December 2009. Pages 24-44.

________. *Unlocking Harry Potter: Five Keys for the Serious Reader.* Wayne, Pennsylvania: Zossima Press, 2007

Guenon, Rene. *The Esoterism of Dante.* Translated by C. D. Bethell. Ghent, New York: Sophia Perennis, 1996.

________. *The Lord of the World.* Translated by Carolyn Schaffer, et alii. Oxford: Coombe Springs Press, 1983.

________. *Fundamental Symbols: The Universal Language of Sacred Science.* Compiled and edited by Michel Valsan, translated by Alvin

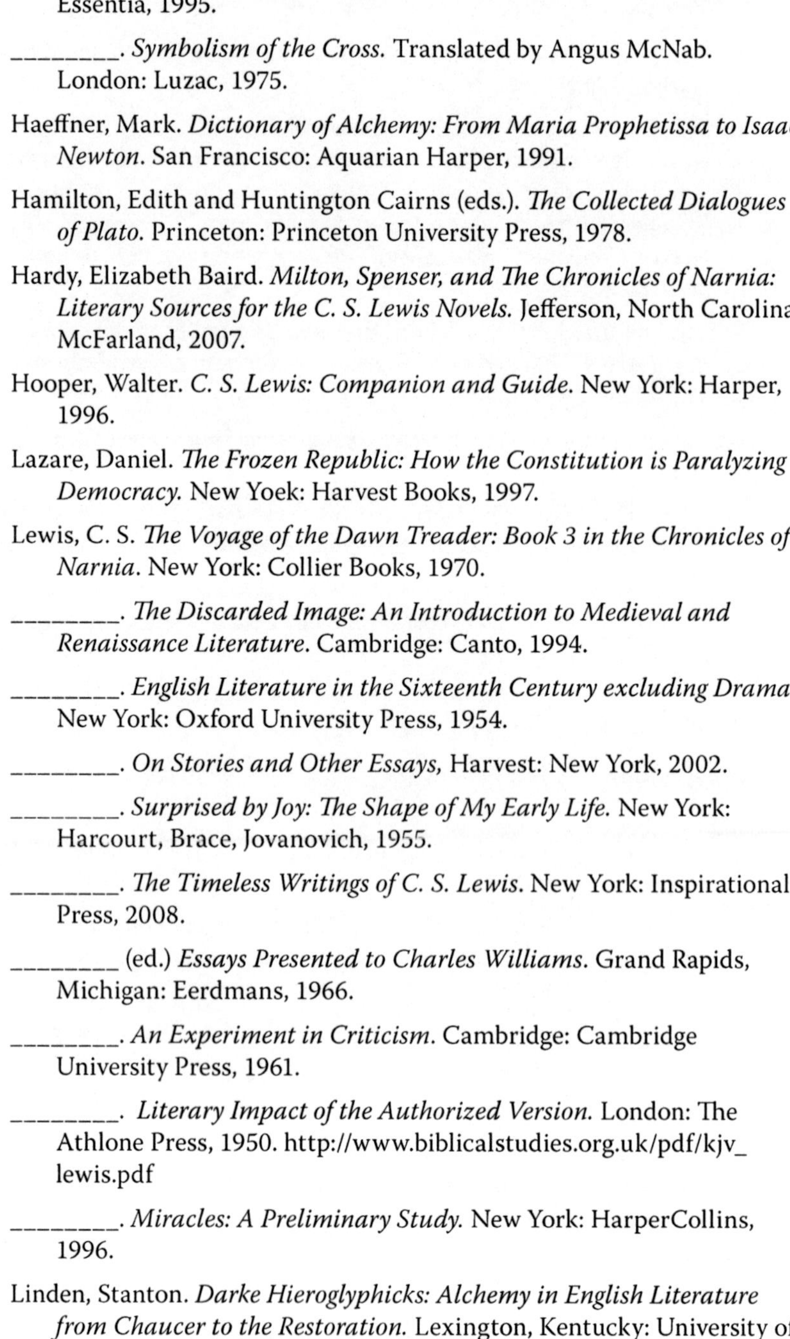

Moore, Jr., revised and edited by Martin Lings. Cambridge: Quinta Essentia, 1995.

________. *Symbolism of the Cross.* Translated by Angus McNab. London: Luzac, 1975.

Haeffner, Mark. *Dictionary of Alchemy: From Maria Prophetissa to Isaac Newton.* San Francisco: Aquarian Harper, 1991.

Hamilton, Edith and Huntington Cairns (eds.). *The Collected Dialogues of Plato.* Princeton: Princeton University Press, 1978.

Hardy, Elizabeth Baird. *Milton, Spenser, and The Chronicles of Narnia: Literary Sources for the C. S. Lewis Novels.* Jefferson, North Carolina: McFarland, 2007.

Hooper, Walter. *C. S. Lewis: Companion and Guide.* New York: Harper, 1996.

Lazare, Daniel. *The Frozen Republic: How the Constitution is Paralyzing Democracy.* New Yoek: Harvest Books, 1997.

Lewis, C. S. *The Voyage of the Dawn Treader: Book 3 in the Chronicles of Narnia.* New York: Collier Books, 1970.

________. *The Discarded Image: An Introduction to Medieval and Renaissance Literature.* Cambridge: Canto, 1994.

________. *English Literature in the Sixteenth Century excluding Drama.* New York: Oxford University Press, 1954.

________. *On Stories and Other Essays,* Harvest: New York, 2002.

________. *Surprised by Joy: The Shape of My Early Life.* New York: Harcourt, Brace, Jovanovich, 1955.

________. *The Timeless Writings of C. S. Lewis.* New York: Inspirational Press, 2008.

________ (ed.) *Essays Presented to Charles Williams.* Grand Rapids, Michigan: Eerdmans, 1966.

________. *An Experiment in Criticism.* Cambridge: Cambridge University Press, 1961.

________. *Literary Impact of the Authorized Version.* London: The Athlone Press, 1950. http://www.biblicalstudies.org.uk/pdf/kjv_lewis.pdf

________. *Miracles: A Preliminary Study.* New York: HarperCollins, 1996.

Linden, Stanton. *Darke Hieroglyphicks: Alchemy in English Literature from Chaucer to the Restoration.* Lexington, Kentucky: University of Kentucky Press, 1996.

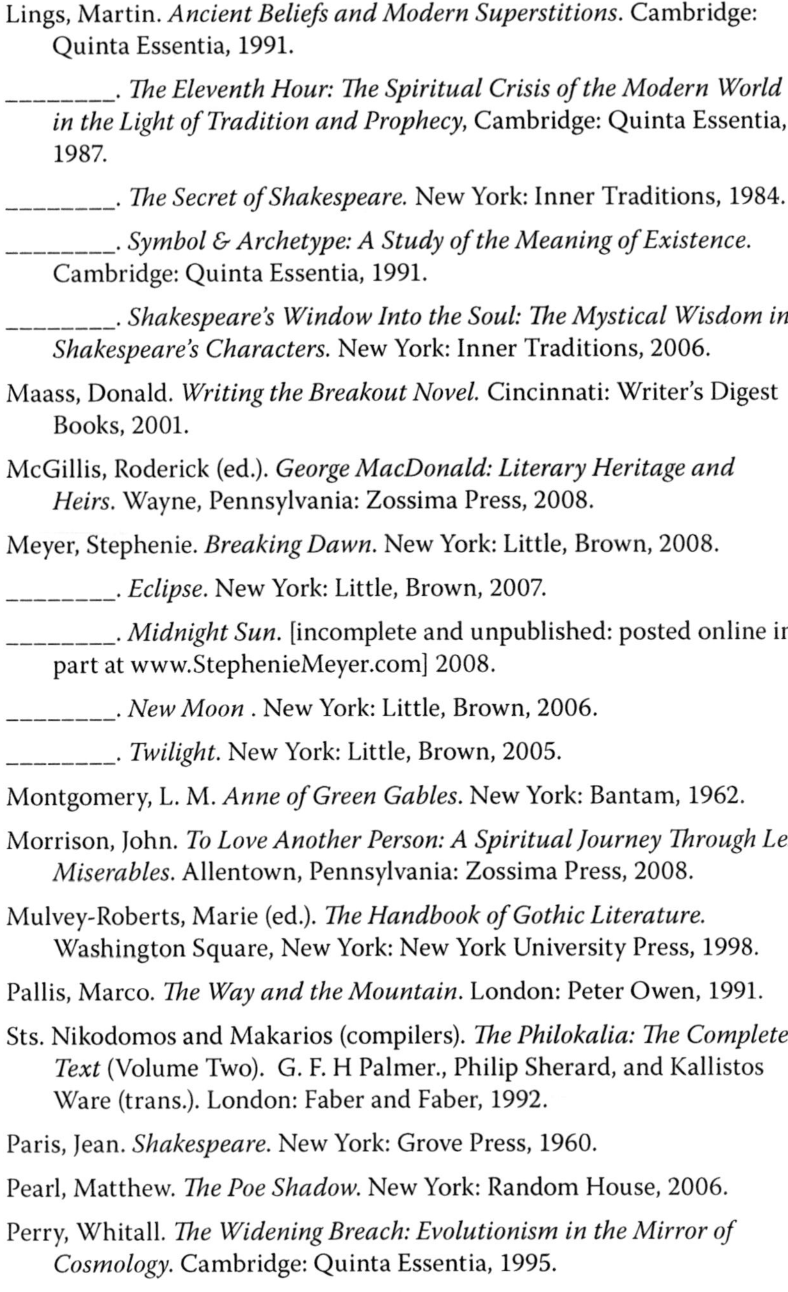

Lings, Martin. *Ancient Beliefs and Modern Superstitions*. Cambridge: Quinta Essentia, 1991.

________. *The Eleventh Hour: The Spiritual Crisis of the Modern World in the Light of Tradition and Prophecy*, Cambridge: Quinta Essentia, 1987.

________. *The Secret of Shakespeare.* New York: Inner Traditions, 1984.

________. *Symbol & Archetype: A Study of the Meaning of Existence.* Cambridge: Quinta Essentia, 1991.

________. *Shakespeare's Window Into the Soul: The Mystical Wisdom in Shakespeare's Characters.* New York: Inner Traditions, 2006.

Maass, Donald. *Writing the Breakout Novel.* Cincinnati: Writer's Digest Books, 2001.

McGillis, Roderick (ed.). *George MacDonald: Literary Heritage and Heirs.* Wayne, Pennsylvania: Zossima Press, 2008.

Meyer, Stephenie. *Breaking Dawn.* New York: Little, Brown, 2008.

________. *Eclipse.* New York: Little, Brown, 2007.

________. *Midnight Sun.* [incomplete and unpublished: posted online in part at www.StephenieMeyer.com] 2008.

________. *New Moon* . New York: Little, Brown, 2006.

________. *Twilight.* New York: Little, Brown, 2005.

Montgomery, L. M. *Anne of Green Gables.* New York: Bantam, 1962.

Morrison, John. *To Love Another Person: A Spiritual Journey Through Les Miserables.* Allentown, Pennsylvania: Zossima Press, 2008.

Mulvey-Roberts, Marie (ed.). *The Handbook of Gothic Literature.* Washington Square, New York: New York University Press, 1998.

Pallis, Marco. *The Way and the Mountain.* London: Peter Owen, 1991.

Sts. Nikodomos and Makarios (compilers). *The Philokalia: The Complete Text* (Volume Two). G. F. H Palmer., Philip Sherard, and Kallistos Ware (trans.). London: Faber and Faber, 1992.

Paris, Jean. *Shakespeare.* New York: Grove Press, 1960.

Pearl, Matthew. *The Poe Shadow.* New York: Random House, 2006.

Perry, Whitall. *The Widening Breach: Evolutionism in the Mirror of Cosmology.* Cambridge: Quinta Essentia, 1995.

Roberts, Alexander and James Donaldson (eds.). *Fathers of the Second Century: Clement of Alexandria (Entire).* Vol. II: *The Ante-Nicene Fathers.* Peabody, Massachusetts: Hendrickson, 1994.

Robertson, D. W. Jr. *A Preface to Chaucer: Studies in Medieval Perspectives.* Princeton: Princeton University Press, 1962.

Romanides, Protopresbyter John S. *Patristic Theology.* The Dalles, OR: Uncut Mountain Press, 2008.

Rowling, J. K. *Harry Potter and the Sorcerer's Stone.* New York: Arthur Levine Books, 1998.

________. *Harry Potter and the Deathly Hallows.* New York: Arthur Levine Books, 2007.

Ruskin, John. *The Queen of the Air.* New York: John Wiley and Sons, 1873.

________. Unto This Last and Other Writings. New York: Penguin Classics, 1986.

Sayers, Dorothy. *Introductory Papers on Dante.* Vol. I: *The Poet Alive in His Writings.* Eugene, Oregon: Wipf & Stock, 2006.

Schuon, Frithjof. *The Eye of the Heart: Metaphysics, Cosmology, Spiritual Life.* Bloomington, Indiana: World Wisdom Books, 1997.

________. *The Transcendent Unity of Religions.* Wheaton, IL: Theosophical Publishing, 1993.

Shakespeare, William. *The Merchant of Venice.* Edited by W. Moelwyn Merchant. New York: Penguin, 1985.

________. *A Midsummer Night's Dream.* Edited by Madeline Doran. New York: Penguin, 1985.

________. *Romeo and Juliet: The Pelican Shakespeare.* Edited by John Hankins. New York: Penguin, 1985.

Tillyard, E. M. W. *The Elizabethan World Picture: A Study of the Idea of Order in the Age of Shakespeare, Donne, and Milton.* New York: Vintage, 1959.

Upton, Charles and Jennifer Doanne Upton. *Shadow of the Rose: The Esoterism of the Romantic Tradition.* San Rafael, CA: Sophia Perennis, 2008.

Upton, Charles. *The System of the Anti-Christ: Truth and Falsehood in Postmodernism and the New Age.* Ghent, NY: Sophia Perennis, 2001.

Ward, Michael. *Planet Narnia: The Seven Heavens in the Imagination of C. S. Lewis.* Oxford: Oxford University Press, 2007.

Ware, Metropolitan Kallistos. *The Orthodox Church.* New York: Penguin, 1993.

________. *The Orthodox Way.* New York: St. Vladimir's Seminary Press, 1995.

Weaver, Richard M. *Ideas Have Consequences.* Chicago: The University of Chicago Press, 1948.

Williams, A. N. *The Divine Sense: The Intellect in Patristic Theology.* Cambridge: Cambridge University Press, 2007.

Yates, Frances A. *Giordano Bruno and the Hermetic Tradition.* Chicago: University of Chicago Press, 1979.

________. *The Art of Memory.* Chicago: University of Chicago Press, 1974.

Zuckerman, Albert. *Writing the Block Buster Novel.* Cincinnati: Writer's Digest Books, 1994.

Mormonism Books

Anderson, Robert D. *Inside the Mind of Joseph Smith: Psychobiography and the Book of Mormon.* Salt Lake City: Signature Books, 1999.

Anderson, Ross. *Understanding the Book of Mormon.* Grand Rapids, MI: Zondervan, 2009.

Andrus, Hyrum L. *Doctrinal Commentary on the Pearl of Great Price.* Salt Lake City: Deseret Book Company, 1969.

Arnaudin, Edwin B. *Mormon Vampires: The Twilight Saga and Religious Literacy.* "A Master's Paper for the M.S. in L.S degree. April, 2008." University of North Carolina, Chapel Hill, unpublished (available online at http://www.ils.unc.edu/MSpapers/3348.pdf).

Bagley, Will. *Blood of the Prophets: Brigham Young and the Massacre at Mountain Meadows.* Norman, OK: University of Oklahoma Press, 2002.

Ben-Dor Benite, Zvi. *The Ten Lost Tribes.* New York: Oxford University Press, 2009.

Bigelow, Christopher Kimball and Jana Riess, PhD. *Mormonism for Dummies.* Hoboken, NJ: Wiley, 2005.

Brodie, Fawn. *No Man Knows My History: The Life of Joseph Smith.* New York: Alfred Knopf, 1993.

Brooke, John L. *The Refiner's Fire: The Making of Mormon Cosmology,1644-1844.* New York: Cambridge University Press, 1994.

Brooks, Juanita. *The Mountain Meadows Massacre.* Norman, OK: University of Oklahoma Press, 1985.

Buerger, David John. *The Mysteries of Godliness: A History of Mormon Temple Worship.* San Francisco: Smith Research Associates, 1994.

Bushman, Claudia Lauper and Richard Lyman. *Mormons in America.* Oxford University Press, New York, 1999.

Bushman, Richard Lyman. *Joseph Smith and the Beginnings of Mormonism.* Urbana, IL: University of Illinois Press, 1984.

________. *Mormonism: A Very Short Introduction.* New York: Oxford University Press, 2008.

________. *Joseph Smith: Rough Stone Rolling.* New York: Vintage, 2007.

Church of Jesus Christ of Latter-day Saints. *Holy Bible* (KJV), *Book of Mormon, Doctrines and Covenants, and Pearl of Great Price* ('The Quad'). Salt Lake City: 1989.

Collings, Michael R. *In the Image of God: Theme, Characterization, and Landscape in the Fiction of Orson Scott Card.* New York: Greenwood Press, 1990.

Denton, Sally. *American Massacre: The Tragedy at Mountain Meadows, September 1857.* New York: Alfred Knopf, 2003.

Godwin, Joscelyn. *The Theosophical Enlightenment.* Albany, NY: State University of New York Press, 1994.

Hansen, Klaus, J. *Quest for Empire: The Political Kingdom of God and the Council of Fifty in Mormon history.* Omaha: University of Nebraska Press, 1974.

Jackson, Andrew. *Mormonism Explained: What Latter-day Saints Believe and Practice.* Wheaton, IL: Crossway, 2008.

Krakauer, John. *Under the Banner of Heaven: A Story of Violent Faith.* New York: Doubleday, 2003.

Laake, Deborah. *Secret Ceremonies: A Mormon Woman's Intimate Diary of Marriage and Beyond.* New York: William Morrow and Company, 1993.

Mann, Charles C. *1401: New Revelations of the Americas Before Columbus.* New York: Vintage, 2006.

McMurin, Sterling M. *The Theological Foundations of the Mormon Religion.* Salt Lake City: University of Utah Press, 1977.

Ostling, Richard N. and Joan K. *Mormon America: The Power and the Promise.* New York: HarperCollins, 2007.

Quinn, D. Michael. *Early Mormonism and the Magic World View.* Salt Lake City: Signature Books, 1998.

Smith, Emma. *Emma Smith's Hymnal: Collection of Sacred Hymns* (reprint). Independence, Missouri: Herald Heritage 1973.

Smith, Hyrum J. and Janne M. Sjodahl. *The Doctrines and Covenants with an Introduction and Exegetical Notes.* Deseret Book Company, 1971 (original 1916).

Smith, Joseph, Jr. (trans.). *The Book of Mormon.* Salt Lake City: Deseret Book Company, 1971.

Smith, Joseph Fielding. *The Way of Perfection.* Salt Lake City: Genealogical Society of the Church of Jesus Christ of Latter-day Saints, 1956.

Solomon, Dorothy Allred. *The Sisterhood: Inside the Lives of Mormon Women.* New York: Palgrave Macmillan, 2007.

Trask, Paul. *Part Way to Utah: The Forgotten Mormons.* Refiner's Fire Ministries, 1997.

Vogel, Dan and Brent Metcalfe, eds. *American Apocrypha: Essays on the Book of Mormon.* Salt Lake City: Signature, 2002.

Vogel, Dan. *Joseph Smith: The Making of a Prophet.* Salt Lake City: Signature Books, 2004.

________. *Religious Seekers and the Advent of Mormonism.* Salt Lake City: Signature Books, 1989.

Walker, Ronald W., Richard E. Turley, and Glen M. Leonard. *Massacre at Mountain Meadows.* New York: Oxford University Press, 2008.

Fiction by Mormon Authors

Card, Orson Scott. *Speaker for the Dead.* New York: Tom Doherty Associates, 1991.

________. *Ultimate Iron Man, Volume 1* (5 issues). New York: Marvel Comics Group, March 2005 – February 2006.

________. *A Woman of Destiny.* New York: Berkley, 1984.

Martindale, S. Michael. *Brother Brigham.* Provo, Utah: Zarahemla Books, 2007.

Perry, Anne. *Come, Armageddon.* New York: Ace Books, 2001.

________. *Tathea.* New York: Ace Books, 2002.

Index

Note: With some exceptions, book titles are listed under the author's name.

X

Y

Z

Zossima Press Titles

C. S. Lewis

C. S. Lewis: Views From Wake Forest - Essays on C. S. Lewis
Michael Travers, editor

Contains sixteen scholarly presentations from the international C. S. Lewis convention in Wake Forest, NC. Walter Hooper shares his important essay "Editing C. S. Lewis," a chronicle of publishing decisions after Lewis' death in 1963.
"Scholars from a variety of disciplines address a wide range of issues. The happy result is a fresh and expansive view of an author who well deserves this kind of thoughtful attention."
Diana Pavlac Glyer, author of *The Company They Keep*

Why I Believe in Narnia: 33 Essays & Reviews on the Life & Work of C. S. Lewis
By James Como

Chapters range from reviews of critical books, documentaries and movies to evaluations of Lewis' books to biographical analysis.
"A valuable, wide-ranging collection of essays by one of the best informed and most astute commentators on Lewis' work and ideas."
Peter Schakel, author *Imagination & the Arts in C. S. Lewis*

C. S. Lewis & Philosophy as a Way of Life: His Philosophical Thoughts
Adam Barkman

C. S. Lewis is rarely thought of as a "philosopher" per se despite having both studied and taught philosophy for several years at Oxford. Lewis's long journey to Christianity was essentially philosophical – passing through seven diffeent stages. This 624 page book is an invaluable reference for C. S. Lewis scholars and fans alike.

C. S. Lewis: His Literary Achievement
Colin N. Manlove

This book is the first thorough analysis of the whole of Lewis's fiction to show that it has behind it a considerable sophistication of literary technique and patterning. The works discussed include *The Pilgrim's Regress*, *The Ransom Trilogy*, *The Great Divorce*, the *Narnia* books and *Till We Have Faces*. Revised and updated from an earlier edition.

The Hidden Story of Narnia: A Book-By-Book Guide to Spiritual Themes
Will Vaus

A book of insightful commentary – Will Vaus points out connections between the Narnia books and spiritual and biblical themes in our world, as well as between ideas in the Narnia books and C. S. Lewis' other books. Each chapter includes questions for individual use or small group discussion.

Harry Potter

Harry Potter & Imagination: The Way Between Two Worlds
Travis Prinzi

Imaginative literature places a reader between two worlds: the story world and the world of daily life, and challenges this reader to imagine and to act for a better world. *Harry Potter & Imagination* takes readers on a journey through the transformative power of those themes by placing Rowling's series in its literary, historical, and cultural contexts.

Hog's Head Conversations: Essays on Harry Potter, Volume One
Travis Prinzi, editor

Sit back and enjoy the ten best Hog's Head conversations of the year, edited into this handy collection. Look for volume two in June 2010.

Deathly Hallows Lectures: The Hogwarts's Professor Explains Harry's Final Adventure
John Granger

In ***The Deathly Hallows Lectures***, John Granger reveals the finale's brilliant details, themes and meanings. Even the most ardent of *Harry Potter* fans will be surprised by and delighted with Granger's explanations of the three dimensions of meaning in *Deathly Hallows.*

Repotting Harry Potter: A Book-by-Book Guide for the Serious Re-Reader
James W. Thomas

Professor Thomas takes us on a tour through the *Potter* books in order to enjoy them in different ways upon subsequent readings. Informal discussions focus on puns, humor, foreshadowing, literary allusions, narrative techniques, and other aspects of the *Potter* books. Dr. Thomas's light touch proves that a "serious" reading of literature can be fun.

Rowling Revisited:
Afterthoughts on Harry, Fantastic Beasts, Quidditch, and Beedle the Bard.
James W. Thomas

Professor Thomas invites readers once again to discover curiosities, droll humorous elements, foreshadowing, and many other matters in Rowling's three ancillary works. These brief books are especially interesting when compared to the complete Potter series.

God & Harry Potter at Yale: Faith & Fiction in the Classroom
Danielle Tumminio

When a course was offered at Yale University on "Harry Potter and Theology" the response was overwhelming. Students included Hindus, Jews, Mormons, Catholics, Episcopalians, Baptists, Methodists, and Agnostics. The aim was not to convert students to Christianity, but to engage their minds with questions that lie at the core of our human experience. In this book the author (and professor of that class) shares her experience.

George MacDonald

Diary of an Old Soul & The White Page Poems
George MacDonald and Betty Aberlin

The first edition of George MacDonald's book of daily poems included a blank page opposite each page of poems. Readers were invited to write their own reflections on the "white page." MacDonald wrote: "Let your white page be ground, my print be seed, growing to golden ears, that faith and hope may feed." Betty Aberlin responded to MacDonald's invitation with daily poems of her own.
Betty Aberlin's close readings of George MacDonald's verses and her thoughtful responses to them speak clearly of her poetic gifts and spiritual intelligence. Luci Shaw, poet

George MacDonald: Literary Heritage and Heirs
Roderick McGillis, editor

This latest collection of 14 essays sets a new standard that will influence MacDonald studies for many more years. George MacDonald experts are increasingly evaluating his entire corpus within the nineteenth century context.
This comprehensive collection represents the best of contemporary scholarship on George MacDonald. Rolland Hein, author of *George MacDonald: Victorian Mythmaker.*

In the Near Loss of Everything: George MacDonald's Son in America
Dale Wayne Slusser

Dale Wayne Slusser unfolds this poignant story with unpublished letters and photos that give readers a glimpse into the close-knit MacDonald family. Also included is Ronald's essay about his father, *George MacDonald: A Personal Note*, plus a selection from Ronald's 1922 fable, *The Laughing Elf*, about the necessity of both sorrow and joy in life.

Other Titles

To Love Another Person: A Spiritual Journey Through Les Miserables
John Morrison

The powerful story of Jean Valjean's redemption is beloved by readers and theater goers everywhere. In this companion and guide to Victor Hugo's masterpiece, author John Morrison unfolds the spiritual depth and breadth of this classic novel and broadway musical.

The Eye of the Beholder: How to See the World Like a Romantic Poet
Louis Markos

This accessible guide to Romantic poetry focuses almost exclusively on short lyrical poems (the exceptions are Coleridge's *Rime of the Ancient Mariner*, Blake's *Marriage of Heaven and Hell* and Wordsworth's "Preface to Lyrical Ballads"). A detailed bibliographic essay on each poet is provided that cites critical studies of their work.

LaVergne, TN USA
19 May 2010
183245LV00003B/37/P

9 780982 238592